The European Union and Democracy Promotion

DEMOCRATIC TRANSITION AND CONSOLIDATION

Jorge I. Domínguez and Anthony Jones, Series Editors

The Construction of Democracy: Lessons from Practice and Research (2007)
edited by Jorge I. Domínguez and Anthony Jones

Democracies in Danger (2009)
edited by Alfred Stepan

Measuring Democracy: A Bridge between Scholarship and Politics (2009)
by Gerardo L. Munck

Regime Change in the Yugoslav Successor States: Divergent Paths toward a New Europe (2010)
by Mieczysław P. Boduszyński

The European Union and Democracy Promotion

A Critical Global Assessment

Edited by
Richard Youngs

The Johns Hopkins University Press
Baltimore

© 2010 The Johns Hopkins University Press
All rights reserved. Published 2010
Printed in the United States of America on acid-free paper
9 8 7 6 5 4 3 2 1

The Johns Hopkins University Press
2715 North Charles Street
Baltimore, Maryland 21218-4363
www.press.jhu.edu

Library of Congress Cataloging-in-Publication Data
The European Union and democracy promotion : a critical global assessment / edited by Richard Youngs.
   p. cm. — (Democratic transition and consolidation)
   Includes bibliographical references and index.
   ISBN-13: 978-0-8018-9732-0 (hardcover : alk. paper)
   ISBN-10: 0-8018-9732-7 (hardcover : alk. paper)
   1. Democratization—Government policy—European Union countries.
2. Democracy—Government policy—European Union countries.
3. European Union. 4. European Union countries—Relations—Foreign countries. I. Youngs, Richard, 1968–
   JZ1570.E9332 2011
   341.242′2—dc22   2010001211

A catalog record for this book is available from the British Library.

Special discounts are available for bulk purchases of this book. For more information, please contact Special Sales at 410-516-6936 or specialsales@press.jhu.edu.

The Johns Hopkins University Press uses environmentally friendly book materials, including recycled text paper that is composed of at least 30 percent post-consumer waste, whenever possible. All of our book papers are acid-free, and our jackets and covers are printed on paper with recycled content.

Contents

	Acknowledgments	vii
1	Introduction: Idealism at Bay *Richard Youngs*	1
2	Unfinished Business: European Political Conditionality after Eastern Enlargement *Geoffrey Pridham*	16
3	The Balkans: European Inducements *Sofia Sebastian*	38
4	Ukraine: A New Partnership *Natalia Shapovalova*	59
5	Organization for Security and Cooperation in Europe: A Paper Tiger? *Jos Boonstra*	78
6	Central Asia: Limited Modernization *Alexander Warkotsch*	99
7	Morocco: A Flawed Response *Kristina Kausch*	115
8	The Gulf Cooperation Council: The Challenges of Security *Ana Echagüe*	135
9	Iraq: A New European Engagement *Edward Burke*	154
10	Nigeria: Conflict, Energy, and Bad Governance *Anna Khakee*	175
	List of Contributors	197
	Index	199

Acknowledgments

The chapters that make up this volume reflect some of the main areas of research undertaken at the FRIDE think tank in Madrid. The chapters began life as separate publications of one form or another. They have been exhaustively updated to provide an overview of European democracy policies as they stood at the end of 2009. Each study has benefited from the input of reviewers for the publisher, series editor Jorge Domínguez, and executive editor Henry Tom, for which we are grateful.

The European Union and Democracy Promotion

CHAPTER ONE

Introduction
Idealism at Bay

Richard Youngs

An apparent duality exists at the heart of European Union (EU) foreign policy. On one hand, most observers argue that the EU has established itself as an international actor strongly committed to idealistic or normative policies. The EU is an arena in which realist interpretations of foreign policy have been most convincingly challenged. It is widely agreed that the EU's credibility as a supporter of democratic norms and human rights has increased in comparison to that of the United States in recent years. Formal European commitments to democracy have strengthened in every region of the world, and unity among EU member states on such aims is widely seen to have deepened.

The EU's 2004 enlargement represented a successful case of democracy support and also brought into the union Central and Eastern European states committed to enhancing the EU's role in democratization. Many analysts have examined the trajectory of EU policy in Central and Eastern Europe during the 1990s and claim it as one of the most influential cases ever of democracy promotion. Accounts differ in the relative importance these analysts attach to the influence of EU conditionality, geopolitical considerations, identity-based convergence, and technical assistance. But most stress the vital anchoring role played by the European

Union in the remarkable transformation of former Soviet states (Schimmelfennig and Sedelmeier 2004; Vachudova 2005).

There are, however, also negative elements. These are clearly challenging times for democracy promoters. In most regions, democratic reversals have occurred, and hopes for an expansion of the community of democratic nations have been dashed. Such disappointments have engendered a process of soul-searching among European democracy promoters. The financial crisis and tighter energy security constraints further complicate the picture. Many skeptics now ask whether support for democracy around the world has any future at all. A growing number of writers argues that the liberal agenda is moribund and that a less idealistic outlook on the world is required (Gray 2008; Hyde-Price 2007; Kagan 2008; Saul 2005). One of the most prominent analysts of democratization doubts that the relationship between enlightened self-interest and democracy support can easily be reconstructed after the failings of the Iraq invasion and occupation (Whitehead 2009). Critical academics most commonly focus now on questioning the whole validity of the democracy agenda (Habermas 2006; Duffield 2007).

It is widely argued that democracy promotion urgently needs to be relegitimized, in particular by making democracy support more demand-driven and tailored to countries' political specificities. This argument is associated with the need for better appreciation of the conditions under which external policies affect domestic political dynamics in nondemocratic or quasi-democratic states. Western donors have been criticized for designing policies that are insufficiently driven by local demands for political reform. If democracy support is to have any future, it is recognized that it must be demand-driven in a tighter and more systematic fashion (Tilly 2007; Diamond 2008; Fukuyama and McFaul 2007; Carothers 2002; Keane 2009). A fundamental redesign of democracy support is called for, imbued with an acceptance of the more modest role international actors are likely to play in the future.

At the same time, doubts have emerged over the prospects for further EU enlargement. The financial crisis threatens a retrenchment in foreign policy positions. Add to this the broader questioning of the legitimacy of democracy promotion in the wake of the Iraq invasion mentioned above, the rise of nondemocratic powers, and the prioritization of counterterrorism, and the constraints on EU normative power appear ever more pressing. Many see trends working so firmly to democracy's disadvantage that European foreign policy should drop the so-called democracy agenda. It is widely suggested that the focus should be on building alliances, in particular with rising powers, and on defending interests as Europe's international power diminishes.

In short, the starting point for assessing European policy is an appreciation of this mix of positive potential and less rosy prognostics. This book examines the balance between these contrasting dynamics within recent EU democracy promotion policies. Is the EU's reputation as a committed supporter of democratic norms justified or overstated? What type of political reform is being promoted within the broad gamut of institutional change pertinent to democratization? How is the EU's democracy strategy responding to the more challenging environment for democracy support? Is European unity on democracy policies increasing or decreasing? European policy documents and statements routinely suggest that the EU should listen to the differing understandings of democracy across regions, but is it really doing so?

These are crucial questions as the administration of President Barack Obama moves into its second year and begins to put flesh on the bones of its foreign policy vision. What prospect is there that transatlantic coordination on democracy promotion can be reconstructed after the divergences of the Bush years? One new volume suggests that the differences between EU and U.S. democracy policies have been exaggerated and that good grounds exist for rebuilding cooperation (Magen, McFaul, and Risse 2009). It clearly matters for the next phase of American foreign policy to understand what Europe is doing in the field of democracy support and how its strategies are evolving.

The present volume addresses these questions across a wide range of case studies. Some of these come from the EU's immediate neighborhood, while others cover the wider span of European foreign policies. We look at European policies toward key states like Morocco, Ukraine, Iraq, and Nigeria and toward strategically important regions such as the Balkans, Central Asia, and the Gulf. We also look at the role of other organizations with significant European participation, like the Organization for Security and Cooperation in Europe (OSCE). EU policies are defined in the broadest sense as incorporating the positions and strategies of individual European governments as well as the initiatives of such Brussels institutions as the European Commission. We understand democracy support or promotion in a broad sense, examining specific democracy assistance aid projects; the use of diplomatic incentives and conditionality; the dynamics of prodemocratic socialization; and the general pursuit of political dialogue and pressure within cooperative security partnerships.

We offer some tweaks to the existing literature on EU foreign policies. We find many (not all) existing case studies of EU democracy policy thin on the detail of European actions, as opposed to general discussion of domestic political developments in the country concerned. We hope here to offer a thicker, more substantial account of the various levels of European strategy. We stress the role of member state national policies that we understand to be a central part of overall EU approaches often neglected in studies that focus on a few commission documents and aid initiatives. We also include case studies on Iraq, the Persian Gulf, Nigeria, and Central Asia, regions and countries that are rarely assessed from the point of view of European democracy support. And as explained below, we hope to move beyond some of the clichés that suffuse studies of democracy promotion.

European Idealism

Recent years have witnessed a pendulum swing in conceptual analysis of European external relations. Such analysis once focused on understanding why EU foreign policy cooperation did not more strongly support common values and norms. Although such analysis continues, by far the largest proportion of work on the EU's Common Foreign and Security Policy has shifted to assessing how the union has developed a common normative orientation. Although such work was initially a challenge to the realist mainstream, it now constitutes the mainstream itself.

A vast array of work falls within this category, the core common concern of which is to examine the identity-driven external replication of internal EU norms. One writer describes the EU as a "liberal superpower" that has "rejected realist interpretations of the international system" (McCormick 2007, 12, 32, 174). Another theorist contends that European foreign policy cooperation represents an international "civilizing process" (Linklater 2005). A raft of constructivist-influenced work argues that EU policies are driven by a commonly shaped democratic identity rather than materialist interest maximization (Christiansen and Tonra 2004; Smith 2004; Checkel 2001). Analysts commonly argue that internal and external legitimacy are mutually constitutive, with democratic values supported externally as a means of embedding their vitality internally.

It is argued that the EU is drawn toward supporting milieu, not possession goals and global public goods that go beyond its own immediate self-interest. It seeks to strengthen "rival" states rather than maximize its own power over the latter. The EU, it is contended, follows a model of inclusiveness, not the pursuit of interests through exclusion. The EU's "worldview is one in which order and the spread of democracy and human rights are assured through rules, regimes, multilateral institutions and values, rather than through power relations, the balance of power, and military force"; the EU is said to "feel globally more responsible for the world's public welfare and global good government" than the United States or any other international actor and thus is more in line with "cosmopolitan values" (Telo 2007, 2, 34). Even studies that take a wider and more measured look at EU democracy promotion still tend toward a celebration of European specificity in this sense (Jünemann and Knodt 2007).

Realist critiques have themselves started from the assumption that EU policies have been too oriented toward liberal values and that this is self-defeating (Hyde-Price 2007). Accounts broadly in line with the call of English School theory for balance between cosmopolitan normative values and power politics also assume that the EU is guilty of veering toward Kant rather than Hobbes (Hurrell 2007). Moreover, from the perspective of critical theory, analysts increasingly berate the EU for what they judge to be an overly vigorous focus on democracy promotion, presuming that the latter can be equated with liberal imperialism.

From a more public policy perspective, external governance has taken root as a concept that highlights the way in which the EU's democracy (and other norms-based) policies are pursued through innovative governance arrangements. External governance extends the increasingly influential concept of governance into the hard case area of foreign policy. A common approach to external challenges is seen as being shaped by the transformative effect of EU institutions on member states' policies. This approach is based on the transfer of European rules. EU foreign policy is seen as an extension of the geographical scope of internal EU rules. In short, complementing ideational accounts, an embedded institutionalist dynamic of rule extension is seen as reinforcing the EU's external support for political norms and values (Schimmelfennig and Wagner 2004; Schimmelfennig and Lavenex 2009).

Our Doubts

In short, several conceptual perspectives concur in underscoring the weight of liberal-normative dynamics in European foreign policy. This collection of case studies suggests that all such perspectives suffer from serious shortcomings. The book points to the lack of strong European commitment to supporting democracy as part of foreign policy, noting an apparent adherence to more traditional concepts of strategic interest and a growing disappointment on the part of reformers in nondemocratic states with the paucity of the support they are offered by the EU. While constructivist accounts shed valuable light on how norms are transmitted, prior account must also be taken of instances where the EU is actively reticent to foster democratic change. We do not claim general relevance for our conclusions. In many policy sectors, the institutionalist and normative dynamics of EU foreign policy might indeed be ascendant; but we maintain that in the area of democracy the detailed evidence does not sustain such a claim.

Despite a plethora of ostensibly firmer prodemocracy commitments, in practice European governments are only weakly committed to promoting political change in most third countries. Overall, the EU is failing to meet the challenges of a more complex international environment for democracy and human rights, having declined fundamentally to reassess its democracy support in either qualitative or quantitative terms. The cases studied in this volume offer a critical mass of evidence to suggest that the EU has failed to fulfill its idealistic commitments to support democratic reform and instead favors a more cautious mix of norms and realpolitik.

Focusing on trends during the last four or five years, the chapters uncover considerable circumspection and in some countries a renewed questioning of democracy support. This is demonstrated across the book's case-study chapters. Most commonly, third countries that do not adopt democratic norms continue to receive aid increases and trade preferences and, under most EU policy frameworks, are allowed to assess their own progress on political reform. Constructivists commonly claim that the EU's prodemocracy discourse has shaped and driven a truly normative content to its foreign policy; but in most cases such rhetoric has also served to mask the EU's hesitancy in supporting democratic reform. Despite much rhetoric to the contrary, in practice there has been no policy shift in the Middle East and North Africa (MENA) away from stability-oriented cooperation with authoritarian rulers. Kristina Kausch's chapter on Morocco (chapter 7) demonstrates that the EU has failed to respond to regimes' "smarter forms of authoritarianism" with a concomitantly smarter democracy promotion. Notwithstanding a growing consensus on the limits of working with MENA governments and the desirability that all social actors be included in politics, the EU has been wary of engaging with Islamists. As the latter reaffirm their status as the most credible and popular of opposition forces in the region, European hesitancy to back a political opening has intensified.

In Iraq, EU bilateral assistance for governance capacity building has increased, but most member states are reducing their presence in on-the-ground governance initiatives. In his chapter on Iraq (chapter 9), Edward Burke points out that, while European governments have stressed their desire to see the European Commission assume a more significant, Europeanized presence, the mandate and resources for this are still lacking. Ana Echagüe (chapter 8) argues that the EU has also failed to develop a comprehensive and coherent policy toward the states of the Arabian Peninsula. The plethora of strategic issues concentrated in the Gulf—energy, regional security, counterterrorism—has led to stability-oriented caution. While there never has been a very notable idealistic European aspiration to support democracy in the Gulf, there was a period of reform commitment after the attacks of September 11. This now appears to have evaporated. The Gulf has been the part of the Middle East where EU approaches have changed least from alliance building with autocratic regimes seen (simplistically) as bulwarks against radical Islam. Such caution is now aggravated by the financial crisis and volatility in international energy markets.

In a case apparently offering the prospect of significant European influence, Sofia Sebastian (chapter 3) argues that in the Balkans the EU has failed to provide a well-defined framework for promoting "democratic stabilization" while assisting in the process of European membership. This is evidenced by the back-loading of democratic conditionality and the shift of European funds in the Western Balkans from democratic stabilization to institution building and economic development. Once again, the focus is increasingly on cautious, stability-oriented reform rather than deep democratization.

In Central Asia, the European Union has increased its resources for democracy promotion since the adoption of the EU's Central Asia strategy in summer 2007. This can be seen first and foremost in plans for a strengthened political and human rights dialogue and increased resources for civil society funding. However, Alexander Warkotsch (chapter 6) argues that at the same time the EU has eschewed diplomatic pressure or highly political aid projects. In Central Asia the aims of EU policy must necessarily be modest; but even in respect to the achievable goal of improving economic governance, Europe has been extremely reticent. Examining another case dominated by energy governance and security concerns, Anna Khakee (chapter 10) points out that European commitment to democracy promotion has not been strong in Nigeria. Here, the complex sources of conflict and strategic judgments have militated against significant prodemocracy engagement on the part of most EU member states.

Hesitancy is seen in other European bodies as well as the European Union. Jos

Boonstra (chapter 5) contends that the OSCE is floundering and risks becoming a paper tiger. Even though the organization has established an impressive body of democracy and human rights commitments, continues to be a lead player in election monitoring, and runs democracy-related activities in a large number of its participating states, many of these states are divided on its function and future. The OSCE further lost relevance during the August 2008 war between Georgia and Russia, when it failed in its core tasks of conflict prevention and early warning.

In pointing to these limits of European democracy support we do not imply that the EU could, on its own and in all cases, ensure successful democratic transition even if its policies were flawless. As is now observed in almost every piece of writing on democracy promotion, change must come from within and be tailored to specific local contexts. Although these are now clichés, they are essentially correct in highlighting that international factors are in most countries a secondary factor. Many of the challenges associated with the democracy backlash and shifting international order may indeed be insuperable in the short term. However, our case studies demonstrate that the EU is far from maximizing the positive potential even of its secondary influence and, in many cases, is having a prejudicial effect on the prospects for internally driven reform.

Explaining Variation

Comparative volumes of European policies commonly focus on a single region. By including a wider range of case studies in this volume we hope to increase the scope for comparison. Our cases do indeed reveal interesting elements of variation. So, how do we explain the differences among the case studies? It is clear that a range of explanatory factors is at work, including the contrasting nature of strategic deliberations across the countries, the role played by distinctive domestic political structures in these countries, and the variation in the EU's leverage over them. The chapters recount how concerns over leverage condition the substance of democracy strategy in terms of the potential for coercive compliance, the setting of meaningful incentives, and the viability for democratic dissemination through institutionalized multiactor frameworks of cooperation.

This reinforces the point that an eclectic lens is required fully to capture the precise nature and extent of variation in EU policy. The tendency of identity-oriented accounts of EU normative power to exclude geopolitical factors militates against this. Detailed case studies, to reveal the precise variations in linkages between domestic and international factors, have been identified as key to advancing understanding of democratization's external dimensions (Severiano 2008). This realization has begun to influence the study of EU policies (Pace, Seeberg, and Cavatorta 2009; Stewart 2009). Such studies have also been suggested as a means of shedding more nuanced analytical light on general concerns now expressed over the backlash against democracy (Burnell and Youngs 2009). Our chapters seek to tease out the extent of such differentiation.

In Central and Eastern Europe, policy has obviously been determined by the link between democratization and accession. In a sense, this renders the region at least a partial exception to the EU's downgrading of democracy promotion. Here, the imposition of strict conditionality has been seen as integrally entwined with EU self-interest. In this region, most academic debate has focused on the question of compliance: why and through which mechanisms the region's new democracies came to converge with EU norms and rules. However, as Geoffery Pridham (chapter 2) shows, in several states the work of democratic conditionality remains unfinished. An additional safeguard clause was applied to Romania and Bulgaria, and it did have some positive effect on outstanding reform commitments in these two countries. Even here, however, full consolidation and deep cognitive change remain elusive, and EU policy deliberations remain far from straightforward.

Natalia Shapovalova (chapter 4) argues that EU policy toward Ukraine increasingly wields the influence of deep integration, increased assistance for institution building, and conditionality. Here, however, such positive substance and leverage continue to be offset by a specific set of concerns relating to Russia. In the Balkans, the EU has an obvious incentive to encourage democratic reforms before letting in the region's aspirant candidate states. At the same time, doubts exist over the relationship between the democracy and conflict resolution agendas. Though the EU has remained a motor for reform in the region, it has failed to adjust the enlargement framework to the different problems that beset Balkan countries and to provide real incentives to persuade them to accept the terms of democratic stability while integrating into the EU.

In the Middle East and North Africa, concerns over the Arab-Israeli conflict, Iran's nuclear program, and counterterrorist cooperation suffice to ensure that the stability focus stays in place. The differing strategic priorities of southern states are reflected in disunity among European governments. There is also a strong link to domestic politics through Muslim immigrant communities. The consensus is that the current situation is not sustainable, but differing views persist regarding possible alternatives. Since no member state can convincingly shift its approach alone, the status quo remains.

It is the growing geostrategic significance and energy importance of Central Asia that has undercut any determination to take a tough stance against this region's authoritarian regimes. In Nigeria, similar reasons lie behind the EU's generally weak commitment to democracy: oil and other economic interests, political concerns related to Nigeria's African great-power status, the fragile internal balance among competing domestic actors, and increasing migration.

The OSCE's problems largely result from the expansion and widening geographical focus of the EU and NATO, which have undercut the OSCE's niche added value in the Balkans and, to a lesser extent, in the countries of the former Soviet Union. Russia's reversal of democratic reform and determination to hinder U.S. and European democracy promotion has also resulted in Russian obstruction within the OSCE, especially in promoting democracy and monitoring democratic commitments.

Extracting from these individual cases, we can hone in on the factors examined in our case studies that help account for variation—and indeed the boundaries of such variance—in European policy across countries and regions. The cases reveal a mix of factors at work in conditioning EU democracy policies. Systematic comparison among the case studies can be organized around three factors. Adding nuance to the role played by these factors in explaining variation in EU democracy strategy is, we believe, our distinctive contribution to the literature.

1. The institutional structure of the relationship between the EU and the country in question is vital but not determinant. The standard observation is that the deeper the institutional relationship, the stronger the EU's leverage and bargaining power. The nature and effectiveness of European policy is then a reflection of how far the particular external relationship is built around prior acceptance of conditionality and the supposition of common European identity as paving the way for participation in the European project. Our case studies, unsurprisingly, offer some corroboration for this standard conclusion. In cases of thin network linkages and attenuated structural European power—as in Nigeria, Central Asia, and the Gulf—the EU is obliged to find less direct ways of influence. Where engagement is weak the EU seeks a more nebulous shaping of political attitudes and presents itself as a normative model, alternative to other great powers. However, the cases also caution that even when the EU enjoys significant bargaining power, its use of conditionality and diplomatic pressure is measured. As explained above (in the case of Central and Eastern European states, the Balkans, and Ukraine), the application of democratic conditionality has been far from uniform and is often molded to the

aims of other policy imperatives. It is too simplistic to assert that the EU merely replicates internal democratic norms as part of a self-sustaining institutionalist logic or an identity-driven normative dynamic. The institutional structure of EU relations with its partners does not entirely account for the variation that does exist between different cases.

2. Instead, the domestic political structures of each country play the most potent role in explaining variation in European policies. The case studies offered here corroborate the importance of reverse direction causality: namely how domestic political dynamics explain the nature of external actors' politics (Youngs 2009). Conditionality worked better in relatively stable Central and Eastern Europe than in the brittle conditions of the Balkans. Morocco has offered productive openings for EU cooperation denied by the specificities of Gulf politics. The vagaries and specificities of conflict in Iraq and Nigeria condition how and in what way the EU seeks to act there. Variation in domestic politics determines the access points for EU policy; the local demand for European democracy support; and the nature of the challenges to be addressed, whether basic liberalization, consolidation, or postconflict political restructuring. Critics ritually accuse democracy promoters of knowing nothing of local political specificities. Our evidence suggests that this is a simplistic and misplaced admonishment: diplomats move pragmatically with the flow of local particularities as they seek traction. The paucity of political will is greater than any insufficiency in nationally specific variation.

3. The varying nature of European strategic concerns is vital and multivariate. Of course, every study on democracy promotion points out how strategic interests often, even overwhelmingly, cut across democracy support. Our case studies again add some nuance to this standard picture. In each case, reasons of strategic self-interest drive as well as inhibit democracy promotion, even if it is the latter dynamic that in most cases has won out. What our studies also demonstrate is that the nature of strategic calculation can differ significantly and is itself mediated through domestic political structures. The implication is that we need to go beyond the standard dichotomy of democracy promotion versus security interest. Rather, work on democracy promotion must give due weight to the complex relationship between these two policy strands; the way in which geopolitics does not exist in isolation from the explanatory role of domestic structures; and the fact that the category of security interests covers a varied range of factors, with differing amenability to the democracy agenda.

Truncated Reform

Our case studies also caution against catchall conclusions in relation to the standard question of whether EU unity is increasing or decreasing. In relation to some aspects of policy, a single European policy can be detected. In other cases, a plurality of policies exists. In Iraq a modest strengthening of unity is in evidence, clearly from a very low base. In the Balkans, EU unity has always been curtailed, and there are few signs to suggest that it will tighten in the near future. The EU is clearly split on the question that could most help Ukraine's democratic consolidation, namely the offer of accession.

However, there is one aspect of policy that does seem to attract unity between member states and a degree of consistency across different regions. Although our case studies reveal variation, they also suggest homogeneity across diverse regions. This commonality is not sufficiently broad to talk in singular terms of the European approach to democracy—a tendency that, we believe, should be resisted. But it is significant that some elements of policy appear to remain constant across differences in domestic political structures and geopolitics.

This constancy is found in the fact that what is labeled democracy policy has in practice generally been aimed at governance changes rather than democratization. This can be said even about the use of conditionality in candidate states. It can be concluded that, through the external extension of EU rules, the EU supports certain aspects of governance reform more assertively than it does the political dimensions of democracy. It might be said that much EU reform activity occurs at the boundary between, on the one hand, governance issues that have little to do with democracy and, on the other, core democratic values. This is why it is often hard to give a straight yes or no answer to the question of whether the EU is indeed committed to promoting democracy through these types of governance rules transfer. However, it would seem safe to suggest that at least a sizable part of the funding that is defined as supportive of democracy is in fact not.

The chapters demonstrate that democracy is a multifaceted concept, consisting of many requisite components, and cannot be reduced to a binary present/not present distinction. Where the dividing line falls between support for good governance and support for democracy is difficult to determine with precision. Some aspects of democracy might be supported through the extension of external governance rules, but others clearly lie beyond this institutionalist model. Support for democracy is in effect divided between two institutional policymaking styles, one relatively technocratic, the other profoundly and increasingly strategic-securitized.

The influence of the latter is at best ambiguous. In short, disaggregating the concept of democracy helps clarify its place within European foreign policy. Recognizing democracy (and democracy promotion) to be multifaceted in nature sheds light on why the standard debate over whether the EU is normative or realist is not always helpful.

The transfer of certain governance rules generally proceeds when there are doubts at the strategic level over the desirability of pushing for wholesale democratization in a particular third country. The two policymaking logics are not necessarily mutually supportive. Support for increasing governance capacity can undermine any objective to open up decision making to popular scrutiny. At the level of democracy, understood as a political regime type, the EU is commonly reluctant to put its structural power to use. The EU is now routinely berated for imposing its one-size-fits-all model. This model might work at the regulatory level, but the evidence suggests it is a questionable way to institute systemic political change. The stress on extending EU governance rules may bring some modest political reform, but such rules merely substitute for a properly political strategy of democracy promotion. In this sense, our case studies shed a sober light on the limited effect of what are ritually painted as the relative strong points of European policies, such as socialization and deeply embedded network governance based on local ownership.

In sum, we contend that the thread running though European democracy policies is one of limited commitment across diverse regional contexts. We detect a fairly strong embedded preference for a truncated form of governance reform, indicative of how European governments conceptualize the process of political reform. At the same time, our case studies reveal variation. In isolating the key elements of comparison, we hope to shed light on the complex relationship among them. Succinctly stated, these elements are international influences, democracy-promoting policy instruments, domestic politics, and geostrategy. This approach certainly calls for a more careful and multifaceted approach to assessing democracy support than is often applied. Our skepticism is not meant to suggest that the EU tacks toward an entirely realist foreign policy, but in the field of democracy support its idealism is certainly at bay. At a time when hope is high for a post-Bush renewal of the democracy agenda, we hope that the observations in the following chapters spur useful policy and analytical debate.

REFERENCES

Burnell, P., and R. Youngs, eds. 2009. *New Challenges to Democratization*. London: Routledge.
Carothers, T. 2002. The end of the transition paradigm. *Journal of Democracy* 13/1: 5–21.
Checkel, J. T. 2001. Why comply? Social learning and European identity change. *International Organization* 55/3: 553–88.
Christiansen, T., and B. Tonra. 2004. The study of European Union foreign policy. In *Rethinking European Union Foreign Policy*, ed. T. Christiansen and B. Tonra. Manchester: Manchester University Press.
Diamond, L. 2008. *The Spirit of Democracy*. New York: Times Books.
Duffield, M. 2007. *Development, Security and Unending War: Governing the World of Peoples*. Cambridge, UK: Polity Press.
Fukuyama, F., and M. McFaul. 2007. Should democracy be promoted or demoted? *Washington Quarterly* 31/1: 23–45.
Gray, J. 2008. *Black Mass: Apocalyptic Religion and the Death of Utopia*. London: Penguin.
Habermas, J. 2006. *The Divided West*. Cambridge, UK: Polity Press.
Hurrell, A. 2007. *On Global Order: Power, Values, and the Constitution of International Society*. Oxford: Oxford University Press.
Hyde-Price, A. 2007. *European Security in the Twenty-first Century: The Challenge of Multipolarity*. London: Routledge.
Jünemann, A., and M. Knodt, eds. 2007. *European External Democracy Promotion*. Baden Baden: Nomos Verlagsgesellschaft.
Kagan, R. 2008. *The Return of History and the End of Dreams*. London: Atlantic Books.
Keane, J. 2009. *The Life and Death of Democracy*. London: Simon & Schuster.
Linklater, A. 2005. A European civilising process. In *International Relations and the European Union*, ed. Christopher Hill and Michael Smith. Oxford: Oxford University Press.
Magen, A., M. McFaul, and T. Risse, eds. 2009. *Promoting Democracy and the Rule of Law: American and European Approaches*. Basingstoke: Palgrave Macmillan.
McCormick, J. 2007. *The European Superpower*. Basingstoke: Palgrave Macmillan.
Pace, M., P. Seeberg, and F. Cavatorta. 2009. The EU's democratization agenda in the Mediterranean: A critical inside-out approach. *Democratization* 16/1 (special edition): 3–19.
Saul, J. R. 2005. *The Collapse of Globalism and the Reinvention of the World*. London: Atlantic Books.
Schimmelfennig, F., and S. Lavenex. 2009. EU rules beyond EU borders: Theorizing external governance in European politics. *Journal of European Public Policy* 16/6 (special edition): 791–812.
Schimmelfennig, F., and U. Sedelmeier. 2004. Governance by conditionality: EU rule transfer to the candidate countries of Central and Eastern Europe. *Journal for European Public Policy* 11/4: 661–79.
Schimmelfennig, F., and W. Wagner. 2004. Preface: External governance in the European Union. *Journal of European Public Policy* 11/4: 657–60.

Severiano Teixeira, N., ed. 2008. *The International Politics of Democratization: Comparative Perspectives*. Abingdon: Routledge.
Smith, M. 2004. Toward a theory of EU foreign policymaking: Multi-level governance, domestic politics, and national adaptation to Europe's Common Foreign and Security Policy. *Journal of European Public Policy* 11/4: 740–58.
Stewart, S. 2009. Democracy promotion before and after the "colour revolutions." *Democratization* 16/4 (special edition): 645–60.
Telo, M. 2007. *Europe: A Civilian Power? European Union, Global Governance, World Order*. New York: Palgrave Macmillan.
Tilly, C. 2007. *Democracy*. Cambridge: Cambridge University Press.
Vachudova, M. A. 2005. *Europe Undivided*. Oxford: Oxford University Press.
Whitehead, L. 2009. Losing "the force"? The "dark side" of democratization after Iraq. *Democratization* 16/2: 215–42.
Youngs, R. 2009. Democracy promotion as external governance? *Journal of European Public Policy* 16/6: 895–915.

CHAPTER TWO

Unfinished Business

European Political Conditionality after Eastern Enlargement

Geoffrey Pridham

Enlargement has been widely recognized as the most influential democracy promotion opportunity of the European Union (EU). The accession process certainly helped to push and entice post-Communist countries in Central and Eastern Europe (CEE) toward democratic consolidation. But the EU's success in bringing about essential political change in this region has not been unqualified. Doubts have remained over the depth and even the permanence of such change, since these countries ceased to be subject to EU leverage over political conditionality once they joined the EU.

The record among the new member states of CEE in completing the requirements of this conditionality is mixed, with significant cross-national variation. There have been some indications of a reluctance to follow up on progress achieved during accession, especially over specific conditions. Concern over this problem of follow-up on political conditionality after entry into the EU has increased since the two Eastern Balkan countries of Romania and Bulgaria joined the EU in early 2007. These two states have substantially failed to address their commitments to fighting corruption, confronting organized crime, and instituting judicial reform.

Official voices in the EU were concerned that this enlargement to the Eastern

Balkans, not long after the mega-enlargement of May 2004 to East Central Europe, would challenge the EU's absorption capacity. Even though a special regime of sanctions was introduced for these two countries—in effect extending conditionality into the first three years of membership, an unprecedented action—there were concerns that authorities in the two capitals would become complacent now that they had achieved their grand objective of EU membership. Such doubts were echoed in some circles in Bucharest, where for instance the editor of the Romanian magazine *Eurolider* noted: "Our politicians are doing their jobs only under pressure from the EU." In particular, these concerns focused on the "corruption, malfeasance, and criminality still so blatant in public life."[1] On the anticorruption drive, it was further reported: "The worry in Brussels is that much of the activity is designed simply to impress EU officials, with little political will to stamp out the culture of bribery or curb the mafia gangs who would take advantage of the new freedoms within the EU. There is a worry that after accession the two countries will have little incentive to continue a campaign that is dangerous and hard to enforce."[2]

There was an uneasy sense that these two new member states were less prepared for the integration tasks ahead than countries joining the EU during previous enlargements had been. This mood of doubt and caution in Brussels was not new, for it followed these two countries' checkered record on conditionality matters during the accession process. On occasion there had been severe criticism from Brussels over political conditionality failures, especially in Romania, and even some scarcely veiled threats to call a halt to the Romanian negotiations.

Some pessimism about the completion of EU conditionality after accession has also been present regarding the post-Communist countries that joined the EU in 2004. Altogether, this has made the question of postaccession compliance over political conditionality—the satisfaction of which was decisive in both opening negotiations and granting membership—a matter that now requires serious discussion. This chapter addresses this problem using selected case studies.

After relevant background on the EU's policy on political conditionality, attention concentrates essentially on the case of Romania, which became notorious shortly after joining the EU for dismissing the reformist minister who had driven judicial reform. Romania had been commonly regarded over the past decade as the laggard of Eastern enlargement, after an incomplete process of democratization following the fall of Ceausescu. But was that negative reputation justified in the light of the country's record on political conditionality? Or did Romania in fact demonstrate an ability to adapt and change, as is required of candidate countries negotiating EU membership? And how did Romania's record look when set against that of other CEE entrants?

For comparative purposes, therefore, the record on following up political conditionality since May 2004 is considered with reference to the two new member states of Slovakia and Latvia. Romania's record on compliance with this conditionality up to its accession in 2007 is discussed as a basis for judging what was still required during early membership. Finally, the case of postaccession Romania is assessed in this comparative light with some reference to developments since that country entered the EU in January 2007.

These cross-country comparisons enable the common institutionalist dynamic of enlargement to be situated within the context of domestic and geopolitical specificities (addressing the three explanatory variables outlined in chapter 1). Conclusions are then drawn about the longer-term prospects for the EU's political conditionality based on this analysis.

Political Conditionality during Eastern Accession

The EU's political conditionality only really began to develop in the mid-1990s in response to pressures over Eastern enlargement. After the original Copenhagen conditions of 1993, requiring candidate countries to have "achieved stability of institutions guaranteeing democracy, the rule of law, human rights, and respect for and protection of minorities," the EU's policy underwent significant changes, with an expansion of its concerns into substantive or qualitative democracy. At the same time, satisfying the political conditions became locked into accession procedural deadlines, while progress in doing so was, after 1998, bureaucratically monitored by the European Commission on an annual basis. These changes strengthened the EU's leverage over candidate countries and routinized the pressure on them to address deficiencies in meeting the conditions (for a fuller discussion, see Pridham 2007a).

It is necessary, however, to highlight certain limitations placed on EU conditionality policy before turning to country responses. First, the conditionality policy did not begin until the CEE countries in question were already some way down the road of democratization. This amounted to a restriction on conditionality's effect on first-order democratization tasks, and it meant that the EU was faced with the emerging imperfections of these new democracies. Second, there were limitations relating to the commission's top-down bureaucratic approach, expressed in its reluctance to engage with political actors like parties and those from civil society. Essentially, the European Commission preferred to deal with national governments in candidate countries and to rely on them to manage other domestic actors. Third, once negotiations were under way, implementation defects became increasingly apparent, leading to a concern about administrative capacity in CEE candidate countries. The relatively short period in which the EU sought to instigate change in candidate countries meant that this problem remained at the time of EU entry, in May 2004. The main achievement of political conditionality during accession was, in short, formal (such as creating new structures and agencies) rather than substantial (that is, creating concrete changes on the ground), which required more time as well as sustained effort.

Brussels' anxiety about the mounting implementation problem in the enlarged EU was one major reason that the new Barroso Commission (formed in late 2004) exercised a tougher conditionality policy for enlargement, beginning with Romania and Bulgaria in their final stage of accession. Due to geopolitical considerations, these countries had benefited from an unusual flexibility in the exercise of political conditionality at the time they were granted membership negotiations in late 1999. Hence there was potential for conditionality problems to arise as negotiations proceeded. They received this invitation in return for their support for NATO in the Kosovo war in spring 1999, despite their failures, especially Romania's, to satisfy political and economic conditions (Commission of the European Communities 1999). Accordingly, the accession treaty of 2005 with Romania and Bulgaria contained a safeguard clause, allowing for a one-year delay in EU entry in the event of final obligations not being met. In this way, Romania and Bulgaria were subjected to the stricter approach of EU conditionality. The Barroso Commission felt that its predecessor had been too relaxed about implementation of the conditions, as indicated in a speech by the enlargement commissioner Olli Rehn soon after assuming office.[3] The view was taken that Romania in particular had been treated too leniently. Additionally, there were indications from inside the Enlargement Directorate-General that Rehn wished to follow a tougher line on Romania so as to differentiate himself from his predecessor, Verheugen.[4] The result was thus a new firmness toward Romania over conditionality in the final stage of accession.

This safeguard clause amounted to an unprecedented extension of conditionality beyond the end of negotiations. According to the EU ambassador to Romania, the safeguard clause was "intended to preserve leverage" on the part of the EU, for the thinking was that "we need to find some instrument that will maintain pressure after the Treaty is signed."[5] While a safeguard clause was also applied to

Bulgaria, similarly providing for a possible delayed entry by one year, the one applied to Romania was much tougher. The clause provided for one year's delay in entry "if serious shortcomings have been observed in the fulfillment by Romania of one or more of the commitments and requirements" relating to four specific items of the competition chapter and seven of the justice and home affairs chapter. The latter included "the acceleration of the fight against high-level corruption," which had meanwhile been included as an item in the *acquis* to reinforce its legal power (Commission of the European Communities 2005).[6]

This novelty in conditionality policy rendered the question of postaccession compliance more visible. Early academic work on this has focused on rationalist and constructivist notions. The former notion envisages unfavorable conditions for postaccession compliance because conditional incentives no longer apply, although the new regime of benchmarks and sanctions for Romania and Bulgaria may be seen as an attempt to extend those conditional incentives to some degree. The latter notion—rather more optimistically—hypothesizes that habit may turn the instrumental approach to meeting conditionality during accession into one of conviction based on European political values. The key point is whether such persuasion and identification, marginalized and superseded previously by conditional incentives, now come to the fore and "acquire a causal impact on compliance," whereby "social" instruments such as socialization effects and peer-group shaming become influential with new member states (Sedelmeier 2006, 147, 160).

Taking account of such different possibilities, four (not necessarily mutually exclusive) scenarios of postaccession dynamics may be hypothesized: routinization and status quo bias, pressure for reversal, monitoring external pressure, and social learning.

1. Routinization and status quo bias are matters of continuity established through habit. They extend beyond EU entry and point to the possible durability of political conditionality. They argue, first, that rules become set and political behavior routinized through the practice of adaptation created during accession and, second, that conditionality-induced change acquires some dynamic quality, so that the implementation of the conditions becomes (perhaps increasingly) difficult to reverse.

2. Pressure for reversal, by contrast, takes the view that impositional Europeanization has its own limitations and risks. The top-down political conditionality of Brussels during accession left little space, and for that matter little time, for value commitment to develop. New member states, having not been involved in or consulted over conditionality matters, are no longer downloaders of EU rules, and

therefore they may seek to overcome at least the less-favored conditions. It is assumed that the constellation of veto players changes somewhat after EU entry and that it is not simply a matter of national governments freely making their strategic choices.

3. Later monitoring of external pressure suggests some limited continuity with accession but is more diffuse and less coercive in the absence of the membership incentive. It is more diffuse in the sense that pressure other than direct monitoring of the political conditions assumes an importance following EU entry. Such pressure may include formal constraints such as those in the Treaty of Amsterdam (1997), which gave contractual force to European political standards and created a new procedure for dealing with a "serious and persistent" breach of these by member states. Provision for sanctions is written into accession treaties, allowing for a form of postaccession monitoring at least for a restricted period, as is the case with Bulgaria and Romania. It should be noted here that some international organizations continued to monitor new member states for a while on some political conditions, such as the Council of Europe has for human and minority rights.

4. Social learning is a question not so much of continuity as of strengthening and even deepening progress on political conditionality in the postaccession stage. Changes may occur in norms and beliefs, with a shift from instrumental to conviction-based behavior on the part of the political elites; these changes possibly involve other actors relevant to the implementation of conditionality. Added to this, the transnational socializing influences of early EU membership, through working regularly and intensively in all of the EU institutions and participating in European policy networks, may increase understanding of European integration. This would favor policy transfer, which would reinforce political conditionality.

Postaccession Compliance in Slovakia and Latvia

Evidence from states that joined the EU in 2004 presents a mixed picture of postaccession follow-up to political conditionality. To some extent, there is cross-national variation; but there is also a significant variation according to the domestic political conditions. As a whole, evidence of a postaccession dynamic developing over conditionality, deriving from advances made during accession, is not overwhelming. Significant social learning from the experience of conditionality during accession has yet to appear. However, over some of the conditionality issues other actors, notably nongovernmental organizations (NGOs), have assumed a role of pressure agents. Furthermore, while some opportunistic relaxation has been evident, there has been no general pattern of backtracking except over fighting corruption in the new member states from CEE.

The record of two new member states, Slovakia and Latvia, on postaccession compliance during 2004–09 provides a useful comparative perspective on the Romanian case. Using bilateral comparison of these two countries, conclusions can be drawn with respect to the four hypotheses presented above. Discussion concentrates on those two difficult EU political conditions, instituting judicial reform and fighting corruption, about which Romania proved wanting for most of its accession period.

Judicial Reform

While external pressure was provided by the commission's regular reports up to 2002, the essential will to produce change came from reformist elements in the governing elites in these candidate countries. In Slovakia the main drive for reform came from the two successive justice ministers in the reformist Dzurinda governments of 1998–2006: Jan Carnogursky and Daniel Lipsic. There is an obvious comparison here with the Romanian justice minister, Monica Macovei, although in the Slovak case the reformist ministers were in office for much longer. Both ministers were committed reformers and benefited from the determination of their own party—the Christian Democratic (KDH)—to fight corruption and make the judiciary transparent. The KDH's determination had an anti-Communist edge that aimed at overcoming legacies from the former regime. At first checked by some internal coalition reservations, this commitment was eventually decisive in carrying through judicial reform even after the commission stopped monitoring it in late 2002 (Pridham 2008, 442).

Thus while the EU was important in setting the agenda and providing bureaucratic pressure, the sustained momentum for this reform came mainly from within Slovakia. As a result, judicial independence was instituted through a constitutional amendment in 2001 with a new judicial council: special courts were created to try major corruption and organized crime cases, and a new system in the administration of justice and criminal law was recodified. Furthermore, each year new judicial appointments were made, gradually reducing the proportion of Communist-era judges (Prochazka et al. 2004, 144). Altogether, much progress was achieved in the first half of the 2000s; but the "purification" of the judiciary remained incomplete on EU entry. The various achievements still needed to be consolidated, focusing on systemic changes and developing human resources

(Prochazka et al. 2004, 144). The new Fico government, elected in 2006, showed rather less sympathy than its predecessor toward judicial reform. Its justice minister, Stefan Harabin, had as a major figure in the judiciary been hostile to this. One of his first initiatives was to propose abolishing the special court, although this effort largely failed because of differences inside the coalition, and eventually its position was weakened through new legislation. Thus a different official attitude to judicial reform had emerged, one not constrained by considerations of EU accession. In June 2007 a report from Freedom House noted that "judicial independence is coming under increased pressure" as a feature of antiliberal trends in Slovakia (Pridham 2008, 443). This became even clearer once Harabin moved from being minister to becoming head of the Supreme Court in 2009 and began using his new position to root out reformist elements in the judiciary.

In Latvia there was a marked slowness in addressing judicial reform. However, in 2004 new administrative courts began to operate with the aim of relieving and speeding up the work of other courts (Kucs and Feldhune 2005, 41–42). These new courts introduced a new cadre of judges who were recruited in a competitive way and were often young, thus largely free from the Communist experience.[7] Judicial independence was based on Article 83 of the Constitution and a law on judicial power, buttressed by several international human rights treaties. Nevertheless, there remained weak points regarding the financing of courts (still under the Ministry of Justice), the general selection of judges, and the quality of judges appointed for life, not to mention periodic attempts by the political executive to influence the judiciary on specific cases. A court administration was created in 2004 to create self-government for the judiciary, but this remained under the supervision of the Justice Ministry. Thus full separation of the judicial and executive powers has not really taken place (Kucs and Feldhune 2005, 37–38).

Sustained political will to reform was less present compared with Slovakia. There was one reformist justice minister in the 2002–04 government of the New Era Party, which was supportive of this reform and of fighting corruption. This government change, together with the EU's persistent push for reform, eventually bore fruit, though mainly after Latvia's EU membership was already granted (in late 2002). Reforms include a new criminal code and new criminal procedures (2005), a law on judicial salaries and pensions (2006), efforts at shortening court proceedings and improving access to courts, as well as provisions for legal assistance and judicial training.[8] In other words, judicial reform did not stop with EU entry. The accession process had created a certain dynamic, but essentially the drive for reform came from individual ministerial commitment and was facilitated by a campaign on this issue by the newspaper *Diena* (Pridham 2009, 74). As with Slovakia, it remains to be seen how much further progress consolidates the changes and overcomes the remaining defects of this reform.

Fighting Corruption

Both Slovakia and Latvia—along with Romania—received severe ratings from Transparency International during the accession period. These three, plus Turkey, were identified as the most corrupt governments in Europe. A tenacious problem undermining the political will for change was close and often corrupting links between the political class and economic interests. This varied somewhat within the CEE, being especially pronounced in Romania.

In Slovakia, EU influence was transmitted through new policies and new agencies. The second Dzurinda government (2002–06) instituted direct measures to fight corruption and also reformed the public finances of the judiciary and the health care system, leading to a decline in corruption in the banking system (Sicakova-Beblava 2006, 611). According to the head of Transparency International Slovakia, a more relaxed attitude toward corruption was later evident in Bratislava (Sicakova-Beblava 2006), and most ministries have reduced anticorruption activity. The new Fico government, in power from 2006, has proved ambiguous over fighting corruption and indeed hostile to international or NGO reports critical of its lack of activity in this area. Accordingly, some promised reforms have lapsed, while in some sectors corruption has remained largely untouched. Although the media have come to play a relevant part in publicizing concrete corruption cases, the outlook after five years of EU membership remains uncertain and sobering (Pridham 2008, 445).

In Latvia the course of fighting corruption has been different from that in Slovakia but also similar in revealing political hostility to the fight. While the political class in Latvia has apparently been more directly involved in corrupt practices than in Slovakia, the Corruption Prevention and Combating Bureau (KNAB)—established under the EU and other outside pressures—developed into an independent actor and became distinctly more assertive than its Slovak equivalent. The EU was decisive in putting corruption on Latvia's political agenda in 1997, for according to a KNAB senior official, "if there had not been accession to the EU, I don't think politicians and government would have been so keen to act."[9] But this agency was not set up until the Repse government (2002–04), which was led by a brand new party committed to the issue. By February 2003 the new agency was fully operational. In short, during the accession process EU pressure set the agenda but did not in fact bring about much change except for the agency's creation. In the words of one Latvian expert on corruption, politicians in that country "followed EU pressure legally, institutionally, but not politically" (Cigane and Karklina 2005, 125).

The establishment of KNAB at the end of the accession period turned out to be the real starting point for change, leading to new laws and to decisive action in corruption cases (Cigane and Karklina 2005, 125). A momentum developed due to the activism of KNAB, to the complementary role of Delna (Transparency International Latvia), to the commitment of Repse's party, to support from State President Vike-Freiberga, and to exposure by the media.[10] For instance, the daily newspaper *Diena* lobbied hard for changes, such as appointing a general prosecutor.[11] However, this very activism of KNAB eventually produced a determined counteraction from the political class and especially from Prime Minister Kalvitis (in office 2004–07), whose own party came under investigation for its corrupt dealings. In summer 2008 the conscientious head of this agency, Aleksejs Loskutovs, was forced out of office under parliamentary pressure, with the intention that someone more compliant would replace him. This action clearly would not have happened during EU accession, for it would have damaged the country's chances of membership. Quite obviously, since EU entry the political class has been acting more freely according to their own political interests, without EU constraints over issues like corruption (Pridham 2009, 76).

The first five years of EU membership, in the cases of Slovakia and Latvia, show no uniform pattern of conditionality follow-up. Although there are similarities between the two countries, such as the difficulty in rooting out corruption even under persistent external pressure, there are also differences, such as progress on judicial reform, largely explained by the timing of reformist commitment. In several instances, real progress began only toward the end of the accession process, as sometimes domestic factors were at work in slowing down change.

By and large, this analysis confirms the overall importance of the EU's leverage with regard to political conditionality during the accession process, despite its limited effects. In particular, the nature of the European and national interaction counts most, as it provides the context in which reform-inclined political leaders may (or may not) seize the opportunity to push for change with European backing. Moreover, even if the EU's main achievement was merely formal—such as new structures and an enlarged statute book to buttress them—a framework for action following accession was formed. Yet the question remains how deep and how permanent EU-promoted political change really is. More time is needed to answer this with any certainty.

While rationalists' fears about unfavorable conditions for postaccession compliance have not been completely borne out, neither have the hopes of the constructivists been fully realized. The dynamics of the accession process, which did much to carry forward conditionality, have obviously disappeared. What has followed instead is a more diffuse situation regarding pressure for change. Given this mixed picture, the following can be concluded regarding Slovakia and Latvia in light of the four hypotheses.

1. Routinization and status quo bias are clearly factors, in that new structures and agencies created to satisfy Brussels during accession have remained in place and, depending on their performance, may continue to provide a pressure point for further action on the conditions. This is also true of the legislation carried out for the same purpose. Furthermore, there is some evidence of EU initiatives bearing belated fruit after EU entry was granted. One might add that being a member state often exposes a country to media glare in other member states as well as at home, and this might continue to act as a pressure—although not always consistently given the sometimes arbitrary nature of media attention.

2. Pressure for reversal does not show a pattern. There are, however, ad hoc examples. The antireform intentions of the new Slovak justice minister in 2006 is a blatant example, as are the hostile maneuvers against the anticorruption agency in Latvia by politicians who resent its actions. Such episodes are worrying; but more time is needed to establish whether they portend real patterns of reversal.

3. Monitoring external pressure shows how diffuse the situation is. Some other international actors have continued for a while to monitor certain conditions (such as the World Bank's reports on administrative capacity in new member states), but they have lacked the power of the EU's preaccession leverage. In addition, any effects of transnational networking as a channel for pressure within the EU have yet to be seen.

4. Social learning has been evident in late accession or postaccession countries that have shown political commitment to introducing reforms, including judicial reform in Slovakia and fighting corruption in Latvia. Such examples demonstrate the importance of committed reformist ministers, who have EU backing and some help from the media. Unfortunately, these leaders represent small sections of the political class, and their effort depends on their remaining in office. Social learning

at a deeper level than that of elites is probably necessary to complete the process of change sought by the EU's political conditionality, but this requires much more time and of course greater consensus.

Romania's Compliance during Accession

The European Commission's annual reports on Romania from 1997 to 2004 track the country's democratic standards during the accession process, thus allowing for an identification of patterns. While some conditionality difficulties were common among CEE candidates, notably judicial reform and fighting corruption, other problems were particular to Romania. Some were problems of degree: for example, Romania was continuously rated by Transparency International as the most corrupt country in Europe. Difficulties unique to Romania include slowness in instituting economic reform (which also might indicate reservations about regime change), low state capacity, a weak policymaking environment, and slowness in meeting European political standards.

Romania's low state capacity was of concern in Brussels during the accession process. Antireform forces in a national bureaucracy hostile to modern management methods were particularly strong. Apart from inherent bureaucratic conservatism, such reform was not helped by the resistance of the Social Democratic Party (PSD, which was in power during most of the negotiations period) to abandoning its political control over the state machine. It was this factor, building on old habits from Communist times, that ultimately checked administrative professionalization—notwithstanding fine-sounding strategies for administrative reform, such as civil service laws produced to please Brussels. In the end, it was pressure for dealing with the EU during negotiations and other accession business that brought about some limited change, in particular in the working methods of those sectors of the administration in regular contact with Brussels. But these changes did not presage wider reform. It remains to be seen whether the everyday experience of being an EU member state eventually brings about the necessary change.

These limited improvements in state capacity were relevant to the implementation of the EU's political conditions, for initially this was a matter of government response or initiative and of legislation. The ultimate problem has been putting these conditions into practice. Here the conditions vary as to what factors—or for that matter, what actors—are responsible. Thus while some conditions are essentially dependent on executive action (as with decentralization, in which Romania was rather slow), other conditions depend on behavioral and cultural compliance as well as executive action.

Throughout the accession period, the two most difficult areas of conditionality for Romania were judicial reform and fighting corruption. Both conditions were inherently complex. Judicial reform involved not merely changing professional structures but also dealing with a judiciary largely appointed under the Communist system and still subject to political influence under the country's post-Communist democracy. Judicial elites were not only innately conservative but also inhibited by a past pattern of political subservience.

Corruption was even more difficult to confront, since it affected several layers of public life, with political elites regarding the state and the economy as a reservoir for furthering personal or party-political interests. Accordingly, the sincerity of the political elites—especially of the PSD during the years of EU negotiations—about embracing reforms was challenged, since embedded party-political interests were in several ways threatened. Above all, the problem of corruption concerned respect for the rule of law, but it also affected other issues of reform (notably administrative and judicial), the professional operation of the public services (notably the health sector), and economic transformation.

The record of the PSD government of fighting corruption is one of persistent reluctance. At the insistence of Brussels, the government drew up the necessary plans and strategies to fight corruption, but their implementation was not forthcoming. This lack of action was the subject of EU concern after negotiations began in 2000 and increasingly as the years of negotiations drew on. The February 2004 European Parliament report was harsh in its criticism of Romania's record and raised doubts about the government's seriousness (European Parliament 2004). There was renewed pressure for suspending negotiations. The EP listed the necessary measures about fighting corruption at the political level, implementing the independence of the judiciary, reinforcing freedom of the media, ending ill treatment at police stations, and action on the moratorium on child adoption. On corruption, the EP demanded that "first and foremost there must be the political will to eradicate corruption, for only this will lead to a change in attitudes" (European Parliament 2004, 5–7, 16).

As the 2004 election approached, with mounting scandals and growing public sensitivity to this issue, EU pressure began to have more effect. One marked difference between the main political forces concerned this very issue of fighting corruption, which by the end of Romania's accession emerged as the most difficult condition to implement. In the December 2004 election, which led to the center-right replacing the PSD in power, fighting corruption was the principal issue. This was mainly due to the PSD's hardly disinterested reluctance to fight corruption while in office during the previous four years. Clearly, the center-right saw political and electoral advantage in exploiting this issue—a case in which partisan interests converged with an EU political demand—although elements of conviction were also present in their position.[12] As negotiations were concluding, and with Brussels requiring some action on conditionalities, the new Tariceanu government made decided efforts to meet several of the political conditions. However, it should be pointed out that the arrival of the new center-right government coincided with the imposition of the safeguard clause on Romania and Bulgaria at the end of 2004. This had a significant influence on Bucharest.

There were some reservations in Bucharest at first over the safeguard clause, although some in government circles, notably in the Ministry of European Integration, saw advantages in it since it helped to maintain accession discipline up to the last possible moment.[13] As it happened, the safeguard clause speeded up reform efforts in some areas, recalling previous Romanian reactions during accession when under pressure. This was most evident regarding judicial reform, in which progress stalled until the EU directly linked it with the safeguard clause (Parvulescu and Vetrici-Soimu 2005, 11). Renewed initiatives for judicial reform owed much to the commitment of the minister of justice, Monica Macovei, a former NGO leader and human rights lawyer turned politician. Her nonhierarchical approach to reform, which also had implications for fighting corruption, was that nobody was above investigation. This approach elicited rancor in political establishment circles, but it had the enthusiastic blessing of Brussels, thus strengthening this last-minute drive to make significant changes in the judiciary, among them a strategy for judicial reform.[14] The revised strategy for judicial reform, adopted in response to the safeguard clause, emphasized efficiency and accountability, improving coordination between the ministry and the EU delegation.[15] As a result, Romania now found itself exonerated over judicial reform for accession purposes.

Nevertheless, fighting corruption continued to be a difficult question. The EC's interpretation of required action on high-level corruption was "serious evidence that high-level corruption is being tackled," with a few notable "big fish," as a sign to the public, to be shown "on the way to prison."[16] But as the legal adviser to the Romanian president on anticorruption noted, catching these big fish was a more political than a legal operation, for normal judicial procedures require operative proof, which is difficult to obtain in corruption cases; and the procedures tend to last a long time—well beyond the schedule of the safeguard clause.[17] At the same time, the fight against corruption ran into problems of political elite consensus. In early 2006 the Romanian parliament resisted passing anticorruption legislation, thus placing the reformist center-right government in an embarrassing position with regard to Brussels, which expressed outrage over this blatant act of parliamentary irresponsibility.

When viewed strictly within the general EU context, the Romanian case reveals a particularly difficult policymaking environment during accession. It demonstrates that, despite EU enlargement being an essentially asymmetrical and top-down process, sufficient account needs to be taken of domestic factors in candidate countries—a lesson to be applied to other accession countries despite the peculiarities of the Romanian case. In Romania, political and party-political interests in particular came to the fore and inhibited implementation of some of the political conditions. In the end, EU pressure and persistence combined with the changing domestic situation to push through some late changes.

What lessons may be drawn from this case of political conditionality? Above all, that conditionality's prospects depended crucially on the specific dynamics of accession. The pressure on candidate countries to satisfy the political and other conditions is relentless and takes advantage of the leverage that Brussels enjoys over them of EU membership. Preaccession conditionality put judicial reform and the fight against corruption on the political agenda, giving these issues a special visibility. It raised the political cost of nonreform, conferring some strength on reformist leaders while putting status quo defenders on their guard (Noutcheva and Bechev 2008, 140). Brussels' hand was certainly strengthened by the extension of conditionality's application beyond the end of negotiations. Persistent and at times interventionist EU pressure—more pressure than was generally true of the other CEE countries that joined in 2004—was decisive in explaining Romania's eventual compliance with, and partial implementation of, political conditionality. Romania was by any definition a difficult accession case; but this was recognized early on and influenced the EU's policy toward that country.

Romania's Postaccession Compliance

The somewhat negative postaccession compliance in Slovakia and Latvia suggests a cautious, even pessimistic, prospect for Romania, which had more difficulty complying with political conditionality during accession than these other two countries. The extra leverage employed by the EU and its unusual interventionism in Romania only underlines that external incentives were crucial in driving Romania's compliance.

Several factors dampen expectations about the safeguard policy for monitoring conditionality during early membership. First, EU leverage is much weaker under this policy than during accession, when the prospect of membership drives the desire to change. On the contrary, Romania's acquisition of membership gave that country equality of status with other member states—a matter of sensitive national pride—which made monitoring politically (and psychologically) more awkward compared with the asymmetric relationship of before. Commission officials admitted in interviews with the author that this demand by Romania (and Bulgaria) for equal recognition created a delicate position for the EU. Second, there are inherent difficulties with the implementation of some of the EU's political conditions due to either elite reservations or problems of wider or deeper behavioral adjustment. Fighting corruption is the issue that most demonstrates this problem. Third, political will and capacity is central. While the change of power in 2004 did open the way for some reformist drive to emerge, particularly over judicial reform, this owed much to individual ministerial commitment and lacked any viable or stable political consensus.

This deficiency came starkly to the fore soon after Romania's EU entry in January 2007, when the justice minister, Monica Macovei (one of the main reformist forces), was dismissed from her post during a government crisis. This move, which almost certainly would not have occurred during accession, caused alarm in Brussels, where Macovei was regarded as Romania's guarantee of continued reform.[18] But political elite resentment against her reformist drive had grown. One may indeed say that an antireform consensus had developed especially over corruption, encouraged by the release from EU accession constraints and notwithstanding the safeguard policy.[19]

Hindrance in the fight against corruption has come consistently from the parliament, such as curtailing the powers of the National Integrity Agency set up in 2007 and restricting the role of prosecutors in modifying the procedural code, despite repeated EU warnings that such actions compromised its ability to fight organized crime (Romanian Academy Society 2008, 5–6). The record of Romanian members of Parliament has led to accusations in the European Parliament and the press in other EU countries that the Parliament in Bucharest was sheltering corrupt politicians.[20]

At the same time, various NGOs in Romania have continued to provide public pressure on this issue, while President Basescu has remained committed to fighting corruption. In September 2008 he suspended the labor minister, the first case of a minister being dismissed over corruption charges.[21] But his very actions on this issue have brought him into serious institutional conflict with Parliament, thus again demonstrating the striking absence of political consensus on reform. This enduring problem has been demonstrated more recently by persistent efforts by Parliament to obstruct the work of the anticorruption agency (DNA)—such as by refusing to allow the investigation of top officials—and to dismiss its assiduous head, Daniel Morar, who had been appointed by Macovei.[22]

Under the safeguard policy, half-yearly reports are issued on Romania's progress in meeting political conditionality demands. These tend to express dissatisfaction and a need for greater efforts in fighting corruption (some progress is admitted in judicial reform). The July 2008 report concludes, "Romania presents a mixed picture. It has put the fundamental elements of a functioning system in place. But the foundation is fragile and decisions on corruption are highly politicized. Each step in the right direction engenders a divisive internal political debate, fostering legal uncertainty. Commitment to reform by Romania's key institutions and bodies as well as with regard to different benchmarks is uneven" (Commission of the European Communities 2008, 6).

Taking into account the rather anodyne wording that sometimes veils problems in such reports, this represents serious criticism indeed. An independent expert report on the anticorruption fight in Romania from a former EU adviser is more direct about the cynicism of that country's political elite. It concludes, "Many of the measures that were presented before accession, to be instrumental in the fight against corruption, have been deliberately blunted by the parliament or government immediately after accession. . . . All major pending trials concerning high-level corruption, started just before accession and only after many years of hesitation, have now been aborted and are, probably definitely, abandoned for all practical purposes" (De Pauw 2007).

A press observation on the 2008 report notes that De Pauw's criticism still applied.[23] The European Commission, though admitting some progress in judicial reform (such as the adoption of new criminal and civil codes) and some positive effects of Romania's National Integrity Agency, concluded: "However, these reform efforts remain fragmented, they have not yet taken root firmly and must still produce practical results for Romanian citizens. The Parliament should show the full commitment to pursuing the fight against high-level corruption. A lack of initiative in addressing local corruption is apparent. Jurisprudence remains contradictory, and a legislative patchwork of emergency ordnances and implementing rules creates legal insecurity. Overall, a broad-based political consensus behind reform and an unequivocal commitment across political parties to real progress has still to be demonstrated."[24]

Altogether, Romania's political conditionality after accession is rather unimpressive. Regarding fighting corruption, Romania's story is a sobering example of failure to carry forward further change in the face of political interests and political cynicism. It was this problem above all that explained the growing view in the EU that the safeguard policy was not working well and was creating frustration among member states that the new members of Romania (and Bulgaria) were "not honoring their commitments."[25]

To summarize postaccession compliance in Romania so far and with regard to the future, the four hypotheses used earlier may be applied.

1. Routinization and status quo bias have been evident with the less complicated conditions, such as the stability of democratic institutions. It could also be seen as embracing formal achievements of judicial reform, even though the commission has warned about the fragility of such institutions. This is illustrated by parliamentary efforts to replace the head of the anticorruption agency, thus drawing a parallel with the Latvian experience. Furthermore, Romania has lacked the partial reformist drive exemplified by Slovakia, where important reforms in other sectors had an indirect effect in reducing corruption.

2. Pressure for reversal, given the sense of "impositional Europeanism" in Bucharest, was to be expected—all the more because of party-political obstacles to embracing genuine reforms already evident during the accession period. It is clear in a way more blatant than in the other two countries that the acquisition of EU membership released supporters of status quo interests from their defensive position during accession and equally helped to isolate reformist figures in Bucharest. But this problem was most evident over fighting corruption and was less pronounced over judicial reform, as reflected in the commission reports. Romania has been lucky not to have suffered from the sanctions regime under the safeguard policy, which provides for freezing EU funds in the event of serious backtracking from reform. The country has benefited from comparison with the worse record of neighboring Bulgaria over political conditions, notably the tough problem of organized crime and greater difficulties with judicial reform.

3. The postaccession monitoring of external pressure on Romania (and on Bulgaria) is subject to a new sanctions regime, which obviously lacks the leverage of the preaccession period and has so far had limited success. Nevertheless, as the

poorest EU member state, Romania would find the blocking of EU funds a painful experience, as has already happened with Bulgaria in summer 2008.

4. Social learning during the short reformist drive for judicial reform (to counter the political cynicism in Bucharest during the accession process) is not evident. Such evidence will depend on the composition and commitment of successive governments in the next few years. The prospects for any development of social learning, in the absence of a change in elite political culture, are not strong. As one reputable publication notes, "Romania has a culture which does not equate corruption with disgrace."[26]

Conclusion

This chapter reinforces the observation that the effect of political conditionality varies in accordance with domestic structures and circumstances. Romania is clearly the worst of the postaccession countries examined in this chapter, thus confirming its unimpressive handling of conditionality matters while negotiating for EU membership. It is clear also that its reputation as a conditionality laggard owes something to the elite culture of stagey opportunism that marked Bucharest's handling of conditionality matters and accession threats up to 2007 and to the shameless cynicism that replaced this opportunism once EU membership was assured. This explains the anger toward Romania among some (especially Northern) member states and their disillusionment with the safeguard policy.

Nevertheless, the case of Romania is not in principle so very different from the cases of Slovakia and Latvia in terms of difficulties with some political conditions and with maintaining a reformist drive in domestic circumstances when EU pressure lessens or disappears. The outcome so far has been that the completion of political conditionality has been only a partial success, while it is becoming increasingly clear that the failure to continue further with fighting corruption is now a cross-national trend among the new member states of Central and Eastern Europe. If Romania stands out it is because of the extent of the problem of corruption and its rootedness in that country's culture.

What about the longer-term prospects for the EU's political conditionality? A number of points may be made, which are all relative but do not altogether support the pessimism that comes from focusing narrowly and perhaps too intensively on the Romanian case. The real achievements of conditionality during accession remain despite attempts to reverse them; ironically, the setbacks since then with the removal of EU leverage over membership confirm the importance of external pressure in propelling change. It should not be forgotten that Romania made some progress concerning political conditions and that it would be politically a more backward country if it had not acceded to the EU. Meanwhile, the Romanian case has become something of an antimodel for accession conditionality and has itself helped to influence the tougher conditionality policy of recent years, especially with regard to implementation. Nevertheless, the EU will face even more difficult countries than Romania (and Bulgaria) if it pursues enlargement to the Western Balkans and then further east, for there the problems of post-Communist transformation are really intractable.

NOTES

This chapter draws on Pridham 2007b.

1. Christopher Condon and Theodor Troev, Romania and Bulgaria celebrate EU entry, *Financial Times,* January 1, 2007.

2. *The Times,* September 25, 2006.

3. Katja Ridderbusch, EU-Kommissar kritisiert Beitrittszusage fur Rumanien, *Die Welt,* December 10, 2004.

4. Interviews with author, October 2005, Brussels.

5. Jonathan Scheele, interview with author, November 2005, Bucharest.

6. Commission of the European Communities, news release, January 5, 2005.

7. V. Terauda, interview with author, July 2005, Riga.

8. I. Juhansone, interview with author, July 2006, Riga.

9. D. Kurpniece, interview with author, July 2006, Riga.

10. D. Kurpniece, interview with author; R. Karklina, interview with author, November 2006, Riga.

11. A. Ozolins, interview with author, July 2006, Riga.

12. A. Ilinoiu, interview with author, November 2005, Bucharest. Ilinoiu, commenting on the corruption issue, said that Basescu's "motivation" was "intrinsic" but was strengthened by "the EU factor."

13. L. Orban, interview with author, November 2005, Bucharest.

14. *European Voice,* April 27 to May 3, 2006.

15. I. Codescu, interview with author, November 2005, Bucharest.

16. O. Simons, interview with author, November 2005, Bucharest.

17. R. Vining, interview with author, November 2005, Bucharest.

18. EC official, interview with author, November 2008, Brussels. Macovei's sacking, this official said, "caused a shock effect, definitely; that would not have happened before EU entry." In April 2007, EC Commissioner Franco Frattini warned that if reforms initiated by Macovei did not continue then the EU might invoke special safeguards against Romania (www.euractiv.com).

19. Erleichterung in Bukerest, *Frankfurter Allgemeine Zeitung,* July 25, 2008.

20. See www.euractiv.com [August 19, 2008].

21. See www.euractiv.com [September 23, 2008].

22. Judith Crosbie, Beacon of Hope: Daniel Morar, *European Voice*, December 11, 2008.
23. Erleichterung in Bukerest, *Frankfurter Allgemeine Zeitung*, July 25, 2008.
24. European Commission, news release, July 22, 2009.
25. EC official, interview with author, November 2008, Brussels. This official commented that the Cooperation and Verification Mechanism was "not a great success; microprogress only was possible through this pressure, but globally it was considered not a success" and was unlikely to be repeated with further enlargement.
26. Mr Too Clean, *The Economist*, August 2, 2008.

REFERENCES

Cigane, L., and R. Karklina. 2005. Minimizing corruption. In *How Democratic Is Latvia: Audit of Democracy*. Riga: Commission of Strategic Analysis and Advanced Social and Political Research Institute, University of Latvia.

Commission of the European Communities. 2008. Report on progress in Romania under the cooperation and verification mechanism.

———. 1999. Regular report from the commission on Romania's progress toward accession.

De Pauw, W. 2007. Expert report on the fight against corruption/cooperation and verification mechanism, November 12–15, Bucharest. European Commission.

European Parliament. 2004. Report on Romania's progress towards accession.

Kucs, A., and G. Feldhune. 2005. The rule of law and access to justice. In *How Democratic Is Latvia: Audit of Democracy*. Riga: Commission of Strategic Analysis and Advanced Social and Political Research Institute, University of Latvia.

Noutcheva, G., and D. Bechev. 2008. The successful laggards: Bulgaria and Romania's accession to the EU. *East European Politics and Societies* 22/1: 114–44.

Parvulescu, S., and B. Vetrici-Soimu. 2005. *Evaluating EU Democratic Rule of Law Promotion: Country Report—Romania*. Bucharest: National Association of the Romanian Bars.

Pridham, G. 2009. Securing the only game in town: The EU's political conditionality and democratic consolidation in post-Soviet Latvia. *Europe-Asia Studies* 61/1: 51–84.

———. 2008. Status quo bias or institutionalization for reversibility? The EU's political conditionality, post-accession tendencies, and democratic consolidation in Slovakia. *Europe-Asia Studies* 60/3: 423–54.

———. 2007a. Change and continuity in the European Union's political conditionality: Aims, approach, and priorities. *Democratization* 14/3: 451–53.

———. 2007b. Unfinished business? Eastern enlargement and democratic conditionality. Working Paper 36. Madrid: FRIDE.

Prochazka, R., et al. 2004. Rule of law, legislation, and application of law. In *Slovakia 2004: A Global Report on the State of Society*, ed. G. Meseznikov and M. Kollar. Bratislava: Institute for Public Affairs.

Romanian Academy Society (SAR). 2008. At stake, the rule of law. Elections Brief 35. Bucharest.

Sedelmeier, U. 2006. Pre-accession conditionality and post-accession compliance in the new member states: A research note. In *Apres Enlargement: Legal and Political Responses in Central and Eastern Europe*, ed. W. Sadurski, J. Ziller, and K. Zurek. Fiesole: Robert Schuman Center, European University Institute.

Sicakova-Beblava, E. 2006. Transparency and corruption. In *Slovakia 2005: A Global Report on the State of Society*, ed. M. Butora, M. Kollar, and G. Meseznikov. Bratislava: Institute for Public Affairs.

CHAPTER THREE

The Balkans
European Inducements

Sofia Sebastian

A decade has passed since the launch of the stabilization and association process (SAP), the framework under which Western Balkan countries are moving closer to European institutions. But the prospect of European Union membership still seems distant for nearly all Balkan states. The European Commission's (EC) most recent (autumn 2009) progress reports remain critical of Western Balkan countries' reform processes. Even if the future of the Balkans lies within the EU, accession is still far off.

The SAP draws heavily upon the accession model used in Central and Eastern Europe, with the addition of a few conflict management policy tools such as refugee return. The accession process in the Western Balkans has, however, been more complex and protracted, as some of these countries have experienced more severe political ethnicization and have faced certain state-building and nation-building challenges in the wake of the Communist collapse (Gordon, Sasse, and Sebastian 2008). In fact, there is concern among European and international officials that the region's ability to move forward with the reform agenda is at risk from ongoing instability and dysfunctional institutions.

Only Croatia seems to be exempt from the spiral of instability, although European officials have warned even that country of the need to speed up reforms if it is to join the European Union before 2012. In Bosnia and Herzegovina (BiH), despite the signing of a stabilization and association agreement (SAA) in June 2008, democratization beyond precarious ethnic power-sharing arrangements remains blocked, and Serb leaders in Republika Srpska (RS) sought in 2009 to undermine the competences of the Bosnian state. Similarly, political infighting both within and between ethnic parties in the former Yugoslav Republic of Macedonia has not only slowed the reform process since the country was given candidacy status in December 2005 but has also put a heavy strain on the functionality of political institutions. Serbia signed an SAA in April 2008, but this was suspended the same day until further cooperation with the International Criminal Tribunal for the former Yugoslavia (ICTY) was forthcoming. Divisions along the nationalist divide and the future of Kosovo cast doubts on the country's direction. Compounding this fragile political scenario, the challenge in Kosovo presents further cause for concern, with potential for instability still running high.

Undoubtedly, the process of European Union accession has helped the Balkan region temper the sources of violent conflict that haunted it in the 1990s. The process has laid the foundations for a more or less stable democratization process, which is well under way in cases such as Croatia. But doubts remain over whether the SAP has been adequately designed to the region's specificities. Even if domestic politics are much to blame for the current state of affairs (political infighting in BiH, for example, has paralyzed Bosnian institutions for a long time), a closer look at the SAP in the Western Balkans is in order.

This chapter argues that, despite the fact that the prospect of EU membership and the concomitant conditionality have made the greatest contribution to stability and democratic development in the region, problems of policy inconsistency, unclear benchmarking, disillusionment over the still remote European perspective, and the gap between rhetoric and practical efforts have undermined EU policies and diminished the effectiveness of EU inducements.

One of the lessons to be learned is that, while the process of enlargement that involved Central and Eastern European (CEE) states offered a practical model for the EU's approach in the Balkans, the integration process cannot be replicated in the Western Balkan region. The EU needs to readjust its framework and take into full consideration the different problems that afflict Balkan countries. The chapter demonstrates how the particularities of these problems explain the different response to EU incentives relative to those seen in other cases covered in this volume, such as Ukraine and Romania. How European institutions respond to these challenges will prove critical for the future stability of the region. At present an abiding fear of recrudescent violence conditions democracy support efforts in a complex and not entirely positive fashion.

The Stabilization and Association Process

Following democratic changes in Croatia and the Federal Republic of Yugoslavia, the EC launched the stabilization and association process at the 2000 Zagreb summit. The process envisioned a new, ambitious agenda for the region. The Zagreb summit also launched a new EU program, the Community Assistance for Reconstruction, Democratization, and Stabilization (CARDS), with an endowment of €4.65 billion over the period 2000—06. CARDS was replaced in 2007 by the Instrument for Preaccession Assistance (IPA), a streamlined mechanism for the disbursement of funds within the SAP.

The launch of the SAP in 2000 represented an attempt to apply a more coherent, comprehensive policy framework in the region both by looking into the process of European membership of CEE and by simultaneously promoting stabilization, transition to a market economy, and regional cooperation. Indeed, the rationale behind the launching of the SAP was threefold (Commission of the European Communities 2006):

1. A credible prospect of European membership, together with a set of conditions attached to membership.
2. The need to encourage bilateral relationships.
3. The need for a more flexible EU approach tailored to the conditions of the Western Balkans.

The SAP was thus created "to accommodate a range of situations, from postconflict reconstruction and stabilization to technical help with matters such as the approximation of legislation to the core elements of the EU *acquis.*"[1] For Western Balkan countries, what was on offer was the chance to establish contractual relations with the EU through the signing of SAAs—along with the prospect of EU membership.

The conditionality framework attached to the SAP was designed to fit the situation of Western Balkan countries. Based on the conditions laid out at the 1997 EU Council, countries had to cooperate with the ICTY; reestablish economic cooperation with one another; respect democratic principles, human rights and minority rights, and the rule of law; privatize state-owned property; and introduce a market economy. Additional criteria were added progressively on an individual basis, depending on the stage or flexibility of the reform process. The SAP also built upon the 1993 Copenhagen criteria to progress toward EU membership, although SAP countries are not required to implement the *acquis communitaire* completely before the signing of an SAA; the SAP rather is the process whereby Western Balkan countries initiate their adjustment to the *acquis* and prepare themselves for EU entry. Only after the conditions laid out for the signing of an SAA are met are the countries concerned given a green light to sign the agreement, the first contractual relationship with the EU. After that, effective implementation of the SAA is a prerequisite for any further assessment by the EU of the country's prospects for accession.

Croatia gained official candidate status in June 2004 and opened membership negotiations with the EU at the end of 2005. While resolute in its efforts to become a member of the EU ahead of neighboring countries, Croatia's border dispute with Slovenia has undermined its prospects of joining the EU before 2012.[2] Croatia also still needs to increase its efforts to fight corruption before it stands a chance of joining the EU.

Other Western Balkan countries are at varying stages in their progression towards EU accession. Macedonia was the first country in the former Yugoslavia to sign an SAA with the EU (in April 2001), but escalating violence between the two major ethnic communities—which brought the country to the brink of open civil war—put the brakes on Macedonia's bid for European integration. Open warfare was avoided thanks to the signing of the EU- and NATO-sponsored Ohrid Agreement in August 2001. Macedonia's progress toward EU integration was delayed, however, and made conditional upon compliance with the agreement, which became a benchmark for assessing the reform process. Macedonia gained the EU's favor again in December 2005 (under the influence of the United Kingdom European Union presidency) when it was granted candidate status in recognition of the progress made.

Notwithstanding the confidence boost provided by this, the fact that membership negotiations have not been opened since then suggests that the granting of candidacy status was more a political gesture than a real concession.[3] The political crisis that followed the 2006 elections, which kept the government hostage to ethnic disputes and led to institutional paralysis for several weeks, cast doubts on the country's political maturity and prompted the EU to hold back on negotiations until further notice.[4] Macedonian hopes of opening membership negotiations have been dashed in successive annual progress reports, which have insisted on the need for the country to engage further in the reform process and have given no clear indication of when accession talks would open. The EC's latest report recommends the opening of accession talks with Macedonia, underscoring "convincing" progress in reform (Commission of the European Communities 2009a).[5] As of now, however, there is no sign that Greece will be willing to unblock the accession process.

In BiH the opening of negotiations conducive to an SAA was approved in November 2005, conditional upon the country taking measures "fully to cooperate with the ICTY, to implement the agreement on the restructuring of the police forces, to adopt and implement all necessary public broadcasting legislation, and to ensure sufficient legislative and administrative capacity to implement the Agreement" (Rehn 2006). The first round of talks for the SAA signing took place on January 26, 2006, and negotiations were completed by the end of that year. Making headway with the SAA was, however, more challenging than expected, primarily as a result of a failure to agree on a police reform package. Indeed, political infighting between ethnic communities and escalating nationalist rhetoric precluded an agreement on police reform before the deadline set by the EU in October 2007, which led to one of the most heated political crises in BiH since the war, with outright frequent confrontation not only between ethnic communities but also between domestic forces and the international community. The country came to a halt when Prime Minister Miroslav Spiric resigned over measures enacted by Miroslav Lajčák, who was serving as both the High Representative and the EU special representative (HR/EUSR) in BiH.[6] Lajčák's measures were meant to speed up the decision-making process in BiH. In November 2007 the Bosnian parties reached an agreement on police reform, putting the country back on the EU track. BiH initialed an SAA on December 4, and the final signing took place in June 2008, following a final agreement on police reform reached in April.

Notwithstanding the importance of this step, little progress has been made since then, and nationalist politics continue to gain resonance. A new crisis unfolded in May 2009, when the RS National Assembly passed a resolution aimed at undoing some of the accomplishments of the peace- and state-building process. The reaction from the international community was divided and slow, but in the end the newly appointed HR/EUSR Valentin Insko used the Bonn powers. These developments put Bosnia back in the spotlight and compelled the EU, by the fall of 2009, to take forceful action. The so-called Butmir talks, jointly supported by the EU and the United States, were set to have Bosnian leaders agree on constitutional changes aimed at easing Bosnia's EU bid and paving the way for the termination of the Office of the High Representative in BiH. As this book goes to press, the Butmir talks had failed to yield any substantive results and the 2009 commission report pointed to the "very limited" progress made by Bosnia in addressing EU accession criteria (Commission of the European Communities 2009b).

Accepted as a full participant in the SAP following the electoral demise of Slobodan Milšević in 2000, Serbia has experienced a bumpy ride toward EU membership, including the emergence of Montenegro and Kosovo as independent countries in 2006 and 2008 respectively. Serbia is the only country to have had SAP negotiations suspended, because of its failure to cooperate with the ICTY. Notwithstanding Serbia's capture of war crimes suspect Radovan Karadžić in July 2008, the issue of cooperation with the ICTY continues to interfere with its European aspirations and divides European countries over how to proceed. Though the EU decided to sign an SAA with Serbia in April 2008, the handing over of war crimes suspect Ratko Mladić to the ICTY became an absolute requirement for some countries before the agreement was ratified. The Netherlands in particular blocked the implementation of the interim trade agreement attached to the SAA until December 2009, when the UN's war crime prosecutor Serge Brammertz confirmed that Serbia's cooperation with the ICTY was progressing (the implementation of this agreement is a prerequisite for moving ahead with Serbia's integration process).

Both Montenegro and Kosovo have conducted SAP negotiations with the EU. Montenegro launched negotiations in 2006, signed the SAA in October 2007, and applied for EU membership in December 2008. Although the commission's 2009 progress report on Montenegro offers a relatively positive assessment of this country's compliance with EU criteria (Commission of the European Communities 2009c), the commission has failed to recommend the opening of accession talks. As for Kosovo, the EU started preaccession negotiations through an SAP tracking mechanism in 2002. This process has stalled, however, following Kosovo's declaration of independence in February 2008, in light of EU divisions over recognition of this country. The local conditions have been particularly cumbersome, including the Serb boycott of Kosovo's institutions and the coexistence of various international organizations (namely the EU Rule of Law Mission, the UN Interim Administration Mission in Kosovo, and the International Civilian Office) with different, and sometimes conflicting, mandates (Sebastian 2009a). The commission's latest report on Kosovo laments Kosovo's "limited progress" in addressing the EU accession criteria (Commission of the European Communities 2009d).

In sum, the process of stabilization and association in the Western Balkans suggests that, even if a merit-based approach—where objective principles are said to apply—has been formally laid out to bring the Balkan countries closer to European standards, in practice political decisions and divisions within the EU have taken primacy. The EU has offered short-term rewards—including the participation of Western Balkan countries in such community programs as the energy and transport markets and such ad hoc benefits as the framework for visa liberalization (approved only for Serbia, Montenegro, and Macedonia, in July 2009)— but three shortcomings have weakened the EU model for the region: the failure to give shape to its priorities with a united voice; the failure to provide a credible European perspective; and the failure to match rhetoric with resources in the promotion of postconflict, interethnic reconciliation.

The Quest for Unity

The postconflict nature of the transition process in the Western Balkans and the challenges associated with it—including the launch of European security and defense policy (ESDP) missions that fall under the council's jurisdiction—have obliged EU policy in the region to traverse the pillar structure and cut across the competences of both the council and the commission. These institutions' differing actors, interests, and working cultures led to the formation of differing priorities and procedures, undermining the EU's ability to speak with one voice and stripping EU inducements of their potential for influence. As a commission official stated, "on paper and formally, it is possible to make the EU speak with one voice, but in practice this is very difficult, and less now with so many members. Messages are not firm, and the EU cannot make clear promises."[7] While the commission should have the leading role in the region, another commission official stresses that the deployment of forces and the conflicting interests of member states tend to make the council's position outrank the commission's.

These problems have been remarkable in the past, with the differing priorities of each institution colliding on numerous occasions, contributing to confusion over the requirements to be fulfilled and weakening the incentive potential of long-term rewards. In BiH, for example, the commission has always advocated an end to the Bonn powers and a return to local sovereignty, as these powers contradict the spirit of the European project, but "the Council has been more cautious and keen on maintaining the international presence."[8] As of late 2009 there was broad agreement on the need to scale down the Bonn powers and to close the Office of the High Representative (OHR). The United Kingdom and the Netherlands, however, remain in favor of maintaining the international envoy for as long as needed. Divisions also remain over the role of the EU special representative in the post-OHR era. The main point of contention centers on the nature and scope of the powers of a "strengthened EUSR" (Sebastian 2009b). While some countries recognize the need to give the EUSR "extraordinary powers," to be used in cases of threats to the country's territorial integrity, others argue that the enactment of such powers will undermine the country's bid for EU accession.

Similarly conflicting approaches can be seen in other situations, such as Macedonia's upgrade to official candidacy under the British presidency in 2005. "This was a political gesture to provide the region with stability, but now, as a result, the Commission has to deal with a very challenging and complex case for EU accession."[9] A similar constraint was forced upon the commission with the creation of the EU-sponsored union of Serbia and Montenegro in 2003. Though the council's interest in promoting security and stability fostered the creation of this union, it soon proved to be ill suited to compliance with the commission's requirements for the implementation of the SAP. One European official recalls that once the union was created, SAP negotiations became unmanageable, involving fifteen members —five from Serbia, five from Montenegro, and five from the union.

While the EU has attempted to tackle the problem of speaking with many voices by addressing institutional rigidity (the Lisbon Treaty is the most recent attempt) and by calling upon its members to ensure consensus, continuing internal divisions have a significant effect on EU policy toward the region. In Serbia, for example, divisions over how to align the country with Europe in the face of clear defiance on the part of nationalist forces have led to tardiness in EU responses to developments in the country. The problem in Serbia has been the need to reconcile two goals that seem incompatible, namely supporting an EU-supervised independent Kosovo and bringing Serbia into the Western fold, which means full compliance with the EU reform agenda and cooperation with the ICTY. Certain European countries, such as the United Kingdom, supported signing an SAA with Serbia without Mladić being handed over to the ICTY, in order to support pro-democratic forces within the country following Kosovo's declaration of independence in February 2008. Other countries, including the Netherlands, remained doubtful about the wisdom of offering too many concessions. It is argued in international circles that lack of resolution over Serbia allowed domestic actors to play EU division to their advantage.

The issue of constitutional reform in BiH is another example of how divisions within the EU have given domestic actors the upper hand, reducing the EU's influence in the country. As a party official in BiH stresses, "domestic actors perceive there is a fight between the major actors within the EU and use it to advance their interests and goals, be it just for the advancement of their goals or simply to buy time and do nothing, denying reality and what needs to be done."[10] The issue of constitutional reform also represents the best example of how unclear benchmarking has left domestic politicians confused over how to proceed. Dino Abazovic laments that the role of the EU has always been ambivalent. "In constitutional reform in BiH, they did not say what needed to be done, what are the standards and what are not. They do not send clear guidelines because it would open debates at home."[11]

Similarly, the head of BiH's Directorate of European Integration, Osman Topcagic, stresses that during constitutional deliberations, "there was no single position from the EU." Now, "you occasionally hear statements from European politicians, members of the EU Parliament, that Bosnia cannot join the EU with the current constitution . . . but it would help to have a better understanding of the requirements, to have a more general discussion." This view is shared by a European official, who states, "there are not really standards in the real key areas where Bosnia needs to move forward, especially in police and constitutional reform."[12] Thus the EU's enlargement policy in the Western Balkans appears to be plagued by some of the same dilemmas that it confronted during the enlargement process in Central and Eastern Europe (CEE), especially in relation to the implementation of the political criteria (as explained in the previous chapter). These include the challenge of operationalization, the lack of clear benchmarks, and imprecise measurements, which politicize the conditionality framework (Henderson 1999; Hughes, Sasse, and Gordon 2004; Sasse 2005).

These criticisms have prompted the EU to adjust its strategy occasionally, although the lack of clear criteria continues to be an issue. As a case in point, criticism over the EU's conduct on constitutional reform in BiH has belatedly compelled the organization to include this issue as an ostensible priority. At the time of writing (October 2009), an attempt to reinject momentum into the constitutional reform debate led by the Swedish presidency at the Butmir negotiations has proven insufficient to produce a breakthrough. The EU has again failed to provide clear guidelines on this question. It is still not apparent what the status of constitutional reform will be within the process of EU integration—whether it will become an express condition for accession or simply a reality that BiH will need to address in the coming years rather than within a specific time frame.

Divisions within the EU have increased as a result of the challenges emerging from Kosovo. Indeed, EU efforts at simulating unity in favor of the recognition of its independence have met with failure, with Spain, Greece, Cyprus, Romania, and Slovakia siding with Serbia. EU divisions over Kosovo set the EU mission in Kosovo (EULEX) off to a difficult start. While EU member states promised to support the mission irrespective of their position on Kosovo's status, in practice, EULEX suffered from these tensions during its early months of operation. Indeed, a question remains over how the EU relationship with Serbia will be affected by developments in Kosovo and by EU divisions on this issue. While some member states insist that Serbia must recognize Kosovo's independence as a condition for entry into the EU, others oppose this position. Such divisions not only exposed the EU's pervasive failure to speak with one voice but also provided Serbian politicians with another opportunity to use EU divisions to their advantage. As President Tadić stated, "One of Serbia's great allies in [the] policy of defending the country's territorial integrity is the fact that there are countries in Europe that have no wish to ever recognize Kosovo. And as long as such countries exist in Europe, it will be nigh on impossible for Europe to set Serbia such a condition."[13] The EU's complex agenda in Serbia has also compelled the EU to devote enormous resources and energy into keeping Serbia on track while supporting Kosovo's independence, often to the detriment of other priorities in the region, such as in BiH (Sebastian 2009b).

Thus although the EU has managed to define its Balkan vision in a much clearer way since the launch of the SAP in 2000, and has also given a European rationale for reform in the region, it continues to send mixed signals, undermining the potential of its inducements to work. As a result, not only is the EU perceived as speaking with many voices, which profoundly affects the way domestic elites regard the process of European integration, it also produces contradictory, conflicting policies in the region, opening the door for politicians to play on EU divisions.

Enlargement or Balkan Fatigue?

In addition to the often conflicting voices within the EU, so-called enlargement fatigue and the failure to deliver on the European perspective offered to the Western Balkans in 2000 also compound the problem of failing inducements. While the decision to offer the prospect of European integration to a rather unstable region in the early 2000s was remarkable, failure fully to engage in the region's reform process has rendered European efforts ineffective in the short to medium term.

There is widespread confusion within the EU not only about the way to approach major challenges in the region but also about the direction the EU should take regarding the next enlargement round. Even if the Lisbon Treaty improves the EU's institutional coherence, the financial crisis has placed further strain on the EU's consensus regarding the issue of enlargement. The formal commitment to Balkan integration remains, and the enlargement machinery rolls on (primarily thanks to the commission's duty to comply with the EU's previous commitments). But there are strong disagreements not only between the commission and the council but also among member states as to how to—or indeed, if to—proceed with the next enlargement round.

Increasingly, positive wording on accession is included in formal EU statements only after acrimonious discussions and pressure from Balkan countries.[14] Member states raised the additional hurdle of the EU's absorption capacity needing to be tested before further enlargement. Some member states even hinted at the possibility of adopting alternative strategies for Balkan integration. German Chancellor Angela Merkel suggested in 2006 a "privileged partnership" for the region as an option for closer ties with the EU.[15] As a result, the enlargement process in the Western Balkans has become not only more uncertain but also more cumbersome than in previous rounds. "The introduction of the absorption capacity [criterion] has meant in reality that there are three new conditions in place, namely the economic absorption capacity, the institutional one, and the preparedness of European public opinion."[16] All of these problems add hurdles to the Balkan accession process, compounding the "moving target" problem that beset the CEE enlargement (see for example Hughes, Sasse, and Gordon 2004).

Notwithstanding the voices firmly supporting enlargement—namely the United Kingdom and new member states—divisions cast major doubts on the prospect of EU membership and affect domestic players' calculations. This has had a major effect on countries such as BiH and Macedonia, whose local politicians have adopted a passive approach toward the EU's reform process, "delaying or avoiding key issues" (Batt 2006). Furthermore, in BiH, "nationalistic rhetoric [has] undermined the country's reform agenda" (Commission of the European Communities 2007b), and politicians such as the RS prime minister, Milorad Dodik, have overtly challenged the European project. In Serbia the EU's inconsistent approach has made almost 50 percent of the population believe that the policy of constant conditioning and blackmailing is the main obstruction in the way of Serbia's European bid.[17]

The continued lack of a timeframe for accession denotes uneasiness on the part of the EU about the next enlargement, with the Turkey impasse contributing to Europe's discomfort. The problem is that there are, as one European official explained, two incompatible agendas.[18] On the one hand, the offer of European accession needs to be clearer and more tangible than ever before in order to soften the effect of Kosovo's independence on the region. The initiation of an SAA with Serbia in November 2007 should be understood in this context. On the other hand, the EU's internal crisis and the reluctance of some member states to deepen the enlargement commitment slow down the pace of the process and leave a big question mark over prospects for the Western Balkans joining the EU in the foreseeable future. A commission official also stresses, "The problem is that the EU and the international community do not have a strategic vision of the region. There are some general goals, like integrating the region into the EU, but with respect to engaging further and dealing with big challenges, the region is moving not because we've thought thoroughly about it but because it's pulled along by previous commitments."

Both the European Commission and the European Parliament, which take a more committed stand than the council on Balkan integration, have criticized the council's ambiguous position. The EC enlargement commissioner, Olli Rehn, voiced concern in a speech delivered to members of Parliament in Strasbourg after the Salzburg meeting: "If we were to go wobbly about the Western Balkans' European perspective, our beneficial influence would be seriously eroded, just when the region enters a difficult period of talks on Kosovo's status."[19] One European official asserted that, while the issue of economics was significant in previous enlargements, "the absorption of the Western Balkans will not cause major economic distress for the Union: it is a relatively small market (the Western Balkan population equals that of Romania), and its absorption into the EU would require a relatively small economic effort compared to the effort made in previous enlargements."[20]

During the last two years there has been a renewed Balkan commitment among some European countries. Both a Greek initiative, presented in November 2007, and France's apparently transformed stance on enlargement indicate a shift within the EU in relation to WB accession. The so-called Greek package was aimed at boosting European progress in the Balkans and at counterbalancing the grim prospects revealed in the commission's yearly progress reports. Aiming to invigorate the Thessaloniki agenda and Greece's role in the region, the measures included the allocation of further European Union funds and a plan for visa liberalization for Macedonia, BiH, Serbia, and Montenegro. The Greek initiative also encouraged the Union to sign SAAs with the remaining countries as soon as possible and grant candidacy status to all countries before 2009. Though most of these initiatives have been partially accomplished, the global financial crisis seems to have now undercut the EU's renewed focus on the Balkans. Indeed, although the Czech Republic and Sweden intended to put the Balkans high on the agenda during their 2009 EU presidencies, the global economic crisis turned out to be of higher priority.

Given that the financial crisis (and the ratification process of the Lisbon Treaty) has diverted the EU's attention to economic and EU matters, it is more pressing than ever for the Balkans to present a credible case for membership. Western Balkan countries have to ensure that so-called Balkan fatigue (that is, the lack of progress in the reform agenda and the ongoing instability in the region) does not prevent member states from disengaging from further enlargement. As a Western diplomat in BiH stated, "even if the danger of the impact of enlargement fatigue in domestic politics is still real, these countries need to do as much as possible, as soon as possible, so as to make it impossible for the EU to say no or to delay entry."[21] The fact that the region continues to suffer complex social, political, and economic problems reinforces the EU's uneasiness about further expansion.

Stabilization and Interethnic Divisions

One of the greatest challenges facing the EU's approach to the Western Balkans is helping the countries in the region to overcome deep interethnic divisions, which are by now institutionally and politically embedded. This particular challenge is most disruptive in cases such as BiH and Macedonia, in which a complex set of power sharing and minority guarantees has been institutionally secured. In contrast to its (reasonably successful) experience in assisting relatively homogenous countries to adjust formally to EU standards, the EU has been less effective in compelling change in contexts in which the state is challenged by interethnic divisions.

Since the first SAP annual report, released in 2002, European officials have pondered the ethnic complexity of the Western Balkans and hinted at the need to adjust the process of enlargement to the particular conditions of the region. The agenda for the Thessaloniki summit, for example, states that "the EU supports activities, initiatives in the Western Balkan countries promoting social cohesion, ethnic and religious tolerance, multiculturalism, return of refugees and internally displaced persons, and combating regressive nationalism" (Council of the European Union 2003). More recently, the council encouraged political parties in the region "to deepen political dialogue and cooperation, including on inter-ethnic relations, in order to move ahead in the accession process" (Council of the European Union 2007a) and to stop nationalist rhetoric (Council of the European Union 2007b). "The region as a whole needs to move forward in building modern democracies and developing a political culture of dialogue and tolerance" (Commission of the European Communities 2007a).

However, there is a gap between the EU's declared goals and its actual efforts on the ground, contributing to a European inability to prompt Balkan societies to move beyond ethnicity as a basis of political and social organization, especially when ethnic divisions are rampant.[22] This gap is revealed in two ways: in the ill-defined formulation of "(democratic) stabilization," the component of the SAP designed to address postconflict issues but that has been practically subsumed under assistance to refugee return (and reconstruction); and in the shift of resources from projects devoted to democratic stabilization to institution building and economic development. This gap confirms that the EU has failed to provide a well-defined framework for understanding and addressing the policy implications of promoting "(democratic) stabilization" while assisting in the process of European membership. As a European official acknowledged, "there is a big institutional problem. We thought at the beginning that this was a postconflict situation. Then we needed to do institution building but we didn't have any recipe for addressing these problems. We didn't know how to do this."[23]

Though the CARDS program had the task of assisting the Western Balkans both in adjusting to European standards and in overcoming interethnic divisions and the legacies of war as a way to "stabilize" the region (Commission of the European Communities 2002a), the EU has fallen short of addressing the latter in a practical manner and with appropriate resources. CARDS allocations for democratic stabilization provide ample evidence of the emphasis placed on refugee return to the neglect of other activities that could additionally contribute to building trust among ethnic communities. From 2001 to 2006, before the IPA's inception, democratic stabilization efforts in the Western Balkans were devoted to two main priority areas, namely refugee return (with a particular emphasis on reconstruction and infrastructure rather than on effective integration of returnees) and civil society. Of these two, refugee return received the great majority of funds available, while civil society figured marginally. In BiH, for example, refugee return received around €25 million, €24 million, and €20 million a year over the 2001–03 period, while civil society and media reform received less than €3 million in 2001, a figure that plummeted to €1 million in 2003. Similar gaps between refugee return and civil society allocations were common in countries where refugee return was a priority. As an official in BiH stresses, "The EU has not been good at investing in civil society. It has been very limited."[24]

There has been a growing disparity between the funds devoted to democratic stabilization and the funds devoted to institution building, administrative reform, and socioeconomic development, showing the EU's preference for replicating models that worked elsewhere. Democratic stabilization received significant resources under CARDS in the early years of its implementation, but these allocations have decreased significantly since 2003. In BiH, for example, allocations for democratic stabilization decreased from around €20 million in 2003 to around €7 million in 2004 and €3 million in 2005 and 2006.

More recently funds dedicated to refugee return have begun to decrease, despite the commission recognizing that the reintegration problems faced by returnees remain acute (Commission of the European Communities 2007a). Furthermore, rather than CARDS and IPA assistance being redirected toward other areas and activities that promote democratic stabilization and interethnic coexistence, it has been readdressed to support formal institutional structures in an effort to help Balkan countries adjust to EU standards and laws. Activities in BiH, for example, are mostly devoted to the development of the private sector and state-level institutions, including the tax and justice administrations and border management. Likewise, in Macedonia, CARDS funds are mostly focused on judicial reform, border management, the fight against crime, and gradual harmonization with the EU's legal framework.

In addition to the allocation gap, civil society programs have fallen short of addressing interethnic deficits in Balkan societies, despite the numerous pledges to devote SAP funds to this end. The 1999 council report marking the launch of the SAP claims that, "Particular emphasis will be given, through civil society organizations, to the post-conflict rebuilding of consensus, to conflict resolution, and to the lightening of the psychological burden consequent to war" (Council of the European Union 1999, 5). Assistance programs have, however, failed to include these goals in their activities. Initial civil society programs in BiH, for example, were mostly devoted to media reform in order "to develop the technical and management capacities of the public broadcasting sector" (Commission of the European Communities 2002b, 3), which suggests an approach to civil society that is institutionally based rather than oriented toward altering patterns of social and political behavior. While the commission reckoned in 2006 that progress in these areas had lagged behind and "greater effort is needed" (Commission of the

European Communities 2006, 5), IPA priorities have not differed from those of CARDS, and civil society programs continue to be funded along similar, circumscribed lines.

Notwithstanding the importance of supporting institution building in the context of the Western Balkans—given the record of dysfunctional and weak administration capacity—and the significant progress made in countries such as BiH, it remains uncertain to what extent these societies have succeeded in building trust across ethnic lines and laying the foundations of functional states. A United Nations Development Program BiH survey, for example, reveals a "virtual breakdown" in social trust, with only one out of fourteen respondents (around 7 percent of the population) expressing trust in others (United Nations Development Program 2007). Furthermore, ethnic divisions are disruptive not only at the social level but also, and more prominently, at the political level and significantly affect the pace of the reform process and the effectiveness of EU inducements. In BiH, for example, ethnic mistrust at the political level often brings the political process to a halt, delaying the government's work. A report published by a local NGO, the Center for Civic Initiatives, reveals that the BiH government has complied with only 25 percent of its annual plan and that the Parliament has passed only 21 of 135 required laws.[25] Similarly, in Macedonia, the council regretted "the delays in reform because of internal political tensions, which diverted the focus of the country's political institutions away from the priorities of European integration" (Council of the European Union 2007a).

In sum, five years since the launch of the first SAP annual report, political and social distrust is rampant and reconciliation remains elusive. The EU should thus readjust the enlargement machinery by diverting further resources toward the promotion of interethnic consensus and devoting more energy to strategic thinking on how to address these issues while integration into the EU takes place. Should European institutions fail to concentrate further resources on this issue, they will miss the opportunity to use their carrots and sticks to prompt Balkan societies to move beyond fixed ethnic quotas as the basis for political organization and social cooperation.

Conclusion

For the EU to induce the Balkans to move ahead with the reform agenda, it should draw three lessons from the stabilization and association experience.

The first lesson is that the EU needs to engage further in the reform process and send clear messages that help prevent leaders from using the EU card for their own political ends. Internal EU divisions, uncertainty surrounding the SAP process as a result of the EU's growing hesitation regarding the next enlargement round, and the lack of benchmarks diminish the effectiveness of EU inducements and allow politicians to challenge the European project in favor of more immediate electoral and nationalistic interests. The EU's sticks and carrots do still possess strong leverage potential, however, and recent developments show how Balkan countries can respond effectively to EU pressure. The 2008 elections in Serbia and the fall 2007 crisis in BiH provide examples of how the EU can be an effective force for change when acting with resolve in the face of instability. While the measures enacted by HR/EUSR Lajčák on October 19, 2007, to speed up the decision-making process in BiH, incited one of the most intense political crises between the international community and the Bosnian Serbs, a determination on the part of the EU and the use of the European card put BiH back on track with Europe. On November 29, the prime minister of Republika Srpska, Milorad Dodik, who had harshly criticized Lajčák over the October measures, stressed that the prospect of EU membership was the reason for ending opposition to the measures enacted by Lajčák. But many challenges still lie ahead, and the EU will need to show similar resolve and determination in Kosovo to avoid further instability in the region and to keep the reform process on track.

The second lesson is that the EU needs to get past any sense of fatigue in its dealings with the Western Balkans and move beyond the wait and see policy. As an official of the commission declared, "We cannot use the wait and see policy; this approach would lead to failure for us and for them too. What we should do is to find ways that increase the sense of responsibility of political elites. This, in practice, is tremendously difficult, but we cannot wait and see." This is particularly important in light of certain upcoming challenges that are not as widely discussed as Kosovo's future status, including the end of the Bonn powers in BiH. Engagement with the situation in Serbia and Kosovo—which is keeping Brussels very busy—will require the EU to undertake early strategic thinking so that its leadership in the post-Bonn powers era is not ill conceived from the start. Judy Batt also calls for caution with regard to the overly optimistic expectations that can result from the signing of SAAs: "The assumption that EU integration along the prescribed SAA path will effect a fundamental political reorientation is as illusory with respect to Serbia as it is for BiH" (Batt 2007). This is particularly relevant in Bosnia, where political infighting among the three major ethnic groups continues to block reform. Further commitment will thus be needed in the face of new challenges associated with Kosovo and the end of the high representative's term in BiH.

The final lesson for the EU is that it needs to adapt the model used in previous enlargement processes, moving beyond restricted support to formal institutional structures. A closer look at the programs and policies in place under the SAP shows how limited the EU's know-how is in relation to the challenges associated with ethnic divisions and the gap between what is called for in print and the real resources on the ground. Even if European officials recognize such complexity in official documents and public statements, and hint at the need to adjust the process of enlargement to the particular conditions of the region, they fail to back up rhetoric with effective programming. The EU thus needs to be more creative in finding ways to build trust across ethnic communities, from the bottom up, and foment a civic sense of democracy to counterbalance the strong divisions that have become entrenched since the war. The EU could learn from projects implemented elsewhere, such as the peace and reconciliation program in Northern Ireland. Implemented with EU structural funds, since the mid-1990s this program has aimed to link socioeconomic and community development with reconciliation at the local level. It may offer important lessons for the EU in devising a holistic strategy for reconciliation in the Balkan region, a strategy not limited to physical reconstruction but rather extending to integration at the community level.

In sum, with Kosovo's independence declared and a new, complex, interpillar mission in place, there is a need for the EU to learn the lessons of its previous experience in the region and to adjust the Copenhagen accession model to one more suitable to the region. How the EU responds to the upcoming challenges, and how perceptive it is regarding the political and social nuances associated with the reform process in the region, will have an enormous effect on how fast the Western Balkans finds its way out of fragile stability and into EU institutions. This is not to suggest that the EU should diminish assistance to institution building and to meeting EU standards but rather that it should take on additional initiatives to shore up EU assistance and direct it to those institutional and noninstitutional challenges associated with the transition process in these countries.

NOTES

1. See The Western Balkan countries on the road to European Union, 2007 (http://ec.europa.eu).
2. The dispute centers on access to international waters, a dispute that has prevailed

since both countries became independent in 1991. In December 2008, Slovenia blocked Croatia's membership talks when Croatia's negotiation team presented various documents and maps that presumably resolved the dispute to the detriment of the Slovenian position. Both countries reached an agreement on an international arbitration mechanism in September 2009; but Croatia's opposition party rejected the agreement in the Parliament on October 31, 2009.

3. EC official, interview with author, June 2006, Brussels.
4. Ethnic Albanian parties boycotted Parliament for sixteen weeks.
5. The European Commission issued a document in early 2008 with a list of priorities that needed to be fulfilled before the start of membership negotiations (known as the 8 + 1 benchmarks). The benchmarks include a constructive political dialogue, effective enforcement of the new police law, political independence of the public administration, the strengthening of the judiciary's independence, and a sustained tracked record of anticorruption legislation (Council of the European Union 2008).
6. The positions of the High Representative in BiH (the international envoy entrusted to monitor the implementation of the Dayton Peace Agreement) and the European Union Special Representative in BiH were joined in 2002 with Lord Paddy Ashdown in order to streamline the reform process in this country.
7. EC official, interview with author, June 2006, Brussels.
8. Commission official, interview with author, June 2006, Brussels.
9. European Council official, interview with author, June 2006, Brussels.
10. Croatia Democratic Union (HDZ) party official, interview with author, July 2007, Sarajevo.
11. Dino Abazovic, interview with author, May 2007, Sarajevo.
12. European diplomat, interview with author, December 2006, Sarajevo.
13. Kosovo no condition for EU, *B92 News*, November 29, 2007.
14. M. Beunderman, EU membership goal clarified under Balkan pressure, *EU Observer*, March 1, 2006.
15. M. Beunderman and E. Krasniqi, Merkel moots privileged partnerships for Western Balkans, *EU Observer*, March 17, 2006.
16. Commission official, interview with author, June 2006, Brussels. See also Emerson et al. 2006.
17. According to an opinion poll conducted in June 2007 by Serbia's EU Integration Office, only 20 percent believe obstruction is due to Serbia's noncompliance with international obligations.
18. Commission official, interview with author, June 2006, Brussels.
19. EP, EC warns European capitals for doubts on accession of Balkans (dtt.net.com, March 16, 2006); UK says EU door must remain open for Balkans (dtt.net.com, March 21, 2006).
20. Commission official, interview with author, June 2006, Brussels.
21. Western diplomat, interview with author, December 2006, Sarajevo.
22. Only Macedonia has presented a framework in which interethnic relations are explicitly included in the overall EU strategy for the country. Compliance with the Ohrid Agreement—a peace agreement oriented toward setting up confidence, building measures between ethnic communities, and guaranteeing minority representation in government institutions—has become a benchmark within the SAP (see for example Council of the European Union 2004).

23. EU official, interview with author, June 2006, Brussels.
24. EU special representative, interview with author, December 2006, Sarajevo.
25. Bosnia: Top institutions slammed, *Birn,* November 29, 2007.

REFERENCES

Batt, J. 2007. Bosnia and Herzegovina: Politics as "war by other means" challenge to the EU's strategy for the Western Balkans. Note IESUE/COPS/INF(07)09. EU Institute for Security Studies, November.
———. 2006. The EU's foreign and security agenda and the Western Balkans. Paper prepared for joint seminar of the EU Institute for Security Studies, November 3, Dubrovnik.
BIRN. 2007. Bosnia: Top institutions slammed. November 29.
Commission of the European Communities. 2009a. *The Former Yugoslav Republic of Macedonia 2009 Progress Report.*
———. 2009b. *Bosnia and Herzegovina 2009 Progress Report.*
———. 2009c. *Montenegro 2009 Progress Report.*
———. 2009d. *Kosovo under UNSCR 1244/99 2009 Progress Report.*
———. 2007a. Enlargement strategy and main challenges, 2007–2008. Communication from the Commission to the Council and the European Parliament.
———. 2007b. *Bosnia and Herzegovina 2007 Progress Report.*
———. 2006. The Western Balkans on the road to the EU: Consolidating stability and raising prosperity. Communication from the Commission to the Council and the European Parliament.
———. 2002a. CARDS assistance program to the Western Balkans. Regional strategy paper 2002–2006.
———. 2002b. Multiannual indicative program. Annex 1, Bosnia and Herzegovina. Country strategy paper 2002–2006.
Council of the European Union. 2008. Council decision of February 18, 2008, on the principles, priorities, and conditions contained in the accession partnership with the former Yugoslav Republic of Macedonia, replacing decision 2006/57/EC. *Official Journal of the European Union,* March 19, 2008.
———. 2007a. Council conclusions on the Western Balkans. 2840th External Relations Council Meeting, General Affairs and External Relations Council, December 10.
———. 2007b. Council decision on the principles and conditions contained in the European partnership with Bosnia and Herzegovina and repealing decision 2006/55/EC.
———. 2004. Council decision of June 24, 2004, on the principles, priorities, and conditions contained in the European partnership with the former Yugoslav Republic of Macedonia.
———. 2003. The Thessaloniki agenda for the Western Balkans. Western Balkans council conclusions, annex A, General Affairs & External Relations Council (GAERC), June 16.
———. 1999. Conclusions of the General Affairs Council of June 21, 1999, based on the Commission communication to the Council and the European Parliament on the stabilization and association processes for countries of southeastern Europe.

Emerson, M., et al. 2006. Just what is this "absorption capacity" of the European Union. Policy Brief 113. CEPS.

EU Integration Office in Serbia. 2007. European integration of the citizens of Serbia: Trends. June 31, in Belgrade, Serbia. www.seio.sr.gov.yu.

Gordon, C., G. Sasse, and S. Sebastian. 2008. *Specific Report on the EU Policies in the Stabilisation and Association Process.* Report in the frame of the FP6 project MIRICO: Human and minority rights in the life cycle of ethnic conflict. Bolzano: EURAC.

Henderson, K., ed. 1999. *Back to Europe: Central and Eastern Europe and the European Union.* London: UCL Press.

Hughes, J., G. Sasse, and C. Gordon. 2004. *Europeanization and Regionalization in the EU's Enlargement to Central and Eastern Europe.* New York: Palgrave.

Rehn, O. 2006. Perspectives for Bosnia and Herzegovina. Speech to the European Parliament, February 15, Strasbourg.

Sasse, G. 2005. EU conditionality and minority rights: Translating the Copenhagen criterion into policy. Working Paper RSCAS 2005/16. Florence: EUI.

Sebastian, Sofia. 2009a. Making Kosovo work. Policy Brief 7. Madrid: FRIDE.

———. 2009b. No time to wind down in Bosnia. Policy Brief 17. Madrid: FRIDE.

United Nations Development Program. 2007. The silent majority speaks: Snapshots of today and visions of the future of BiH.

CHAPTER FOUR

Ukraine
A New Partnership

Natalia Shapovalova

In March 2007 the European Union and Ukraine opened negotiations for a new agreement. This will replace the Partnership and Cooperation Agreement (PCA), which was signed in 1994 in the aftermath of the fall of the Soviet Union. The prospective Association Agreement (AA) is inspired by EU agreements with acceding Central European countries in the 1990s.[1] It is designed to be a comprehensive cross-pillar agreement for integration, convergence, and cooperation in such areas as political reform, the rule of law, human rights, justice, home affairs, the Common Foreign and Security Policy (CFSP), and free trade between Ukraine and the EU (Emerson 2008, 26; Emerson et al. 2007, 12–13; Hillion 2007, 169–82). In addition, in May 2009 the EU launched the Eastern Partnership, which included Armenia, Azerbaijan, Belarus, Georgia, Moldova, and Ukraine. This policy offers the potential to increase EU engagement in the region.

The EU was widely seen as having played a significant role in Ukraine's 2004 Orange Revolution. But will these new initiatives be sufficient to help Ukraine with its faltering democratic consolidation? Will a new partnership serve as a better model than the loose European Neighborhood Policy (ENP)? This chapter outlines this latest phase of relations between the EU and Ukraine, examining the possible advances under the AA. It is often argued that the EU's most potent influence lies in the extension of its rules to partners under the rubric of highly institutionalized partnerships. So examining this most recent stage of post–Orange Revolution relations with Ukraine represents an important test case for EU democracy support. In this light, the chapter argues that, even though the EU may be offering strong democracy support, the AA is likely to have little effect on Ukraine's democratic consolidation.

Ukrainian Support for Accession

EU-Ukraine relations have developed rapidly since 2005 as a result of the EU's Eastern enlargement. The accession of Ukraine's neighbors—Poland, Slovakia, Hungary, and Romania—extended the EU's border to Ukraine.

With the 2004 Orange Revolution, Ukrainian society demonstrated its desire to be part of a united Europe, based on democracy, rule of law, and human rights. "We have chosen Europe: it is not just a question of geography, but a matter of shared spiritual and moral values," stated the new Ukrainian leader in the European Parliament two months after the revolution (Yushchenko 2005).

Although the Ukrainian population is regionally divided in terms of geopolitical orientation, with the western part of the country historically and culturally tied to Europe and the eastern and southern regions favoring close relations with Russia, there has been continuous countrywide majority support for Ukraine's membership in the EU.[2] This fact cannot be ignored by the political parties in Parliament. As a result, projects contradictory to Ukraine's European future, such as economic and political reintegration with Russia within the group called the Single Economic Space, have not been pushed by the major political forces since 2005.

All the political parties in the Ukraine Parliament except the communists are in favor of European integration. Our Ukraine Party, the political force of President Viktor Yushchenko, is the most consistent in its support for integration, making the issue a priority in its electoral campaigns, with repeated promises of achieving EU associate member status. It is the only political force supportive of Ukraine membership in NATO as a step on the road to EU accession. Although Bloc Yulia Tymoshenko (BYT) has not focused on EU integration issues in recent campaigns, nonetheless, the BYT is fully supportive of EU-related initiatives in Parliament and within the governing coalition.

The Party of the Regions (PR), led by Viktor Yanukovych, Viktor Yushchenko's rival for the presidency in 2004, is slightly more ambiguous in its European policy.

This is especially true during election campaigns, when it promises both closer ties with the EU and better relations with Russia. This reflects the makeup of its voters, who are generally from eastern and southern Ukraine, where pro-Russian sentiment is strong. PR's leadership considers EU membership a strategic and long-term prospect. Moreover, PR represents varied business interests, including both those who would benefit from European markets opening up to Ukraine and those who would suffer from the increased competition that EU integration would bring.

Regardless of their political orientations, Ukraine's largest business groups would be the main beneficiaries of economic integration into the EU. As such, they are interested in achieving improved conditions for international trade and investment and a more stable and transparent economic environment in Ukraine—for example, through better protection of property rights (Makobriy 2006; Puglisi 2008).

The wide support among Ukrainian parties for EU membership was confirmed by the adoption of the Verkhovna Rada Resolution "on the start of negotiations between Ukraine and the EU on a new basic agreement." Some 399 deputies, covering all parliamentary factions, voted in 2007 in favor of the resolution. Ukraine's legislature called for negotiations on an agreement leading to EU membership, with Ukraine's participation in the EU single market as an intermediate goal. Ukraine's legislature sought a legally binding agreement based on Europe's experience with CEE countries.

The consensus among the political elites, which is mirrored by popular support, is that EU integration is a strategic choice for Ukraine not just in terms of foreign policy but also in terms of Ukraine's internal development, representing a model for the country's modernization. Ukraine's future within the EU has come to be viewed as a guarantee of the country's further development as a consolidated democracy and market economy.

Democracy Promotion in Ukraine

The Orange Revolution was a breakthrough not only in Ukraine's transition to democracy and "Europeanization" but also in European policy toward Ukraine, as the EU played a crucial role in the resolution of the postelectoral political crisis (Youngs 2008). Due to the position taken by Poland and Lithuania, the CFSP High Representative Javier Solana was involved in mediating negotiations between the government and opposition parties to prevent the use of force. Before the second round of elections, the EU sent a special envoy and a record number of election monitors. As Ukrainian analysts argue, "the swift and strong support of the European Union in Ukraine's internal struggle for a democratic election highlighted a shift in the EU's attitude toward its neighbor. From a cautious and primarily economic partner that was wary of aggravating Russia unnecessarily, the EU suddenly became a proactive, lively defender of the democratic movement in Ukraine" (International Center for Policy Studies 2004, 8–9).

Encouraged by the visible shift in the EU's approach and hoping to benefit from Ukraine's "fifteen minutes of fame" in Europe, the new leadership even considered applying immediately for membership. New member states advocated rewarding Ukraine's democratic achievement with a membership prospective. This position was also adopted by the European Parliament (European Parliament 2005).

While EU states managed to act unanimously to back democratic change in Ukraine, they appeared divided on the issue of further support of Ukraine's emerging democracy. Some long-standing EU members—Germany, France, Belgium, Spain, and the Netherlands—opposed making any commitments, even long-term ones, regarding Ukraine's accession (Youngs 2008, 16). The commission advised Ukraine not to apply and instead to concentrate on reforms.

After consultations with its supporters among EU member states, Ukraine's Ministry of Foreign Affairs decided not to apply for membership in 2005 but to make diplomatic efforts to win a membership prospect in the new agreement, which would replace the expiring PCA in 2008. To encourage Ukraine's democratization efforts without making a new membership commitment, the EU offered Ukraine several new instruments within the ENP. Its main implementation tool, the EU-Ukraine Action Plan, signed in February 2005, was revised to include issues raised by Ukraine's new government. The Ukrainian side put significant effort into including conditions in this document. Previously, the EU had not applied any democracy promotion conditions to Ukraine. The PCA combined minor economic and financial incentives with a low-credibility threat to withhold them in the case of political noncompliance or promises regarding further relations (Schimmelfennig and Scholtz 2007, 11). The ENP's EU-Ukraine Action Plan made the future of EU-Ukraine relations and further integration dependent on progress in the implementation of the plan's priorities, including those regarding democracy and the rule of law. For example, the initiation of consultations on the new enhanced agreement was conditioned on Ukraine's fulfillment of the political priorities of the plan, helping to ensure democratic conduct in the 2006 parliamentary elections.

New opportunities for socialization emerged. The EU-Ukraine political dialogue was intensified due to the action plan. Parliamentary contacts between the EU and Ukraine have intensified since 2005 and have been extended beyond the PCA arrangements. Three Ukrainian parties—Viktor Yushchenko's Our Ukraine, Yulia Tymoshenko's Batkivshchyna, and another member of the Orange coalition, the People's Movement of Ukraine—have become observer members of the European People's Party. The EU introduced visa facilitation for Ukraine in exchange for an agreement on the readmission of illegal migrants.

In late 2005 the EU finally granted Ukraine market economy status, thereby putting Ukrainian exporters in a more competitive position. Furthermore, Europe offered Ukraine a prospective of deep free trade with the EU, conditioned on the country's accession to the World Trade Organization (WTO). In addition, Ukraine and the EU signed several agreements launching sectoral cooperation in the fields of energy, aviation, and satellite navigation. Ukraine was also given access to lines of credit in the European Investment Bank. In 2006 the European Commission cleared the path for ENP countries to participate in certain EU agencies and programs.

As with Central European and Western Balkan states, such external incentives with considerable short-term rewards have proved effective even when domestic factors are not favorable. Despite the complex domestic debate and stalled legislation process due to a political crisis in 2007, Ukraine's parliament gave significant support to WTO-related legislation.

EU assistance has been strengthened by new instruments and increased aid. From 2007 onward the EU introduced the European Neighborhood and Partnership Instrument (ENPI), which includes national, regional, cross-border, and thematic components and had a budget of €494 million in 2007–10 (Commission of the European Communities 2007, 4). One of the three priorities for ENPI funding, "Support for democratic development and good governance," accounts for 30 percent (€148 million) of the budget. Cooperation tools borrowed from the enlargement policy, like the twinning program and the Technical Assistance and Information Exchange, were offered to Ukraine to help implement the plan. The first governance facility allocations (€22 million) were made to Ukraine in recognition of progress in reform.

The EU enhanced its direct support to civil society organizations in Ukraine under the reformed European Instrument for Democracy and Human Rights (EIDHR). Unlike U.S. aid to civil society in Ukraine, EIDHR support was largely apolitical, mostly supporting social rights projects. Aid available to Ukrainian civil society is still very small: in 2007–08 the European Commission made €1.2 million available via the EIDHR, but only about €650,000 were actually granted to Ukrainian NGOs. In addition, EU member states, especially those expressing greater interest in Ukraine's future within the EU, have bilateral democracy aid programs covering a spectrum of agents of change, including civil society, media, political parties, Parliament, and local politicians (Solonenko and Jarabik 2008, 93–95). ENPI aid under the democracy and good governance priority supports effective public administration (particularly in energy, trade, border management, and migration) and the fight against corruption, rather than the political foundations of democracy. The promotion of good governance under the ENPI is output oriented and has mainly relied on intergovernmental cooperation, with only a modest shift toward input legitimacy and the involvement of nonstate actors (Borzel 2009, 32–33). In contrast with U.S. democracy aid, the EU does not focus on parliamentary and political party development.

Despite increased EU engagement in Ukraine's democratic development, its tools for democracy promotion are weak. In contrast to the European Commission's evaluations of ENP results, in which Ukraine appears to be among the most successful of EU neighbors, the country is, since the Orange Revolution, failing to consolidate its new democracy.

Democratic Consolidation in Ukraine

The Orange Revolution was a turning point in Ukraine's transition from a semi-authoritarian regime to democracy. Through the establishment of free and fair elections and political freedoms, Ukraine made its shift to democracy. However, this new democracy has yet to be consolidated. It has been characterized as "vibrant" but "nonetheless fragile and dysfunctional" (Emerson 2008, 27) and not a democracy "in the European meaning of the term" (Solonenko 2007, 140). Ukraine lacks democratic institutions and a civic political culture. Institutional weakness is the main cause of political instability in Ukraine and thus is the main issue to confront. Since 2005 Ukraine has gone through two parliamentary electoral campaigns (including early elections followed by the dissolution of Parliament in April 2007) and several elections at the local level, among them early elections in Kiev. In autumn 2008 the president dissolved Parliament for the second time, but a preterm election was canceled as Ukraine experienced the deepest economic recession in Europe.

During the five years following the Orange Revolution, Ukraine had four governments and an even larger number of political coalitions in Parliament. Since 2006 the government has been run by the president and the prime minister, both of whom have executive powers. This "cohabitation" has hindered all areas of public policy. Ukraine's political instability is mainly caused by strong political competition, with unreformed and weak political institutions. Government machinery can still be used for administrative leverage in political struggles. From 2005 to 2007 the Constitutional Court was paralyzed and lost its credibility as a result of pressure from political actors and corruption scandals involving judges. The judiciary is used as a political instrument by other branches of power, and top officials do not execute its decisions. The opposition's rights are not enshrined in law, the organization of political parties and electoral party lists falls far short of democratic standards, and the levers of political influence available to civil society exist only formally.

Political instability stems from institutional weakness, and since the competing political elites remain focused on the short term, and since institution building and capacity building yield dividends only in the long term, institutional weakness will not be remedied. As a result of short-term thinking, the policy agenda is dominated by populist issues, such as increasing social expenditure or compensating Soviet Oshchadnyi Bank deposits.

Ukraine's poor record in democratic institution building is confirmed by the evidence in evaluations of the EU-Ukraine Action Plan by the Ukrainian government and the European Commission (Commission of the European Communities 2009, 2008b; Commission of European Communities and Ministry of Foreign Affairs of Ukraine 2008a) and by Ukrainian NGOs (Razumkov Center 2007, 2008; Laboratoria 2007). The monitoring reports published by the Parliamentary Assembly of the Council of Europe regarding Ukraine's accession commitments paint a pessimistic picture of Ukraine's democratic progress (Parliamentary Assembly of the Council of Europe 2008, 2009).

All of the evaluations show limited progress in the implementation of action plan priorities in the fields of democracy, rule of law, human rights, and the fundamental freedoms detailed in the Political Dialogue and Reform chapter of the plan. The NGO consortium assessment shows that none of the priorities spelled out in the chapter has been fully implemented (Razumkov Center 2008, 4). Experts conclude that "the nature of government in Ukraine actually did not change. Moreover, the political crisis that arose in April 2007, at the end of the second year of the Action Plan's implementation, revealed not only the shortcomings of the amendments to the Ukrainian Constitution but also the critical state of the judicial system, law-enforcement bodies, the absence of a system of checks and counterbalances in the organization of governance in Ukraine" (Razumkov Center 2007, 11). Electoral law, public administration, corruption, state mass media—the list of the crucial issues in which Ukraine has failed to make progress is long.

The need for democratization reform in Ukraine, unchanged since the Orange Revolution, is demonstrated by several government collapses since then. Notwithstanding the 2010 presidential election, there is little chance of substantial reform in the coming years, as internal political divisions remain strong. Moreover, the economic crisis reinforces public demand for stability rather than deeper democratization, especially as the word *democracy* has been discredited in citizens' eyes due to the irresponsibility, impunity, and lack of accountability of democratically elected governors. Still, institutional reforms are crucial to Ukraine's EU membership bid. Kiev will have to achieve internal political consolidation to make progress through the new agreement.

Ukraine's Membership Prospects

Negotiations between the EU and Ukraine on the Association Agreement officially opened in March 2007. The talks focused on general principles and institutional arrangements; political dialogue and foreign and security policy; justice, freedom, and security issues; and economic cooperation.

In February 2008, when Ukraine was invited to join the World Trade Organization, negotiations for a free trade area were launched as part of the AA process. A comprehensive and deep free trade area will be a core part of the AA. Encompassing liberalization of trade in goods and services, deep free trade refers to the harmonization of the regulatory environment with that of the EU. According to the impact assessment, deep free trade will induce rapid and sustainable economic growth in Ukraine and will contribute to prosperity, stability, and democracy (Emerson 2006, 126–28).

Ukraine declared its desire to become a full-fledged member of the EU in 1998 and views the AA as equivalent to those signed between EU and CEE countries in the 1990s, granting a clear membership path for Ukraine.[3] In the Ukrainian government's view, the new agreement is not limited by the parameters of the ENP and would be built on the principles of political association and economic integration. This position is shared by all of the political parties in Ukraine, which despite deep divisions regarding other foreign policy issues, are united regarding Ukraine's European vocation.

Ukraine's expectations of a membership prospective are not echoed by the EU. The Council of the European Union did not include a membership prospective in its agreement and stipulated that "this agreement shall not prejudge any possible future developments in EU-Ukraine relations" (Council of the European Union 2007). The EU position is that the new agreement has to aim at building "an increasingly close relationship with Ukraine, aimed at gradual economic integration and deepening of political cooperation." Moreover, the EU regards the AA as part of the ENP and will probably use the agreement as a model for other ENP partners.

During the council's discussions on a mandate for the commission, a division among EU member states over Ukraine's membership possibilities became apparent. New member states—together with the United Kingdom, Sweden, and Finland—expressed their support for a long-term prospect of membership for Ukraine. France, Germany, the Netherlands, Belgium, and Spain opposed a firm commitment.

In February 2008 France made an informal offer to sign an associated partnership agreement with Ukraine. The offer included a number of other attractive rewards, such as visa liberalization dialogue and possibilities for Ukraine to participate in EU policymaking processes. As a result, the French EU presidency of 2008 obtained the council's consent to sign the AA and to launch a dialogue on the establishment of a visa-free regime for Ukrainian citizens travelling to the Schengen Agreement countries. However, according to some critics, the generous French offer should be regarded as a formula to discourage Ukraine's leadership from striving for EU accession, similar to the Mediterranean Union in the case of Turkey's accession. Moreover, France badly needed the ENP eastern dimension to be strengthened in order to get the new member states' support for its initiative toward the EU's southern neighborhood.

The European Parliament expressed the most positive opinion of the AA. In its recommendations to the council, it called for the AA to include, in the long term, "the attainment of EU membership" and such instruments for integration as abolition of the visa regime and increased financial assistance (European Parliament 2007). In another report, the European Parliament offered to fill "the conceptual, political, and legal gap existing between the Union's Enlargement Strategy and its Neighborhood Policy" in order to respond to expectations of the EU's eastern neighbors, while differentiating between the enlargement policy and the accession of the candidates (European Parliament 2008).[4] The European Parliament emphasized the "integration capacity" of the EU as an indispensable condition for the latter. Additionally, the European Parliament encouraged the commission and the council further to differentiate the ENP by establishing a free trade area, to be followed by close relations along the lines of the European Economic Area Plus and even a European Commonwealth. One EU commissioner remarked of Ukraine accession that "Nothing is ruled out and nothing is ruled in."[5] The EU's enlargement policy remains the most successful tool it has for promoting democratization and economic modernization in third countries.

The crucial issue seems to be whether EU accession conditionalities will be applied to Ukraine. Member states are divided on this. The preamble to the agreements with Central and Eastern European countries explicitly refer to a prospect of membership, recognizing that "the final objective of the respective country is to become a member of the Community and that this association, in the view of the parties, will help to achieve this objective." Some EU member states try to avoid reference to article 49 of the Treaty on European Union, according to which "any European State," if it respects the principles of liberty, democracy, human rights and fundamental freedoms, and the rule of law may apply for membership. For example, Germany did not even want to refer to six non-EU members of the Eastern Partnership as "European" countries, preferring the phrase "countries of eastern Europe" or "Eastern partners."[6]

The withholding of a membership prospective would be painfully disappointing to Ukraine, which has invested political and diplomatic capital in this issue. The Ukrainian president has repeatedly declared that his country will sign the Association Agreement with a prospect for membership, and the main parliamentary parties expect that the EU will "finally overcome its internal divergence of opinion and give a concrete prospect to Ukraine and start a serious dialogue."[7] Following the EU's blocking of Ukraine's and Georgia's efforts for a NATO membership action plan and its soft response to Russia's interventions in its neighbors' affairs (culminating in the 2008 invasion of Georgia and Gazprom's 2009 cut-off of energy supplies to Ukraine and seventeen other European countries), the EU's denial of Ukraine's accession prospect would constitute a further defeat for Ukrainian supporters of a European choice. An overly pragmatic EU approach could lead Ukraine to believe that Europe values gas more than democracy. Ukraine does not want the AA as a substitute for a membership prospective but as a step toward it (Ministry of Foreign Affairs of Ukraine 2008).

The Association Agreement

In the event that democracy promotion based on accession conditionality cannot be applied to Ukraine, the question arises as to what extent the EU will be able to promote democracy though other instruments within the AA. The ENP policy combines two basic models to promote democracy in the neighborhood. Together with political conditionality, which appears in the EU-Ukraine Action Plan, the EU aims to promote democracy through assisting social and economic development and socialization in its neighborhood. The EU achieves this by offering ENP partners "deep and comprehensive FTAs" and "support for reforms to improve trade and the economic regulatory environment and the investment climate," along with extension of the EU transport and energy networks and enhanced dialogue in key sectors (Commission of the European Communities 2006).

The ENP concept envisages the promotion of socialization through greater mobility (visa facilitation, removing obstacles to travel); educational, research, and civil society exchanges; enhanced civil society participation in the ENP; and the strengthening of political dialogue at the diplomatic and political levels on other issues within bilateral and multilateral frameworks. Both concepts of democracy promotion, applied together with the aforementioned instruments, are incorporated into the AA.

Under the AA framework, the EU continues to apply to Ukraine a conditionality model developed within the ENP in which the partner is offered deeper political and economic integration on condition of its "commitments on rule of law, democracy, human rights, market-oriented economic and sectoral reforms, and cooperation on key foreign policy objectives" (Landaburu 2006). For example, the opening of the EU internal market to Ukrainian producers will depend on the Ukrainian government's implementation of its commitments on the approximation of legislation. Ukraine's progress in implementing the AA within the areas of justice, freedom, and security will likely have an effect on the EU-Ukraine dialogue on visa issues.

Moreover, ENP conditionality is increased through the AA. In contrast to the action plans of the PCA and the ENP, which are both political documents, the AA will be legally binding in many of its provisions. A dispute settlement mechanism for binding provisions will be established, which will define a time line for implementation, consequences if provisions are not implemented or are delayed, and responsive measures to be taken.

In addition, the institutional architecture of the AA will be similar to that of other EU association agreements. This means that the Ministerial Council will be empowered to make legally binding decisions about the provisions of the AA. Benchmarking, monitoring, and evaluation mechanisms, all crucial elements of conditionality, will be implemented under the AA. The commission will develop an implementation tool for the AA, which will be reviewed and monitored jointly on an annual or biannual basis. The monitoring and evaluation system that exists under the ENP is inefficient, as benchmarks are absent, and ENP action plans have been criticized for being "shopping lists" of very diverse items without a hierarchy, time frame, or link to EU funds. This has made monitoring and evaluation of action plan implementation difficult. ENP progress reports remain general in their evaluation and do not specify how so-called significant progress is measured. These progress reports reflect political relations between the EU and the ENP country concerned, rather than the state of reforms. Moreover, as the ENP is largely unpopular with non-EU partner countries, including Ukraine, its progress reports are not taken seriously by the government, political parties, and the press, and as a result, citizens do not take them seriously either.

In this regard the European Commission has proved responsive. The EU-Ukraine Association Agenda, a successor to the EU-Ukraine Action Plan and a tool to prepare and facilitate the entry into force of the Association Agreement, enlists concrete, precise, and demand-driven priorities for political reforms in Ukraine. These priorities reference the norms of the EU and other European and international organizations as standards. Such reform priorities, together with improved monitoring and evaluation mechanisms in the AA's institutional arrangements, will strengthen EU leverage over Ukraine's government.

Two parts of the AA—those concerning political dialogue and cooperation in the field of CFSP and justice, freedom, and security—will contain provisions directly referring to the further consolidation of democracy and the rule of law. These will include provisions for cooperation on a wide range of issues, inter alia joint efforts to promote respect for democratic principles, the rule of law and good governance, and human rights and fundamental freedoms. Also included are domestic reforms, legislation related to the International Criminal Court, and cooperation on combating money laundering, organized crime, and terrorism (Commission of the European Communities and Ministry of Foreign Affairs of Ukraine 2007, 2008b). The AA will be built on the positive experience of the EU-Ukraine Action Plan on Justice, Freedom, and Security but will go even further.

As well as increasing conditionality, the EU will intensify socialization processes through the AA. In spirit, the AA is an integration agreement and goes much further in substance than the Europe Agreements of the 1990s. It enhances institutional links and provides more opportunities for people-to-people contacts through trade and sectoral integration of Ukraine into the EU and multifaceted cooperation in fields such as energy, transport, education, research, culture, civil society, common foreign and security policy, and justice, freedom, and security. Along with improving the trade and business environment, the trade strand of the AA will require legislative approximation and institutional reforms in the governance system (in such sectors as customs, corporate governance, taxation, and public procurement), resulting in the establishment of more transparent administrative procedures and reduced corruption (Emerson 2006, 98–108; Shumylo 2007, 175–213). The EU will extend sectoral policy dialogue with Ukraine. This will assist the promotion of democratic governance as a side effect of transgovernmental cooperation, in which ENP country state actors gradually familiarize themselves with democratic practices (Freyburg, Skripka, and Wetzel 2007, 8).

Deeper integration of Ukraine's air transport sector into the EU's common civil aviation area could be a powerful catalyst for the expansion of people-to-people contacts, business travel, and tourism (Emerson 2006, 171–76). Access for European low-fare airlines to the Ukrainian market and increased competition in the sector will give Ukrainian citizens more opportunity to travel to EU member states. Smoothly functioning borders will also facilitate people-to-people contacts in the frontier regions between Ukraine and EU countries. The major obstacle to people-to-people contacts between the EU and Ukraine is the visa regime for Ukrainian nationals. Although the effect of the AA on the visa facilitation agreement that entered into force in 2008 has been largely positive, the margin of improvement has been relatively small due to the new visa "curtain" that appeared after the entry of new member states to the Schengen zone in December 2007 (Stefan Batory Foundation 2009).[8] The Ukrainian government advocated a visa-free travel regime as a part of the AA and sought to establish an EU-Ukraine visa dialogue similar to those the EU launched with Western Balkan countries in early 2008. The European Commission adopted a positive position on this issue, but some member states opposed the idea for economic and political reasons. Nevertheless, the French European presidency managed to reach an agreement in the council. As a result, in October 2008 the EU and Ukraine launched a dialogue on the establishment of a visa-free regime.

However, the EU-Ukraine visa dialogue differs from that under way with the Balkan countries. First, "a long-term perspective" means that the EU is not able to offer a visa-free reward to Ukraine in the foreseeable future. Member states are divided on the issue: some that were initially against it now support the visa dialogue in order to ease diplomatic pressure from Kiev and the capitals of some EU states. Moreover, in the declaration produced during the first Eastern Partnership summit in Prague, EU members diluted the commission's offer of "visa-free travel to all cooperating partners" to a vague promise of "visa liberalization." Unlike the Western Balkan states, Ukraine does not have a road map defining the objectives of reforms and the evaluation matrix of their implementation. Since the beginning of the visa dialogue, Ukraine has been negotiating unsuccessfully with the EU over the possibility of receiving a road map.

The experience of the Western Balkan countries shows that a clear and time-limited prospective and conditions for a visa-free travel regime could serve as a powerful "carrot" for reforms to the justice, freedom, and security sector and could be used by the EU to encourage successive Ukrainian governments to proceed with other reforms. Visa-free travel, one of the few AA priorities explicitly backed by all Ukrainian political parties, could galvanize political and public support for reforms promoted by the EU.

Through the AA framework, the EU has an opportunity to implement an initiative presented in the enhanced ENP on strengthening "civil society exchanges, reaching beyond governmental contacts to build bridges in many areas." It also aims to "allow appropriate participation by civil society representatives as stakeholders in the reform process, whether in the preparation of legislation, in the monitoring of its implementation, or in the development of national or regional initiatives related to the ENP" (Commission of the European Communities 2006). The EU is beginning to engage more closely with Ukrainian civil society. In 2004 the European Economic and Social Committee (EESC), a consultative body to the EU institutions that represents economic, social, and civic organizations in EU member states, established the Contact Group on European Eastern Neighbors in order to contribute to the Eastern dimension of the ENP. Since 2005 the EESC has organized several visits to Ukraine, has held joint seminars with Ukrainian civil society, and has established cooperation with Ukraine's National Tripartite Social and Economic Council, which represents trade unions, employers' organizations, and the government. The EESC advocates institutional representation of Ukrainian and European civil society under the AA. Bearing in mind the experience of candidates and associated countries, the EESC offered to establish a joint body composed of an equal number of members from the EESC and a body representing organized civil society in Ukraine. It also offered to provide consultation to the Joint Ministerial Council (European Economic and Social Committee 2008).[9]

The European Commission pays increasing attention to nonstate actors in ENP countries. At the regional level, it offered to launch a Civil Society Forum within the Eastern Partnership "to promote contacts among civil society organizations and facilitate their dialogue with public authorities" (Commission of the European Communities 2008a, 14). At the bilateral level, it organized an international conference on civil society issues in Kiev aiming to strengthen interaction between Ukrainian civil society and the commission. Further, Ukraine's civil society organizations are invited to consultations on EU initiatives for Ukraine, such as the review and planning of ENPI funds for Ukraine. The 2009 EIDHR national call for proposals was more locally demand-driven and demonstrated a shift from the strict rights promotion and protection approach to the more complex approach of supporting civil society initiatives, including dialogue with state actors and public advocacy.

As it turns out, both foreign democracy promoters and domestic advocates had unrealistic hopes for Ukraine's new government after the Orange Revolution, while they underestimated the role of civil society in democracy consolidation. As the political reform process stagnates, the European Commission, along with many other international donors, is trying to diversify support for democracy by enhancing the capacities of nonstate actors and promoting civil society engagement in the reform process and EU integration policies. The EU tries to balance its largely top-down intergovernmental approach to democratization by promoting civil society development and empowering its actors through the new agreement. The AA will be the first agreement between the EU and a European third country containing a chapter on civil society.[10]

The Eastern Partnership brought few novelties to Ukraine. The content of the EU's contribution to the new agreement with Ukraine—EU association, deep free trade, cooperation on energy, enhanced political dialogue, and visa liberalization—is to be offered to the whole EU Eastern neighborhood. To finance these new instruments, the commission increased assistance to Eastern partners from €450 million in 2008 to €785 million in 2013. However, this sum will not significantly change Ukraine's share: €494 million for 2007–13. Funds for ENP countries remain lower than those of candidate states: the EU's offer of €600 million for implementation of the Eastern Partnership in 2009–13 is almost five times less than aid to Turkey. Another financial problem is Ukraine's budget: without improvements in budget transparency and accountability, the EU must question whether to increase its funding for Ukraine governance. In this regard, the issue of AA implementation between the EU and Ukraine becomes critical. While the ultimate goal of integration is not given clearly to Ukraine, the costs of deep integration and legal approximation will be considerable for both the country's government and its private sector. The economic benefits of free trade and adoption of EU regulations are long term, but the costs are immediate. Based on the World Bank's 2006 report, Ukraine would need a hundred billion dollars during 2006–15 to comply with EU norms and standards (Mayhew 2008, 41–42).

Conclusion

The Association Agreement between the EU and Ukraine is an example of a narrowing of the EU's enlargement policy. The agreement envisions the integration of Ukraine into the EU through deep free trade, but the agreement does not provide for democracy promotion. The most potent tool for democratic transformation is EU accession policy in which a membership prospective is combined with accession conditionality. But this prospective is not offered at this stage, and other political incentives appear weak.

Unlike in some other cases discussed in this volume, the EU's commitment to democracy in Ukraine is not in question. Shortcomings to EU democracy promotion stem from the lack of a common vision of Ukraine's future in Europe. Enlargement has benefitted the "insiders" but may be leaving a trail of negative consequence in those countries now left on the outside. Ukraine's domestic specificity within the scope of this volume is the degree of raised, and frustrated, expectation invested by the country's reformers in the anchoring potential of EU membership. The EU remains internally divided on such strategic issues as Ukraine's EU accession prospect and EU engagement in the region where its influence is continuously contested by Russia. The EU is also divided on other issues indicating the level of openness of the EU to Ukraine, such as a visa-free travel regime for Ukrainian nationals.

The AA has the potential to influence democratization in Ukraine, as it enhances both conditionality and socialization. Unlike the ENP Action Plan, the AA will be legally binding, with a stronger monitoring and evaluation system. Trade liberalization with the EU can promote good governance by being conditioned on reforms in many sectors of public administration. Moreover, deep free trade will lead to a multiplication of personal and institutional contacts, namely intensification of business contacts as a result of enhanced economic activities, and greater mobility as a result of easier access to cheap travel operators. The agreement envisages intensified political dialogue as well as more opportunities for people-to-people contact in the areas of culture, education, research, and civil society. The AA will be the first agreement between the EU and a European country to include a separate article on civil society, which will be empowered to provide its recommendations.

Notwithstanding all this, the agreement still relies heavily on a top-down, government-to-government approach toward democratization—a model borrowed from enlargement policy—and inherits the ENP's ambiguity in terms of the final goal of integration. This weakens the EU's leverage over Ukraine. Therefore, despite the reinforced democracy promotion tool kit of the AA, the agreement will not serve as an alternative effective enough to substitute for accession-driven Europeanization. The AA's comprehensive and cost-intensive reform agenda is unlikely to be implemented in Ukraine—where no major democratization reforms have been implemented since the democratic breakthrough in 2005—unless a final goal of integration into the EU is clearly defined. Only a strong political incentive such as an accession prospective is likely both to compel divisive political elites to restrain their personal ambitions in favor of a common policy agenda and to justify the high costs of EU-driven reforms.

NOTES

1. The New Enhanced Agreement was the provisional name for the EU-Ukraine agreement until September 2008, when the EU and Ukraine agreed on Association Agreement.
2. Polls across all regions, regularly conducted since 2000, show consistent public support for Ukraine joining the EU (support is greater in western and central Ukraine than in the east and south). The 2008 polls (conducted by the Razumkov Center, the Institute of Sociology of the National Academy of Sciences, and the Democratic Initiatives Foundation) show 44–56 percent support for EU membership, depending on the formulation of the question. A significant proportion (20–27 percent) were undecided. Support for Ukraine membership in NATO is very different: 58–59 percent against, 18–22 percent in favor.
3. In 1998 President Leonid Kuchma approved the strategy for Ukraine's integration into the European Union by a decree that proclaimed Ukraine's midterm goal to be an associated EU member and its final objective to become a full-fledged one. The Ukrainian Parliament declared this goal even earlier, in 1993, through the adoption of the Resolution on Basic Directions of Foreign Policy for Ukraine.
4. Also see European People's Party–European Democrats Group in the European Parliament, news release, July 10, 2005.
5. Benita Ferrero-Waldner, EU commissioner for external relations and the ENP. EU wants "targeted deepening of relations" with neighbors, *EU Observer*, April 3, 2008.
6. Big names to stay away from Prague summit, *EU Observer*, May 5, 2009.

7. Member Ukrainian Parliament, interview with author, April 2008.

8. The number of visas issued by the new member states to Ukrainian nationals in 2008 dropped significantly from 2007. In the case of Poland, Ukraine's largest EU neighbor, the number fell by 60 percent. Additionally, a visa fee was introduced by new member states that previously issued national visas free of charge.

9. The problem of proper representation of Ukrainian civil society prevails in this body and in its partner, the National Tripartite Social and Economic Council.

10. The EU-Chile Association Agreement (2002) contains an article on civil society.

REFERENCES

Borzel, T. 2009. Transformative power Europe? The EU promotion of good governance in areas of limited statehood. Paper prepared for ERD workshop, Transforming political structures: Security, institutions, and regional integration mechanisms. April 16–17. Florence.

Commission of the European Communities. 2009. *Implementation of the European Neighborhood Policy in 2008: Progress Report Ukraine.*

——. 2008a. *Eastern Partnership.*

——. 2008b. *Implementation of the European Neighborhood Policy in 2007: Progress Report Ukraine.*

——. 2007. *Ukraine: National Indicative Program 2007–2010.*

——. 2006. *Strengthening the European Neighborhood Policy.*

Commission of the European Communities and Ministry of Foreign Affairs of Ukraine. 2008a. *Joint Evaluation Report on the EU-Ukraine Action Plan.*

——. 2008b. *Second Joint Progress Report: Negotiations on the EU-Ukraine New Enhanced Agreement.*

——. 2007. *Joint Progress Report: Negotiations on the EU-Ukraine New Enhanced Agreement.*

Council of the European Union. 2007. Council conclusions concerning the negotiation of a New Enhanced Agreement between the EU and Ukraine. 2776th External Relations Council Meeting. January 22. Brussels.

Emerson, M. 2008. Policies toward Ukraine, 2005–20: Status quo unintended. In *The European Union as a Normative Foreign Policy Actor.* Brussels: CEPS.

——. 2006. *The Prospect of Deep Free Trade between the European Union and Ukraine.* Brussels: CEPS.

Emerson, M., et al. 2007. European Neighborhood Policy two years on: Time indeed for an "ENP plus." Policy Brief 12. Brussels: CEPS.

European Economic and Social Committee. 2008. *EU-Ukraine Relations: A New Dynamic Role for Civil Society.*

European Parliament. 2008. *Report on the Commission's 2007 Enlargement Strategy Paper.*

——. 2007. *Committee for Foreign Affairs Report.* With a proposal for a European Parliament recommendation to the council on a negotiation mandate for a new enhanced agreement between the European Community and its member states on one side and Ukraine on the other.

Freyburg, T., T. Skripka, and A. Wetzel. 2007. *Democracy between the Lines? EU Promotion of Democratic Governance via Sector-Specific Cooperation.* Zurich: National Center of Competence in Research.

Hillion, C. 2007. Mapping out the new contractual relations between the European Union and its neighbors: Learning from the EU-Ukraine "enhanced agreement." *European Foreign Affairs Review* 12: 169–82.

International Center for Policy Studies. 2004. Political commentary 12/18. Kiev.

Laboratoria zakonodavchych initsiatyv. 2007. *Ukraina: Evropejskyi Soyuz: naperedodni ukladannia novogo bazovogo dogovoru.* Kiev: *Materialy kruglogo stolu.*

Landaburu, E. 2006. From neighborhood to integration policy: Are there concrete alternatives to enlargement? Policy Brief 95. Brussels: CEPS.

Makobriy, O. 2006. Vplyv yevropeyskoyi integratsiyi Ukrayiny na dial'nist' velykogo vitchiznianoho biznesu. Report 9. Kiev: National Center for Euro-Atlantic Integration.

Mayhew, A. 2008. *Ukraine and the European Union: Financing Accelerating Integration.* Warsaw: UKIE.

Ministry of Foreign Affairs of Ukraine. 2008. Comment on the communication from the European Commission on implementation of the European neighborhood policy in 2007 to the EU Council of Ministers and the European Parliament.

Parliamentary Assembly of the Council of Europe. 2009. Honoring of obligations and commitments by Ukraine. Information note by the co-rapporteurs on their fact-finding visit to Ukraine (5–8 April 2009).

——. 2008. Honoring of obligations and commitments by Ukraine. Information note by the co-rapporteurs on their fact-finding visit to Ukraine (14–16 January 2008).

Puglisi, R. 2008. A window to the world? Oligarchs and foreign policy in Ukraine. In *Ukraine: Quo Vadis?* ed. S. Fischer. Paris: European Union Institute for Security Studies.

Razumkov Center. 2008. Ukraine-EU action plan: Results and prospects. *National Security and Defense* 6/100.

——. 2007. Assessments of the Ukraine-EU action plan implementation in 2005–2006. *National Security and Defense* 5/89.

Schimmelfennig, F., and H. Scholtz. 2007. EU democracy promotion in the European neighborhood: Political conditionality, economic development, and transnational exchange. Working Paper 9. Zurich: National Center for Competence in Research.

Shumylo, O., ed. 2007. *Free Trade between Ukraine and the EU: An Impact Assessment.* Kiev: International Center for Policy Studies.

Solonenko, I. 2007. The EU's impact on democratic transformation in Ukraine. In *Ukraine, the EU, and Russia: History, Culture, and International Relations,* ed. S. Velychenko. New York: Macmillan.

Solonenko, I., and B. Jarabik. 2008. Ukraine. In *Is the European Union Supporting Democracy in Its Neighbourhood?* ed. R. Youngs. Madrid: FRIDE.

Stefan Batory Foundation. 2009. Changes in Visa Policies of the EU Member States. Warsaw.

Youngs, R. 2009. Europe's inconsistent support for democratic reform in Ukraine. *International Politics* 46/4.

Yushchenko, V. 2005. Ukraine's future is in the EU. Address to the European Parliament. *Neighborhood Watch* 1. Brussels: CEPS.

CHAPTER FIVE

Organization for Security and Cooperation in Europe

A Paper Tiger?

Jos Boonstra

While the Organization for Security and Cooperation in Europe (OSCE) is a less high-profile body than either the European Union or NATO, the world's biggest regional organization has established an impressive body of democracy and human rights commitments, runs democracy-related activities in a large number of member states, and continues to be a lead player in election monitoring.[1] However, the OSCE is floundering. Participating states from Vladivostok to Vancouver are divided over the OSCE's function and future. The organization's last five Ministerial Councils have concluded without agreement. The insignificant role the OSCE played in the war between Georgia and Russia is telling: in South Ossetia the OSCE failed to fulfill its core tasks of conflict prevention and early warning, and it did not play a substantial role in the aftermath of the conflict.

Although all EU member states recognize the importance of the OSCE's track record in building a regime of political agreements on security issues, they have become less active in pushing non-EU members to comply with these agreements. This is particularly evident compared with the organization's human rights and democracy-related achievements of the early 1990s. The conviction that the OSCE is a mechanism actively pursuing democracy promotion is dissipating. EU assistance for democratic reform in OSCE member states in Eastern Europe, the Southern Caucasus, and Central Asia now mainly exists on a national basis or through EU institutions, even if EU documents and strategies that deal with Eastern Europe, the Southern Caucasus, and Central Asia do often refer to OSCE commitments.

The OSCE's problems result from two main trends. First, the expansion and widening geographical focus of the EU and NATO have undercut the OSCE's niche added value in the Balkans and to a lesser extent in the countries of the former Soviet Union. This general trend affects the OSCE's activities as a whole, not only its democracy promotion activities. However, EU and NATO democratization efforts—through the European Neighborhood Policy (ENP) and the Partnership for Peace, respectively—have encountered particular difficulties in recent years.

Second, Russia's reversal of democratic reform and, indeed, its determination to hinder U.S. and European democracy promotion initiatives have resulted in Russian obstruction within the OSCE and an unresolved debate about internal reform. A complete overhaul to adapt the OSCE to the current Atlantic-Eurasian security context is blocked. According to most Western states, a more technical reform process embarked upon by OSCE participating states is now completed. However, Russia and several Commonwealth of Independent States (CIS) allies want more—not in order to strengthen the OSCE's effectiveness but rather to deepen its impotence, especially over democracy promotion activities.

Whether the OSCE will be able to remain relevant is highly questionable. It risks becoming a paper tiger, leaning heavily on political agreements but lacking the power to enforce them. The OSCE will need to reinvent itself to safeguard its place in regional security. In 2010 Kazakhstan will chair the organization: for the first time, a non-European country that has been critical of the OSCE will take the lead. Although Kazakhstan does not meet all OSCE requirements in the field of human rights and democracy, it might be able to build bridges and remove some of the new divides between East and West. This is also an opportunity for the EU to be involved with Kazakhstan. Astana's position as chair, along with a concerted EU effort, could help the troubled OSCE get back on track, both by providing a forum for security dialogue and by aiming for a renewed common understanding of past democracy and human rights–related agreements.

In the context of this volume, this chapter on the OSCE demonstrates that the structure of the multilateral organizations within which the EU seeks to pursue its democracy policies is a powerful, and at the moment complicated, variable. The multilateral route might have potential, but in the OSCE's case it can also explain a decrease in attention to effective democracy support. In this case, an institutional structure of multilateral partnership has reinforced a security dynamic more than it has (so far) energized the transnational networks and socialization alluded to in the opening chapter and some other case studies covered in the volume.

Reform and Divergent Interests

The OSCE has always been under pressure to adapt to contemporary needs. In the period between the end of the cold war and the start of the Yugoslav conflicts, what was then the Conference on Security and Cooperation in Europe (CSCE) was able to transform itself from a discussion forum into a practical, hands-on organization. During the cold war, the CSCE enabled East-West debate and introduced the notion of comprehensive security (including economic and social aspects). The CSCE evolved into the OSCE, a broad-based organization focusing on a wide range of topics and issues: security dialogue, conflict management, standardization and monitoring of commitments, and democratization assistance.[2]

Unfortunately, the OSCE has not adapted to current needs, and the cooperative spirit of the 1990s has been lost. Since 2000 many former Soviet republics have either given up on democracy or have chosen an authoritarian path. Apart from the case of Russia, the Central Asian republics, Azerbaijan and Belarus, are the clearest examples of this trend. Today the OSCE member states that are scrutinized on human rights and democratic principles feel stigmatized and have lost a sense of ownership and thus interest (Dunay 2006, 78). The OSCE has always been a battlefield for states to thrash out differences, but after many years of debating institutional reform and implementing changes to increase organizational effectiveness, doubts about the OSCE remain in the minds of discontented members. The Georgia-Russia war worsened matters; some consider it to be the final nail in the OSCE's coffin.

Still, it is unlikely that the OSCE will cease to function or lose relevance completely. More than thirty years of security cooperation have resulted in a robust body of shared values and agreed commitments. Another asset is the inclusive character of membership. All European, Eurasian, and North American countries are members, hence the OSCE's relevance to neutral countries such as Switzerland. Every country has an equal voice and may bring their security concerns to the table. The OSCE has built up an impressive track record and is able to assist states through its many institutions: the Office of High Commissioner for National Minorities, the Office of the Representative for Freedom of the Media, the Vienna-based secretariat, the Office for Democratic Institutions and Human Rights (ODIHR), and its many field offices. In addition, the OSCE performs activities that other organizations are unwilling or unable to perform due to insufficient experience, such as policing and antitrafficking (Lynch 2006). Moreover, the OSCE is a forum in which a broad spectrum of governments and civil society organizations meet and engage with each other.

In 2003–04 it became clear to all members that it was imperative to revitalize the OSCE. Not only did the organization have to deal with new threats such as terrorism, trafficking, and corruption, but issues such as Euro-Atlantic enlargement, decreasing U.S. attention toward Europe, and Russia's regained assertiveness on the international stage also made change necessary.

Russia was active during the OSCE's growth in the 1990s, when Moscow still sought to link security and democratic reform. But most of Moscow's proposals, which aimed at strengthening the pan-European organization at the expense of NATO, were rejected. From 2000 onward, the Putin administration gradually changed course after concluding that the OSCE had been unable to prevent NATO's campaign against Serbia. President Boris Yeltsin's signing of the OSCE Istanbul Charter, which demanded more of Russia than it would get in return, was also a factor (Ghébali 2006). Due to its decreasing influence on its "near abroad" and Georgia's democratic revolution, Russia's position moved from disinterest to sharp criticism. From 2004 onward, CIS members have presented documents demanding reform.[3] Russia and its partners objected to "imbalances" among "the three dimensions," claiming that the human dimension was overdeveloped at the expense of the political-military and economic dimensions. Russia also accused the OSCE of applying "double standards," pointing out the OSCE's focus on countries "east of Vienna" and its "subordination to NATO and EU interests" due to its lack of political control and its insufficient institutionalization (Ghébali 2005).

In reaction to these objections, a series of technical reforms were agreed upon and implemented between 2005 and 2008 that sought to strengthen the institutional framework of the OSCE, for instance by giving a more influential role to the secretariat in Vienna and limiting the organizational role of the chairman in office (CiO). After several cosmetic changes (which did marginally improve the OSCE's effectiveness), most countries felt that the technical demands of reform had been met and wanted to return to business as usual. But Russia and its allies urged further reform, seeking to impose more onerous unanimity requirements, which in turn would weaken the decisiveness of the organization and its ability to address democratic deficits.

The United States and most EU countries wish to emphasize human rights and democracy in the OSCE's third (human) dimension, while taking up hard security issues within NATO and to a lesser extent the EU. Russia's severest complaints about the OSCE are clear: double standards, imbalances among the dimensions, and insufficient institutionalization. Russia's position is that OSCE ambitions regarding the human dimension should be lowered and that the use by the EU and NATO of the OSCE to violate Russian or CIS countries' sovereignty should be stopped. In the words of Foreign Minister Sergey Lavrov, "The CIS space has turned into a sphere for geopolitical games, which involve such instruments as 'democratorship.'" In blunt terms, the main criterion used to measure a nation's level of democracy seems to be its readiness to follow other countries' policies (Lavrov 2007, 5). Vladimir Putin argues that "the balance in the OSCE has been disturbed. The OSCE has been transformed into a vulgar instrument that aims to defend the supranational interests of a group of countries against other countries."[4]

Despite such harsh statements and objections to OSCE's human dimension mechanisms, it is doubtful whether Russia has given up on the OSCE altogether. Moscow knows that the OSCE will never play a leading role in European security by replacing NATO. In its disregard for the OSCE it felt confident enough to suspend its participation in the overarching, though obsolete, 2007 Conventional Forces in Europe (CFE) Treaty. Nonetheless, Russia, together with other like-minded countries, has a significant influence in the organization in comparison to its budget contribution. It is also notable that Russia recently started to send better-qualified personnel to the OSCE for contracted positions. Russia chooses to be critical through an active position rather than by abstaining from participation and playing a low-key role. Moscow has now proposed a pan-European security pact, which would not only surpass the OSCE but also sideline NATO. It is unlikely that Western and new EU members, the United States, and Canada would be willing to second track NATO or do away with the earlier OSCE commitments in order to establish a new security pact.

The United States has been a somewhat hesitant supporter of the OSCE. Although it fully supports the dialogue aspects of security, it objects to the implication that the OSCE is a full-fledged pan-European security and defense organization. U.S. interests seem to be the exact opposite of Russia's. According to Washington, the OSCE's main significance lies in the human dimension, especially ODIHR's democracy promotion and the work of field missions. A senior U.S. Department of State official even referred to ODIHR election monitoring as the "international gold standard" in this field (Kramer 2007). Under the Bush administration, the OSCE was seen as a welcome extension of the U.S. democratization agenda. Although the United States is currently having second thoughts about robust democracy promotion, it remains a strong supporter of OSCE commitments, monitoring possibilities, and institution building. This is unlikely to change under the Obama administration, although Washington might be somewhat more inclined to work with Russia within OSCE structures. Still, the United States does not see much merit in internal OSCE reform and prefers to keep the organization as it is—vaguely defined, with practically oriented and independently functioning institutions. Over the last three years U.S. financial support through extrabudgetary funds dropped, and the United States has been pushing to reduce its general contribution to the budget. The OSCE certainly does not play a significant role in U.S. foreign policy, but without U.S. support a revitalization of the organization is unlikely.

The EU tries to occupy the middle ground between Russia and the United States, although most countries clearly lean toward the U.S. position, especially when it comes to the human dimension. However, the EU attaches more importance to the political-military dimension than the United States does. Euro-Atlantic unity in the OSCE might be strengthened under the Obama administration, to the extent that the latter is more open to taking Russian views into account. In its bridging function the EU "should seek to foster the return to co-operative security in the OSCE, recognizing that it is impossible to achieve the desired transformation without addressing the alienation experienced in those countries where it is hoped the transformation will take place" (Dunay 2006, 73). In this sense, synergy between EU eastern policies and OSCE activities is imperative. Almost half of OSCE members are also EU members; the EU pays 70 percent of the OSCE's budget and accounts for more than half of the personnel. Commission assistance funds, for instance through the European Instrument for Democracy and Human Rights (EIDHR) are sometimes channeled through OSCE missions. Although EU country representatives at the OSCE meet weekly in order to agree on joint positions for the Permanent Council, the EU's voice within the organization is not clearly heard.

EU members differ in their approach to the OSCE in two respects. First, countries differ on the degree of importance attributed to the organization. Countries with an Eastern European–oriented foreign policy due to proximity are more interested and active than countries in the southwest of Europe. The smaller northern European countries that combine an active interest in Balkan, Eastern

European, and Eurasian affairs with active human rights and democratization policies have an especially important stake in the OSCE. Second, countries position themselves at different points along the Russia-U.S. scale. Whereas German OSCE policy is sometimes perceived as giving in to Russian demands, believing that Russia will at some point be satisfied with the OSCE's work and act constructively again, the UK is closer to the U.S. position, emphasizing the human dimension and cautioning over supporting reform according to Russian wishes. With five EU member states holding the chairmanship in succession, the EU had the opportunity to set a clear line for the reform and development of the organization. It failed to do so.[5] Differences in emphasis and interest in EU countries' approaches to the OSCE, along with insufficient planning for EU-OSCE division of labor in postconflict management, resulted in a shortsighted stance.

After the technical reforms of recent years, the OSCE remains an organization of fifty-six states that manages twenty-six institutions and field missions. Reforms so far have not diluted the human rights and democracy commitments. However, other factors harm the OSCE's third dimension and OSCE democratization promotion in general: opposition to monitoring, declining extrabudgetary contributions, a stagnant general budget, insufficient expert staff, and antidemocratic action from Russia. The result of this is frustration among EU and NATO countries.

Democracy Promotion

OSCE democracy promotion policies are broad and difficult to define since they are an integral part of the security dialogue, cooperation, and mechanisms the organization aims to promote. Through the Helsinki Accords of the 1970s and several landmark documents in the early 1990s the OSCE has built up an extensive *acquis* in the human dimension that is larger in scope than any other regional intergovernmental organization can boast. In essence, the sum of political agreements that deal with democratic governance is largely completed. Most of the essential ingredients of democracy—good governance, the rule of law, parliamentary oversight, election standards and procedures, civil society, freedom of the media, and civil-military relations—are included.

The participating states went so far as to say that "they categorically and irrevocably declare that the commitments undertaken in the field of the human dimension of the OSCE are matters of direct and legitimate concern to all participating states and do not belong exclusively to the international affairs of the State concerned" (Office for Democratic Institutions and Human Rights 1991).

Today agreement on such formulations would be impossible, and referring to this phrase in cases of concrete breaches is seen by several members as unwelcome interference in domestic politics. Whereas nowadays it is difficult to envisage additional commitments or democracy updates, there are other fields in the human dimension that do allow cooperation to create improved standards, such as antidiscrimination, gender issues, and human trafficking.

The golden years of democracy promotion in the 1990s began when the CSCE ceased to be a dialogue mechanism between two ideological blocks and former communist countries opened up to the idea of building democratic societies. While the commitments on democratic principles and practice were shaped, the CSCE/OSCE became deeply involved in conflict management during the Yugoslav breakup. These factors resulted in the OSCE setting up large missions in the Balkans that also focused on institution building, the rule of law, and civil society. In this context, it was logical that the OSCE would perform the same tasks in the post-Soviet space, where states were being built in an insecure environment. Today broad agreement on democracy has evaporated, but the commitments made have endured and can be referred to when a state's democratic credentials sink. In this sense consensus decision making, which currently stops progress, also has some benefits. The human dimension documents were agreed upon by all member states, including those that have not ratified all UN treaties and the Central Asian states that are not members of the Council of Europe. The all-inclusive character of the OSCE is essential because Russia and several CIS countries signed up to democracy monitoring in the past and can be reminded of their duties. Unfortunately, reminding countries of their obligations is done halfheartedly, as evidenced by the human rights violations in Chechnya and the curtailing of NGOs and fraudulent elections in many CIS states.

Monitoring Capacities

The OSCE has several institutions that monitor the commitments of participating states. One of the most noteworthy of these instruments is the Moscow Mechanism, which allows a group of states to investigate a specific human dimension concern in a particular member state, for instance by asking a rapporteur to investigate. This is one of the few mechanisms that do not require consensus decision making. But pressure on the human dimension has stopped states from using it since 2003 (Baker and McMahon 2006, 63). Even the 2005 Andijan massacres in Uzbekistan did not compel member states to use the mechanism, revealing a lack of political will to use the OSCE to its full capacity to address serious human rights violations.

The responsibility for monitoring human dimension commitments is scattered across the organization; the High Commissioner on National Minorities in The Hague; the Representative on Freedom of the Media in Vienna; the ODIHR, through several mechanisms; the OSCE Parliamentary Assembly in Copenhagen; and the field missions.[6] The latter report to the CiO and the Permanent Council on violations of commitments in specific countries. There has been criticism that the reports by the heads of mission differ in quality and are not uniform. Since missions have differing mandates, as well as differing in size, monitoring by the field offices cannot be regarded as a coherent mechanism, although such monitoring provides important information that can appear on the agenda of the Permanent Council's weekly meetings.

The High Commissioner on National Minorities and the Representative on Freedom of the Media fulfill some monitoring tasks in areas closely linked to democratization. Because most work is carried out through quiet diplomacy, the monitoring aspects of these institutions are weak. The Representative on Freedom of the Media mostly works through other OSCE institutions, providing them with information on threats to and violations of media freedom.

Best known for monitoring human dimension commitments is the ODIHR. Its monitoring task is threefold: following human rights developments without publicly confronting members with shortcomings; organizing annual human dimension implementation meetings, supplementary meetings, and seminars, in coordination with the CiO; and its core business of election observation. Each human dimension meeting reviews implementation and gives national delegations the opportunity to debate the human dimension. Although independent experts are invited, the meetings are now essentially political. Even the agenda needs to be agreed upon by consensus beforehand by the Permanent Council in Vienna. Often it proves difficult to set the agenda because countries that are resistant to the democratization aspects of the human dimension try to downplay the issue—and often succeed.

The most high-profile part of the ODIHR's work is election assessment and observation (Erler 2006). The OSCE benefits from eighteen years of experience in this field and the commitments laid down in the 1990 Copenhagen document. These now are a source of tension between several CIS members, on the one hand, and the United States, the EU, and countries with a Euro-Atlantic integration perspective, on the other. The critical group holds that election observation by a largely uncontrolled entity like the ODIHR—which reports on the quality of procedures immediately after elections—leads to instability and tends to undermine these countries and their governments. The examples of the democratic revolutions in Georgia (2003) and Ukraine (2004) stand out. In contrast, after the result of the April 2009 Moldovan election was declared by international observers as "positive on the whole," riots broke out and the opposition demanded new elections; Moldova got a change of government in the autumn of 2009 following fresh elections.

Those in support of election observation see the work of the ODIHR as being of a high professional standard, while arguing that "democratic changes of government are based on the results of elections, not the observation of electoral processes" (Erler 2006, 8). The quality of election observations always leaves room for improvement. A focus on strengthening longer-term observer missions, as opposed to the well-known, short-term observers that flood a country for a few days, is especially necessary to help countries improve the quality of elections. Ballot stuffing is out of date, and most regimes resistant to change commit fraud through electronic techniques that are difficult to trace.

For Russia the ODIHR is the most negative part of the OSCE. ODIHR interim election reports, which come out immediately after elections, can shame countries that hold elections only as a façade to cover up authoritarian rule. Countries that do not respect OSCE democratic standards see monitoring as more than a nuisance—as indeed an institution with the ability to destabilize power transfers and term extensions. The consolidation of Putin's regime around 2004 empowered Moscow to publicly complain about monitoring: "The question of the monitoring activities of the ODIHR, which has shown itself to be an instrument of shamelessly applying 'double standards' for purposes of political pressure, merits special attention" (Ministry of Foreign Affairs of the Russian Federation 2004). The Russians kept the ODIHR out of their December 2007 parliamentary elections and their March 2008 presidential vote by imposing certain restrictions, which caused the OSCE to forfeit monitoring Russian elections.

The Russians complain that elections are not monitored west of Vienna, and in fact Russia has a point. U.S., UK, and Canadian legal systems do not allow external observers full access to their electoral processes and provide for only a shallow assessment of their elections. Full election observation in mature democracies would, however, be a costly enterprise with few benefits. The current, shallower, assessments provide some useful information on electoral processes in democracies and offer technical advice to countries "west of Vienna" where necessary.

Important information was provided, for instance, by ODIHR experts in Belgium and the Netherlands in 2006, who noted possible flaws in electronic voting.

In a paper on election observation, the Russian delegation to the OSCE holds that the procedure should be conducted in all member states without differentiating (Delegation of the Russian Federation to the OSCE 2007). In addition, the paper advises that the number of observers should not exceed 50. Considering that the 2007 elections in Kazakhstan involved 36 long-term and 400 short-term observers, one can appreciate the limited effect 50 observers would have during elections in a country the size of Russia (Office for Democratic Institutions and Human Rights 2007). In most proposals made by Russia, the country emphasizes the importance of bringing decision making—on everything from the mandate to reporting by the ODIHR—to the Permanent Council. If these proposals were to be accepted, it would end election observation altogether, as council agreements must be unanimous and no consensus on any mission report would ever be reached.

The OSCE Parliamentary Assembly also plays a substantial role both in the monitoring of OSCE human dimension commitments and in election observation. Whereas all OSCE institutions have a certain level of independence, the assembly is placed mostly outside the organizational structures and has its own budget. As national legislators are not constrained by diplomacy or consensus, the Parliamentary Assembly has a lot of freedom for maneuver in monitoring commitments. In addition, the political differences that partly paralyze the OSCE have a less severe effect on the assembly. It carries out fact-finding missions and drafts resolutions concerning democracy and human rights. Nevertheless, assembly reports are taken into account by the Ministerial Council only once a year and not by the Permanent Council. Over the last few years it has become clear that the Parliamentary Assembly is seeking an increased role. In a report on the future of the OSCE, the assembly proposed that it should approve the OSCE budget as well as confirm the secretary-general after nomination (Organization for Security and Cooperation in Europe Parliamentary Assembly and Swiss Institute for World Affairs 2005). Over the years there has been some tension between the assembly and OSCE's Vienna institutions, the assembly arguing that its elected president is equal to the CiO and that its secretary-general is equal to that of the OSCE. However, such equality is not recognized by the Permanent Council and the Vienna institutions (Nothelle 2007).

A bitter argument took place between the ODIHR and the Secretariat of the Parliamentary Assembly regarding election observation. The ODIHR and Western diplomats claimed that parliamentarians often made politically motivated statements after elections, resulting in Russian accusations of bias. It was argued that the legislators were short-term observers and mostly ignorant about the countries they briefly visited, while ODIHR observers were well informed and familiar with local legislation and traditions. The secretariat, on the other hand, refers to the 1997 cooperation agreement between the ODIHR and the assembly, which the secretariat claims grants it political leadership in election observation missions. The secretariat wants to strengthen this position (Organization for Security and Cooperation in Europe Parliamentary Assembly 1997). Currently its participation is often regarded as symbolic. Secretary-General Oliver Spencer—the Parliamentary Assembly's fiercest exponent—argues that members of Parliament are better suited to make a fair judgment because they have experienced the election process themselves. In the end, the Parliamentary Assembly agrees with Russia that election observation should be held in all member states. Without ODIHR logistical support, however, this would be difficult to implement. The ODIHR—supported by Western countries' representatives in the Permanent Council—argues that election monitoring in mature democracies would be useless and too costly.

The row has already resulted in each side delivering its unique take on elections—assembly judges noting whether the elections were "free and fair," ODIHR judges making technical points. Insiders say that the resultant lack of clarity is almost more serious than Russian attempts to weaken OSCE election observation.

While this conflict unfolds, the Russians, who despise the ODIHR but would probably be even more resistant to maverick members of Parliament, sit back and observe. The monitoring of OSCE commitments in the human dimension is diverse and complicated. There is certainly room for improvement, but due to countries' differing motives for reform, no substantial change is to be expected. In the field of election observation the OSCE is on the defensive due to the Russian proposals, while in-house fighting between the Parliamentary Assembly and the ODIHR weakens its credibility. Nonetheless, commitments have not been watered down and election observation in transitional countries is still being conducted.

Promoting Democracy in Practice

Even though the monitoring of democracy commitments risks falling into decline, the OSCE also promotes democracy through assistance programs. The main actors are again the ODIHR, the Secretariat of the Parliamentary Assembly, and field missions. The ODIHR focuses on institution building, offering tailored advice on legislation and support to civil society. The secretariat in Vienna performs a number of functions related to democratization; for example, its Strategic Police Matters Unit assists states in transforming their police forces into transparent and accountable structures. And field missions are responsible for a whole host of democratization activities, including activities with a political-military dimension.

The 1994 Code of Conduct on Politico-Military Aspects of Security is a guideline for member states on how to run defense and security structures in a democratic fashion. It tackles issues such as democratic control of the armed forces and international transparency on defense matters. Although the code is comprehensive and refers not only to the armed forces but also to police and intelligence services, recent events have made it seem out of date. For instance, it does not take into account terrorism and its implications for civilian control of security. Security sector reform goes somewhat further than the Code of Conduct and is currently being crystallized in EU and Organization for Economic Cooperation and Development (OECD) documents.[7]

Under current circumstances it will be difficult for the OSCE to follow suit and reach an agreement on security sector reform. Nonetheless, that does not prevent it from addressing such reform. The OSCE is free to attach importance to this reform in the work of its field missions as long as the activities do not conflict with the mandate. A good example of this might be the cases of Armenia and Azerbaijan, where OSCE missions supported projects on democratic control of armed forces and security sector governance.[8] These are examples of addressing issues of democracy and security in transitional societies that only recently opened up their security sectors to public debate. In practice, it will be a challenge to pursue security sector reform in addressing the democratic governance of security in Central Asia, where the armed forces and internal security structures safeguard the regime instead of the population. This is a field in which the OSCE can grow, using its experience by carefully debating security issues from a democracy and governance angle.

Through field operations, the OSCE is currently active in seventeen countries, ranging from the Balkans to Central Asia.[9] The missions differ in size and tasks. They were often set up in postconflict situations and mostly focus on assistance in democratic transition and, in countries such as Moldova, in conflict resolution. The mandates and their extension are often controversial. To Russia's disappointment, the missions to Estonia and Latvia that focused on the rights of Russian minorities were closed at the end of 2001. Russia argues that this issue is far from resolved and that the missions were terminated because the two countries were to become EU members.

On the other hand, Western countries could not endorse Russian demands in 2003 to limit the mandate of the small mission in Chechnya to humanitarian assistance and exclude any competence for the mission to report on human rights violations. The extension of mandates and their contents remain in constant threat of erosion. In 1999 the mission to Ukraine was downgraded to an OSCE project coordinator who lacked a monitoring and reporting mandate. This inspired authoritarian states: in 2006 Uzbekistan succeeded in downscaling the OSCE Tashkent Center, leaving only a project coordinator, unable to meet freely with NGOs and with a limited staff and limited mandate. Other Central Asian regimes are currently contemplating limited options like these. In contrast, Tajikistan approved a strengthened mandate in 2008, which resulted in more funds, projects, and OSCE staff being engaged in the republic. Meanwhile Kazakhstan has a significant stake in the OSCE due to its 2010 chairmanship.

In June 2009 the OSCE's most important mission in the Caucasus was closed. The mandate of the mission to Georgia could not be extended because of disagreement over the status of South Ossetia, where the OSCE acted through mediation and observers on the ground. The Russians argued that the OSCE could work in South Ossetia only through a new and separate mission, thus forcing other members indirectly to recognize South Ossetian independence. Most OSCE members wanted access to South Ossetia through the Georgia mission, as they had until the August 2008 conflict. A Russian veto ended the OSCE's work in Georgia. It remains doubtful whether the EU will take the OSCE's place. The EU Monitoring Mission has in broad lines replaced the monitoring functions concerning South Ossetia, although its focus is on Russian troop withdrawal, while the OSCE's task was to monitor tensions between South Ossetians and Georgians. The United States might even contribute to this EU-led initiative. Meanwhile the ENP and its new Eastern Partnership might partially take over those OSCE tasks in Georgia focused on democratization, human rights, and training.

A more general problem of OSCE field operations is the lack of qualified personnel. Because the OSCE is currently a noncareer organization, which mostly attracts personnel through secondments, working for the OSCE is less attractive than working for other international organizations. Staff quality and pay vary greatly, and turnover is high. Some of the field staff lack knowledge about the region they work in and are simply not credible to local interlocutors and authorities. Although several countries do send qualified staff, secondment contracts are being extended to somewhat longer ones, and the OSCE has been able to offer a few fixed contract positions, nevertheless, greater professionalization is still required.

Field staff in the Balkans implements democratization-related projects in all three categories through capacity building and good governance in national and local authorities, parliamentary oversight, the rule of law and the judiciary, the development of political parties, civil-military relations, gender issues, media, and civil society support. In Albania, for example, good governance is promoted through projects focused on increasing budget transparency under the economic and environmental dimension. In Bosnia and Herzegovina the political-military dimension is focused on projects for democratic defense reform and democratic control of armed forces. In Serbia good governance projects were implemented to strengthen the oversight role of Parliament in the human dimension.[10]

In Eastern Europe OSCE missions focus less on democratization. In Belarus the mandate and the regime's restrictions scarcely leave room for this. In Moldova emphasis is on settlement of the Transnistrian conflict. The offices in Baku and Yerevan undertake projects related to freedom of the media, electoral reform, and civil society capacity building. Democratization activities in Central Asia are limited. While there has been some progress in democratization projects in Kazakhstan, the work of the OSCE in other Central Asian republics has been seriously curtailed.

In 2008 the OSCE spent about 70 percent of its €164 million budget on field operations (Organization for Security and Cooperation in Europe 2009, 110). The lion's share of these funds went to operations in the Balkans and, more specifically, operations in Bosnia and Herzegovina (18 percent of the total OSCE budget) and Kosovo (9 percent). The OSCE works in Central Asia on budgets of between €1.3 million (Turkmenistan) and €5 million (Kyrgyzstan). Taking into account that personnel are mostly seconded by member states, a large share of OSCE funds go to project implementation, often directly or indirectly related to democratization. Nonetheless, the budgets for most field operations and their work on democracy promotion are dwarfed by other donors' efforts. There exists the possibility for member states and associated countries such as Japan to support projects through extrabudgetary donations, although these are said to be around only €20 million to €25 million a year, excluding a few very cost-intensive technical projects. These small funds are important since they do not have to be approved by the Permanent Council, which might have objections to, for instance, the OSCE actively promoting democracy in Central Asia.

Russia is trying to increase the powers of the Permanent Council in this area in order to regulate extrabudgetary funds and make every single project subject to consensus approval. Together with Belarus, Kazakhstan, and Kyrgyzstan, Russia has objected to the fact that missions are deployed only east of Vienna, that they mainly focus on the human dimension, and that they are intrusive in the internal affairs of member states (Dunay 2006, 61). To remedy these perceived imbalances, proposals for reform have been made to limit the duration of mission mandates to one year, to give the host nation a veto over the nomination of the head of mission, and to increase control over budgets. Setting up thematic missions was also discussed when it became clear that most member states were not willing to address the geographical imbalance by setting up expensive missions in the Basque region or Northern Ireland. The thematic missions that would address pressing cross-border issues would also involve activities in countries without a standing mission. Most countries are not enthusiastic about creating new mechanisms, fearing they will overlap with existing institutions. They argue that the OSCE has enough tools to address new security challenges. Furthermore, several member states wonder how these missions would be funded, given the fact that the OSCE budget is in relative decline.

Field operations are the OSCE's most cost-intensive assets and are often used as its calling card. From a practical democracy promotion point of view, this is reassuring. It is worrying, however, that funds for democratization projects are diminishing and that the offices in Central Asia, where assistance is most needed, are too small to have a significant effect. Although these countries are earmarked by the OSCE as democratic but in need of further transformation, in reality authoritarian regimes are busy consolidating their positions through gas and oil revenues.

OSCE democratization is not aimed at regime change but is intended to make a contribution over the long term. And although its democratization work has not come to a halt, it does not show any sign of intensifying. Given this, it will be important for OSCE missions to work closely with the EU, NATO, and the United Nations Development Program in situations where the OSCE's main advantages—its experience and its eyes and ears on the ground—add value.

Challenges and Expectations

The 1990s showed a substantial growth of OSCE participating states' commitments toward democracy and human rights. The organization could boast of its transition success stories—in the Balkans but also further east. The positive attitude toward democratic change in Eastern Europe at that time seemed to provide a steady wind in the sails of OSCE cooperation. Unfortunately, agreements on democracy are no longer in touch with reality. Several member states have lost their appetite for transforming their societies into democracies. For the OSCE it would be logical to step up activities in Central Asia, especially given the precarious balance between regional security threats and lack of democratic reform. However, resistance to democracy by Russia and several CIS countries makes the monitoring of commitments and democracy promotion problematic.

The challenge for the countries in the OSCE that do believe in its democracy commitments lies in continued investment in the organization's monitoring and project capacities. EU member states have a key role to play here and should act jointly to prevent member states from defaulting on their commitments. The OSCE is a useful mechanism for the EU and its member states, being an institution responsible for democratic commitments and the implementation of democracy promotion programs. Unfortunately, declining funds, staffing problems, and lack of confidence in the OSCE's capacity to push reform where needed undermine the organization, and the unity surrounding democracy in the early 1990s is unlikely to return any time soon. The fact that the OSCE is the only regional organization in Europe that has confirmed democratic commitments and that has all authoritarian European and Eurasian states as members is an asset. That seems enough for the time being to secure its importance.

A complete overhaul to adapt the OSCE to current security challenges is out of reach. Few innovative ideas exist, and a deadlock among member states prevents action. EU members have not come up with ways to revitalize the OSCE and have, for the last few years, increasingly given preference to other channels of democracy promotion. Moreover, restructuring the three dimensions into one list of clearly defined objectives would risk watering down commitments in the human dimension. The OSCE will have to be satisfied with a modest role in comparison with the roles of other international actors, such as the EU and NATO in the field of security and the EU in the area of democracy promotion beyond its borders. The OSCE has undergone a process of technical and organizational reform that may increase its effectiveness. Western countries have worked to ensure that these reforms allow room for maneuver when OSCE institutions need to act. For example, reforms aimed at increasing consensus decisions by the Permanent Council would be disastrous for democracy promotion. The OSCE will be able to perform its role in democratization only if institutional reform is regarded as largely completed and if

Russian proposals for further reforms are judged by members on the merit of increasing effectiveness, not downplaying commitments or limiting projects.

In sum, the variables presented in chapter 1 play themselves out in complex ways within the OSCE. The body's overarching institutional structure accords Russia far greater sway than the policies of other organizations do. The all-inclusive membership of the OSCE has not facilitated democracy support, as was predicated in the 1990s. EU strategic interests remain a multifaceted variable within the OSCE. Strategic interests can drive democracy promotion, as in Georgia. But they can also weaken EU efforts to promote democracy, as for example in Turkmenistan. A case-by-case assessment is required. Compared to other cases examined in this volume, structural and institutional factors play a relatively prominent role in explaining the OSCE's recent record. Some of the OSCE's democratic members have lost the appetite to push the democracy agenda; but those that wish to keep it alive find themselves hamstrung by institutional arrangements agreed upon during the rosier 1990s.

The monitoring of democratic commitments, and election observation in particular, will remain sensitive topics. The ODIHR has the opportunity to improve the quality of its work, one of the demands made in the reform process. The ODIHR will remain the world's leading organization in election observation, but it needs continuous support from those countries that deem free and fair elections to be at the heart of democracy. Meanwhile, an important challenge for the OSCE is to solve the disputes between the ODIHR—already under attack from Russia— and the Parliamentary Assembly, which is looking for increased influence in election observation. Both sides need to compromise, as long as their internal functioning is not threatened. Internal disputes could be disastrous for OSCE democracy promotion at a time when member countries are already divided.

Democracy promotion through field operations shows a little more flexibility. The monitoring role of missions has declined, but there is still room to implement new projects. The closure of the mission in Georgia was bad news for OSCE democracy promotion efforts. It will also be difficult to step up activities in Central Asia, although there may be scope for initiatives on good governance of scarce water resources or democratic control of security forces. Extrabudgetary funds are crucial for this, because the OSCE's general budget is small and the budgets of the missions in Central Asia and the Caucasus states are, in most cases, insignificant compared to those of other donors. In these regions, it will be necessary to look for synergies between the ENP, the Eastern Partnership, and the EU's Central Asia policy—as well as some Partnership for Peace programs. The OSCE missions remain important for conflict resolution and prevention as well as human rights, good governance, and the rule of law.

The OSCE will continue to be a platform for dialogue but also for disagreement. This is nothing new. However, it is unfortunate that important security challenges are mostly taken up elsewhere and that the system of democracy promotion is under attack. OSCE democracy promotion has not come to a grinding halt, but it is slowing down. The organization is unable to maintain its members' commitment to all that was agreed upon in the 1990s in the fields of security, democracy, and human rights. In that sense, the OSCE has become a paper tiger. Meanwhile the number and size of democracy-related projects has shrunk. The OSCE should look for new challenges, maintain a comprehensive approach to security, and pursue democracy promotion through patience and perseverance. It can do so only if it receives moral and financial support from member states to fulfill its mission of building a community of peaceful, prosperous, human rights-respecting, and democratic societies.

NOTES

1. Some of the information presented in this chapter draws upon interviews by the author with officials from OSCE institutions in Vienna and Warsaw and with national Permanent Representative Missions to the OSCE in Vienna, May 2007 and July 2007, respectively.
2. The OSCE's work is divided into three dimensions: political-military, economic and environmental, and humanitarian.
3. The Moscow Declaration was signed by Armenia, Belarus, Kazakhstan, Kyrgyzstan, Moldova, Russia, Tajikistan, Ukraine and Uzbekistan. The so-called Astana appeal of September 2004 was signed by the same members, with the exception of Moldova. In the following years, similar documents have been presented by some of these countries.
4. Author's translation, The OSCE outlived, *Moscow News*, May 10, 2007.
5. The following EU countries held the chairmen-in-office position: Slovenia in 2005, Belgium in 2006, Spain in 2007, Finland in 2008, and Greece in 2009.
6. For an overview of OSCE Human Dimension monitoring mechanisms and proposals on how to improve these, see Narten 2006.
7. For more detailed information on security sector reform and the OSCE see, Law 2006, 83–106.
8. Organization for Security and Cooperation in Europe, news release, August 3, 2007, www.osce.org/item/25853.html.
9. For further details on field missions, see Legutke 2006; Semneby 2005.
10. Organization for Security and Cooperation in Europe, news release, August 3, 2007.

REFERENCES

Baker, S. H., and E. D. McMahon. 2006. *Piecing a Democratic Quilt? Regional Organizations and Universal Norms.* Bloomfield, Conn.: Kumarian Press.
Delegation of the Russian Federation to the OSCE. 2007. Basic principles for the organization of OSCE observation of national elections. Paper PC.DEL/458/07.
Dunay, P. 2006. The OSCE in crisis. Chaillot Paper 88. Paris: EU Institute for Security Studies.
Erler, G. 2006. Germany and OSCE reform. Working Paper 158. Hamburg: Centre for OSCE Research.
Ghébali,V-Y. 2006. The reform of the OSCE: Problems, challenges, and risks. In *The Reform of the OSCE Fifteen Years after the Charter of Paris for a New Europe: Problems, Challenges, and Risks,* ed. V-Y. Ghébali and D. Warner. Oxford: Program for the Study of International Organizations.
———. 2005. The Russian factor in the OSCE crisis: A fair examination. *Helsinki Monitor* 16/3: 185–87.
Kramer, D. 2007. Speech, Baltimore Council on Foreign Affairs, May 31, in Baltimore, United States.
Lavrov, S. 2007. The present and the future of global politics. *Russia in Global Affairs* 2/5.
Law, D. 2006. Rethinking the code of conduct in the light of security sector reform. In *Consolidating the OSCE,* ed. Daniel Warner. Oxford: Program for the Study of International Organizations.
Legutke, A. 2006. The reform of field activities: Technical or political necessity. In *The Reform of the OSCE Fifteen Years after the Charter of Paris for a New Europe: Problems, Challenges, and Risks,* ed. Victor-Yves Ghébali and Daniel Warner. Oxford. Program for the Study of International Organizations.
Lynch, D. 2006. The basic challenges facing the OSCE. In *Consolidating the OSCE,* ed. Daniel Warner. Oxford: Program for the Study of International Organizations.
Ministry of Foreign Affairs of the Russian Federation. 2004. *A Survey of Russian Federation Foreign Policy.* www.mid.ru/Brp_4.nsf/arh/89A30B3A6B65B4F2C32572D7002 92F74?OpenDocument
Narten, J. 2006. Options for a general OSCE human dimension monitoring instrument. Hamburg: Center for OSCE Research.
Nothelle, A. 2007. The OSCE parliamentary assembly: Driving reform. In *OSCE Yearbook 2006.* Hamburg: Center for OSCE Research.
Office for Democratic Institutions and Human Rights. 2007. Interim report of the Election Observation Mission to the 2007 Parliamentary Election in the Republic of Kazakhstan (16 July-4 August). www.osce.org/documents/odihr/2007/08/25894_en.pdf.
———. 1991. Document of the Moscow meeting of the conference on the human dimension of the CSCE. October 3. Moscow. www.osce.org/documents/odihr/1991/10/13995_en.pdf.
Organization for Security and Cooperation in Europe. 2009. *The OSCE Annual Report 2008.* Vienna.
Organization for Security and Cooperation in Europe Parliamentary Assembly. 1997. *Cooperation Agreement between OSCE PA and ODIHR.*

Organization for Security and Cooperation in Europe Parliamentary Assembly and Swiss Institute for World Affairs. 2005. Colloquium. The future of the OSCE. June 5–6. Washington. www.osce.org/documents/pa/2005/06/15378_en.pdf.

Semneby, P. 2005. Ten lessons for running OSCE field missions in the future. *Helsinki Monitor* 16/3: 232–37.

CHAPTER SIX

Central Asia
Limited Modernization

Alexander Warkotsch

Central Asia provides one of the toughest tests for Europe's commitment to democracy. The political structures in the region offer little ground for successful democracy promotion. Neither the European Union nor any other Western actor has so far had any discernible impact on democratization. On the contrary, democratic rights have deteriorated since the late 1990s: in its June 2009 report, Freedom House ranks the Central Asian republics as "consolidated authoritarian regimes" (Freedom House 2009). Against this background, many experts see talk of democratization in Central Asia as entirely fanciful (Blank 2004, 133). European influence in Central Asia is relatively limited compared to that of other external players. The combination of complicating domestic and external variables means that it is hardly surprising that EU democracy promotion efforts have made little headway. But the EU can be admonished for failing even to use what influence it does have to advance the more modest aims of promoting good governance and widening the space for civic activity.

In most Central Asian states presidents rule by decree, and parliaments and courts are weak and routinely ignored. Opposition has been circumscribed, co-opted, or repressed. Elections have had dubious legitimacy, and the emergence of independent mass media has been hindered. In short, substantive democracy is absent. Of course, the picture varies: a formal democratic opening in Kyrgyzstan, some liberalization in Kazakhstan and Tajikistan, little reform in Uzbekistan and Turkmenistan. Turkmenistan in particular is a sobering example of Central Asia's failed postcommunist transformation. It has deteriorated to a tragic yet farcical restaging of Stalinism's worst excesses.

Formally, the promotion of human rights and democracy has been incorporated into the network of EU agreements in Central Asia, purportedly as a shared value and objective. For example, Central Asian Partnership and Cooperation Agreements (PCAs) start with a declaration on "general principles," which states that "respect for democracy, principles of international law and human rights . . . as well as the principles of a market economy, underpin the internal and external policies of the Parties and constitute an essential element of partnership of this Agreement." Moreover, article 1 of all PCAs explicitly refers to the "consolidation of democracy" as a main objective of cooperation. The stated aim of the EU's technical and financial assistance is to promote a "democratic mentality" (Commission of the European Communities 2004, 26). Since 2007 the new Development Cooperation Instrument (DCI), an aid program managed by the European Commission, defines "the promotion of democracy, good governance and respect for human rights" as an "overarching objective of cooperation."

In June 2007 the EU raised new hopes that it could live up to its rhetoric and finally help set the Central Asian republics on a path toward democracy. With the European Council's adoption of a new Central Asia strategy, the EU doubled its Central Asia assistance, with some €750 million allocated for 2007–13 under the DCI. Though the strategy sets out a broad range of general objectives, it also highlights "good governance, the rule of law, human rights, and democratization" as "key areas" for EU support (Council of the European Union 2007, 1). Only one year after the adoption of the strategy, the council and the commission claimed in their first progress report on the implementation of the strategy that a "new quality of cooperation has evolved between Central Asia and the EU" (Council of the European Union and Commission of European Communities 2008).

But is it really the case that the EU has enhanced concrete policy and assistance initiatives in support of human rights and democracy? Is the EU's current approach to human rights and democracy promotion likely to trigger tangible political change in the Central Asian republics? This chapter critically examines the EU's policy instruments, the types of projects that are being funded, and who are the addressees of democracy projects in Central Asia. In addition, it looks at the tradeoffs between short-term interests and democracy objectives. The chapter argues that the EU's commitment to democracy support has been weak in Central Asia, weaker indeed than in most of the other areas examined in this volume. The EU should, nonetheless, hone in on the more achievable aims of good governance and civil society reforms in a more systematic fashion.

Democracy in European Strategy

The adoption of the EU's Central Asia strategy represents an ambitious project to upgrade EU–Central Asia relations. However, it is hardly a strategy in the true sense of the word; rather, it is a general framework setting out the goal of increased cooperation in such policy areas as energy, organized crime, the economy, the environment, and democracy and presents new initiatives and instruments to address them.

In the section on "human rights, rule of law, good governance, and democratization," two directions are apparent. First, it follows a comprehensive notion of security by stressing that "the development of a stable political framework and of functioning economic structures are dependent on respect for the rule of law, human rights, good governance, and the development of transparent, democratic political structures" (Council of the European Union 2007, 5). Second, it addresses the challenge of promoting the rule of law, transparent political structures, and a human rights culture. It does not emphasize strengthening democratic political institutions, such as the Parliament and the courts. Though the strategy briefly mentions increased support for the "creation and development of an independent judiciary," this support is not further specified. Legal cooperation instead builds on a new "rule of law initiative" that "will support the Central Asian States in core legal reforms, including reform of the judiciary, and in drawing up effective legislation, for example in the fields of administrative and commercial law" (Council of the European Union 2007, 6).

The strategy emphasizes dialogue as a means of human rights and democracy promotion. It outlines certain dialogue commitments: starting a regular regional political dialogue at a foreign ministers' level with the EU troika, holding annual meetings of its heads of mission, and establishing a bilateral, results-oriented human rights dialogue (Council of the European Union 2007, 2). While the form and the modalities of such dialogue are not defined, its objectives and contents are specified as "enhancing cooperation on human rights, inter alia in multilateral fora such as the United Nations and the OSCE" as well as "raising the concerns felt by the EU as regards the human rights situation in the countries concerned, information gathering and initiatives to improve the relevant human rights situation" (Council of the European Union 2007, 6). The strategy also briefly mentions financial and technical cooperation and projects to be funded under the new European Instrument for Democracy and Human Rights (EIDHR) for improving the human rights situation in Central Asia.

Increasing cooperation in justice through a rule of law initiative as well as fostering a human rights culture through dialogue certainly take center stage in the strategy's norms agenda. The rule of law initiative was officially launched at a ministerial conference in Brussels on November 27–28, 2008. The key outcome of the conference was commitment from the Central Asian republics to allow discussions and assistance on the rule of law at the regional and bilateral levels. Agreement was also reached to hold two rule of law conferences in autumn 2009 in Bishkek and Tashkent. Another conference is scheduled for 2010 in Central Asia (Isaacs 2009, 2). To a certain extent the EU also emphasizes the importance of an active civil society and media independence for "sustaining a culture of human rights" and establishing a pluralistic society. However, contrary to the two focuses of justice and human rights cooperation, the strategy does not suggest a new initiative or instrument for the implementation of civil society and media support. The model of truncated governance reform expounded in the opening chapter to the volume has particular resonance in Central Asia.

All in all the strategy's approach toward human rights and democracy promotion seems to be relatively soft. Contrary to prior EU documents on Central Asia, the principle of conditionality is absent. While the partnership and cooperation agreements—the closest thing to a strategy for Central Asia the EU had before the adoption of the 2007 strategy—include so-called human rights clauses and therefore provide for the reduction or even suspension of cooperation in cases of noncompliance (article 92), similar provisions have not been made within the EU's new Central Asia strategy. Rather, the EU's plans for a human rights dialogue, increased political dialogue, and a rule of law initiative favor instruments of persuasion over mechanisms that build on political and material incentives or pressure.

Europe's Policy Instruments

In reality there is remarkably little European support for democratization processes in Central Asia. EU democratization assistance for Central Asian states is negligible, concentrating mainly on good governance instead of democratization in the narrower sense. Strong instruments of sanctions are hardly used, and the principle of positive conditionality, which has been laid down in almost all EU strategy documents and agreements with Central Asian countries, has not been implemented. In sum, EU democratization policy in Central Asia can be described as highly cautious and tame. Put into a larger theoretical framework, the EU's preferred mechanism for democracy promotion in the Central Asian republics is less a rationalist bargaining approach, which builds on incentives and cost-benefit calculations on the side of the target elites, and more an approach that relies on deliberation and discourse. Looking in detail at the EU's several policy instruments—political and human rights dialogue, technical and financial assistance, democratization aid, and political conditionality—commitment appears if anything to be wavering rather than strengthening.

First, political and human rights dialogue is not a significant part of the EU's formal agreements with Central Asia. The PCAs are documents of some sixty pages but contain only a brief section (one page) on political dialogue. This brevity is at odds with the pride of place given to political issues in the PCAs' declaration of principles and in article 1, describing the character of the partnership (MacFarlane 2003, 149). Moreover, the goals of political dialogue are outlined only very vaguely (article 4): "A regular political dialogue . . . shall support the political and economic changes under way . . . and contribute to the establishment of new forms of cooperation." Only the Uzbek PCA adds that "The political dialogue . . . shall foresee that the Parties endeavor to cooperate on matters pertaining to the observance of the principles of democracy, and the respect, protection, and promotion of human rights, particularly those of persons belonging to minorities and shall hold consultations, if necessary, on relevant matters."

Dialogue between the EU and the Central Asian republics has not been intensive. Pursuant to the PCAs, dialogue rests mainly with the Cooperation Council. However, while the Euro-Mediterranean Committee for the Barcelona Process meets on average every two to three months, the Cooperation Council in Central Asia meets only once a year. Moreover, council talks are conducted in a cautious manner, and sensitive subjects are seldom discussed in detail (Von Gumppenberg 2002, 39). It has long been a struggle to find high-level EU officials to attend the Cooperation Council meeting, while many Central Asia delegations are often composed of the prime minister or the foreign minister (International Crisis Group 2006, 18).

Not only is dialogue relating to reform commitments under the PCAs half-hearted; until recently, other high-ranking diplomatic contacts have been limited.

For example, former EU External Affairs Commissioner Chris Patten's March 2004 tour of Central Asia was the only trip to the region by an EU commissioner in ten years.[1] With only a four-person delegation in the Kazakh capital of Almaty and otherwise only the commission-run Europe House in Tashkent, the EU's on-the-ground representation cannot pay more than marginal attention to Central Asia's transition to democracy.

Dialogue as a democracy promotion instrument has recently begun to increase in importance. An EU special representative for Central Asia was appointed in July 2005. Though mainly a response to earlier political upheaval in Uzbekistan and Kyrgyzstan, this step represented an increase in the EU's capacity to promote human rights and democracy goals through dialogue. The EU's strategy for Central Asia outlines concrete dialogue commitments, including strengthening political dialogue in particular and starting a high-ranking, regular regional political dialogue as well as the bilateral, results-oriented human rights dialogue.[2]

However, so far the enhanced dialogue follows a top-down approach. Meetings are confined to discussions between EU officials and representatives of the Central Asian regimes, while local civil society organizations and representatives have not been targeted by the EU for enhanced political dialogue (Boonstra and Melvin 2008, 3). Regarding regular participation by high-ranking officials, the strategy's ambitious rhetoric is undercut by a more prosaic reality. Between June 2007 and late 2009 the EU troika met only four times with Central Asian representatives. In addition to continued Cooperation Council meetings, High Representative Javier Solana last visited the region in October 2007 and Foreign Affairs Commissioner Ferrero-Waldner followed in April 2008 (Council of the European Union and Commission of the European Communities 2008, 3).[3]

Second, technical and financial assistance remains limited in magnitude and political reach. The EU has frequently stated that the OSCE functions as its primary organization for security cooperation in Central Asia (Swanström 2004, 48). Since the OSCE pursues a concept of comprehensive security with a strong "human dimension," EU officials have always been tempted to believe that the body functions as the ideal forum to deal with issues of democratic transition and human rights in Central Asia. With respect to the EU's technical and financial democracy assistance, this "outsourcing" of sensitive issues has led to a concentration on "good governance" (open and accountable decision making, efficient and effective management of public administration) instead of fostering democracy in its more political sense (civil and political rights, institutions of democratic representation, and democratic civil society) (Warkotsch 2006, 515).

As noted, new technical and financial assistance projects have been introduced through the DCI, although most of the currently active projects are still running under the old TACIS scheme. Within the area of good governance, the Policy Advice Program (PAP) is the EU's flagship project. The specific objectives of PAP are to assist high-ranking decision makers in the development of reform-oriented, sustainable economic and social policies, supporting the implementation of these policies by appropriate institution building. Funding concentrates on Kazakhstan, Kyrgyzstan, and Tajikistan. In 2007 financial support for ongoing projects was between €1.2 million for Tajikistan and €1.4 million for Kazakhstan.[4] Uzbekistan and Turkmenistan receive only sporadic, small-scale PAP support. The EU's equivalent for policy reform on the local level is the Institution Building Partnership Program (IBPP). IBPP supports social nongovernmental organizations (NGOs) and local authorities at the province and district levels in the fields of economic development, urban management, environment, and public administration. In 2007 IBPP support ranged from €0.6 million for Turkmenistan to €1.7 million for Kazakhstan. The bulk of PAP and IBPP support for good governance goes to capacity building of national and local administrations. Less then 20 percent is spent on strengthening government accountability. This expenditure in 2007 was €1.9 million for all of Central Asia.

These amounts are negligible. PAP and IBPP support for Central Asia is meager. For example, the 2007 IBPP allocation for Ukraine was more than double the amount of support for all five Central Asian republics put together. With the new strategy this discrepancy is likely to be reduced. Still, even with the EU's increased Central Asia budget for technical and financial cooperation, EU support for Central Asia lags massively behind its support for other regions. For the period 2007–13 EU per capita support will be €9, compared to €17 for the Western Newly Independent States, €29 for the southern Mediterranean countries, and €237 for the Balkans for 2007–10.[5]

Third, overtly political democratization aid is even more curtailed. Democracy in its narrower sense is promoted first and foremost through the European Instrument for Democracy and Human Rights (EIDHR). Before 2005 the Central Asian republics were not included as eligible recipients and received only very limited and sporadic support from EIDHR. Funding concentrates, again, on Kazakhstan, Kyrgyzstan, and Tajikistan, with the bulk of cooperation being microprojects (since 2007 officially called country-based support scheme projects) of between €10,000 and €100,000 each. These projects, which are managed by the European Commission Delegation to Kazakhstan, Kyrgyzstan, and Tajikistan, focus on local civil society organizations. Recent examples of grants include €22,379 for the International Foundation for the Protection of Speech Fund Adil Soz in Kazakhstan and €99,995 for the Interbilim International Centre in Kyrgyzstan for the inclusion of youth in the democratic processes. Larger projects are managed from Brussels, with €900,024 for support of the democratic process in Uzbekistan, through the German Konrad Adenauer Stiftung, being the largest amount allocated to a single project. Other large grants include €762,597 for Freedom House, €423,697 for the International Helsinki Federation for Human Rights, €333,275 for the International Step-by-Step Association, and €224,814 for the OSCE's Office for Democratic Institutions and Human Rights. Finally, €100,000 for projects on constitutional reform in Kazakhstan and Kyrgyzstan have been made available through the Council of Europe. Considering large and small grants together, there is a clear focus on human rights promotion and minority rights protection. Only about one-third of expenditures concentrate on strengthening the democratic process as such.

Expenditure from the EIDHR in 2006 was €6.4 million and in 2007, €6.5 million. The Central Asia strategy has not had much impact on EIDHR allocations. Increased project commitments can probably be expected only from 2010 onward.[6] Between 2005 and 2007, the bulk of EIDHR expenditures were relatively equally distributed among national and international NGOs. Only about 5 percent of project expenditures is implemented by intergovernmental organizations. With the exception of one large project in Uzbekistan, the EU concentrates on less authoritarian Kazakhstan, Kyrgyzstan, and Tajikistan.

Fourth, the EU eschews political conditionality in Central Asia. The principle of positive conditionality is formally enshrined in many of the EU's Central Asia strategy documents. For example, the Central Asia Indicative Program 2007–2010 states that "assistance . . . will depend on the aspects needed for continued cooperation in particular respect of democratic principles and human rights and fulfillment of PCA obligations. Democratic evolution and the human rights situation in the countries of the region will be taken into consideration in the preparation of the annual Central Asia Action Programs and as a parameter for the final budget allocation" (Commission of the European Communities 2006, 25). In practice, however, compliance with liberal-democratic rules does not seem to be an important factor determining EU aid allocations. The EU's bilateral aid programs amount to nearly €220 million, of which Tajikistan receives €66 million (30 percent); Kyrgyzstan, €55 million (25 percent); Kazakhstan, €44 million (20 percent); Uzbekistan, €33 million (15 percent); and Turkmenistan, €22 million (10 percent) (Commission of the European Communities 2006, 5). This translates into the following per capita allocations: Kyrgyzstan (€10.6), Tajikistan (€10.0), Turkmenistan (€4.6), Kazakhstan (€2.9), and Uzbekistan (€1.2). These figures reveal a somewhat erratic picture of the principle of positive conditionality. Especially surprising is the high per capita amount for dictatorial Turkmenistan, which receives almost 70 percent more per capita aid than Kazakhstan, one of the region's relatively reform-minded and less illiberal regimes. Of course, one might explain Kazakhstan's relatively low level of assistance by its promising economic development. However, this argument does not hold for Uzbekistan.

Provisions for the use of negative conditionality—that is, the reduction or suspension of benefits should the recipient not comply—are evident in the Partnership and Cooperation Agreements. For example, article 2 includes respect for democracy and human rights as an "essential element" of the bilateral relationship between the EU and the Central Asian countries. Article 95 continues, "if either Party considers that the other Party has failed to fulfill an obligation under this Agreement, it may take appropriate measures," thus enabling the EU to suspend the agreement in the event of a breach.

Between 1993 and 2006 the Central Asian states saw thirty-seven cases of electoral manipulation in national elections and incidents of presidential power consolidation. The EU responded in only eleven cases and then used only soft responses, like declarations condemning the violation (Warkotsch 2008). Tough instruments like the reduction of aid or sanctions were not applied. So far the EU has imposed sanctions only on the Uzbek regime after its 2005 violent crackdown on the Andijan uprising, which caused hundreds of civilian casualties. Sanctions involved the suspension of PCA Cooperation Council meetings, travel restrictions for members of the ruling elite, and an arms embargo; they did not affect gas sales or trade and investment flows. However, the EU's toughness on human rights issues did not last long. By late 2008 the main sanctions had been removed, at the behest of the German government in particular. In October 2009 EU governments agreed to remove an arms embargo, the last remaining measure in place against Uzbekistan. After a meeting shortly before the September 15, 2009, EU–Central Asia ministerial conference in Brussels, EU and Uzbek senior officials were eager to downplay differences and focus on pragmatic cooperation. Frank Belfrage, secretary of state at the Swedish Foreign Ministry, who chaired the meeting, called the bilateral relationship "broad and deep" and sidestepped questions asking for an assessment of the recent Uzbek human rights record.[7]

With regard to the essential elements clause, the EU claims that "the principal rationale for the clause is to form a positive basis for advancing human rights in third countries through dialogue and persuasion" (Commission of the European Communities 2007, 13). In other words, the preference is to use positive action rather than penalties to avoid cutting off constructive dialogue and losing influence altogether. In practice, as shown above, such dialogue remains thin.

Explaining the Rhetoric-Reality Gap

In sum, implementation of the EU's human rights and democracy policy in Central Asia has not lived up to the expectations created by European rhetoric. While EU positions assert that political reform is necessary for security, in practice short-term strategic calculations have cut across democracy support. Three issues are germane: first, the special relations of some member states with Russia; second, the participation of member states in the war against terrorism; and third, energy security.

From the outset of his presidency, Vladimir Putin took a strong and decisive hand in retaining control over Russia's near neighbors. In dealing with Putin's policy of a "Greater Russia," the EU, urged by its bigger member states (Germany, France, Italy), sought to reassure Moscow that its intention was not to question Russia's position in its traditional backyard. Russia's former defense minister asserted that Moscow's interests in CIS countries were a strategic priority and that Russia would therefore "react very sharply to the export of [democratic] revolutions to the CIS countries" (Eder and Halbach 2005, 7). An aggressive EU democratization policy would certainly be considered an assault on this position, since the single most important factor in spreading the Kremlin's influence in the region has been the degree to which the Central Asian trajectory parallels that of Putin's authoritarianism. For the Central Asian elites, in turn, it is reassuring that Russia publicly announced that parliamentary democracy is inapplicable in Central Asia (Laruelle 2009, 5).

Central Asia's strategic importance in the war against terror also overrides many human rights and democracy concerns. The participation of EU member states in the International Security Assistance Force requires military cooperation with Central Asian regimes. Most significantly, Kyrgyzstan, Tajikistan, and Uzbekistan have provided overflight rights and air bases and have agreed to host foreign troops, including German forces in Uzbekistan and French troops in Tajikistan. While many Westerners have been forced out of Uzbekistan after the tragic events in Andijan, the German army continues to operate its base in the border city of

Termez.[8] This continued cooperation comes with a trade-off: it was Germany that for some time prevented EU sanctions against Uzbekistan in the EU Council of Ministers following the Andijan massacre.[9] It was also Germany that undermined the credibility and symbolic value of these sanctions when Uzbek Interior Minister Zokirjon Almatov, who was at the top of a visa ban list, received medical treatment in Germany.

Energy security has become a more prominent part of the European policy agenda, and the EU has begun to consider Central Asian resources as an "additional filling station." The EU's new Central Asia strategy is explicit about establishing a new Caspian–Black Sea–EU energy transport corridor. Hopes rest on three of the five Central Asian states. Kazakhstan has by far the largest energy reserves: oil in the global top ten, gas in the top fifteen. Turkmenistan has large unexplored gas reserves, maybe even the third-largest in the world. Uzbekistan is also a significant gas producer, though of minor importance compared with Kazakhstan and Turkmenistan (British Petroleum 2007, 6, 22). Now that the EU is getting serious about diversifying energy imports by endorsing the Nabucco pipeline project (at its May 8, 2009, Southern Corridor summit in Prague), the strategic importance of Central Asian states has grown even more.

Europe's business interests in the oil and gas sector in Central Asia are enormous, most notably in Kazakhstan, where about 80–90 percent of total European foreign direct investment (about €1 billion a year) is allocated to the energy sector. The main investment partners are British Gas (UK), Eni (Italy), Shell (Netherlands), and TotalFinaElf (France) (Warkotsch 2006). It is hard to imagine that EU democracy promotion efforts are not influenced by such energy issues, not least because the EU is in direct competition with Russia and China.

The effect of these strategic calculations is compounded by the nature of domestic political structures in Central Asia. A widely held assumption is that the EU is especially active in countries that provide a favorable context for democracy promotion, above all by their regimes showing a certain willingness for reform. This is in accordance with the council's position that increased democracy support is to be considered where positive changes have taken place and democratization aid falls on fertile ground (Council of the European Union 1998). Given the character of Central Asian regimes, this should be considered an important factor in the relatively low level of democratization resources that the EU has allocated to the region.

EU democratization projects are complicated by the way Central Asian societies are structured. The social fabric of Central Asia is a mixture of traditional institutions, like kinship and clan affiliations. Regional experts differ in their assessment of how important such customary structures are, with some arguing that their role can be overstated. But at the very least, such considerations present the EU with complex policy challenges in terms of which local organizations to support. For some experts, the culture of patronage and personalism associated with traditional networks militates against internationally supported democratic norms (Collins 2004).

Refocusing Strategy

Asked about achievements of recent EU–Central Asian relations, a European Commission official optimistically named as a particular success "the new engagement by the countries of the region to cooperate in sensitive areas like reform of the judiciary, legal reforms, or even civil society, including Uzbekistan or Turkmenistan, which were recently on the brink of cutting off any cooperation." The commission attributes this to increasingly "consistent and constructive dialogue and cooperation" since the adoption of the strategy. Though there is so far no real sign of increased cooperation in terms of new technical and financial assistance or EIDHR projects, dialogue may play a decisive role in future EU–Central Asian relations. A second feature, which has become more apparent since the adoption of the strategy, is a focus on good governance instead of on the establishment of democratic institutions. As said, the centerpiece here is the EU's rule of law initiative for Central Asia.

EU assistance for strengthening the democratic process in Central Asia comprises a standard portfolio of power redistribution efforts similar to what is offered to other post-Communist regions: above all, judicial reform, parliamentary strengthening, political party development, and electoral programs (Commission of the European Communities 2004; European Community 2006). Such an approach may have worked in Eastern Europe, where authoritarian structures were already broken up, elite commitment to democratic reform was strong, and material incentives were high. In Central Asia, however, it is unlikely to succeed.

So far the EU has provided only limited incentives for the opening up of Central Asia's authoritarian regimes (Carothers 2000). Like the U.S. Agency for International Development and other international donors, much effort has been expended encouraging the growth of alternative centers of power by, first and foremost, concentrating on civil society support. For example, the EU—through TACIS/DCI projects and a few EIDHR seminars—teaches NGOs the basic values of freedom, democracy, the rule of law, and liberal individual rights. The problem with civil society support is, however, that it largely depends on the good will of the target government. Central Asian governments are irritated by not only the NGOs' oppositional stance but also the fact that outsiders finance their activities. NGOs are often seen as agents of Western imperialism. Throughout 2005, in particular, Central Asian governments demonstrated how quickly NGO support can be brought to a halt. Their ability to function effectively was virtually nonexistent in Turkmenistan and Uzbekistan, was very limited in Tajikistan, and was constrained in Kyrgyzstan and Kazakhstan (Matveeva 2006).

A focus on good governance is often criticized as a convenient way to avoid tough decisions on human rights and democracy in strategically significant countries. However, from the perspective of transition theory—and given the difficulty associated with civil society support—the EU's good governance focus is a practicable strategy to contribute to the breakup of authoritarian structures. The notion of good governance is subject to not only narrow definitions focusing on public administration (with the goal of increasing the capacity and efficiency of executive institutions) but also a broad approach stressing the normative dimensions of openness, accountability, and transparency of government institutions. The broader approach tends to support the values of democratic government. Strengthening certain lines of government openness and accountability (for example, increasing financial accountability through an independent auditor or introducing ethics statutes and codes of conduct for public officials, outlining unacceptable practices) reduces regime autonomy and therefore imposes power costs on the ruling elites. However, these measures are far less challenging for the incumbent regime (and therefore less costly) than, for example, the promotion of free and fair elections or the support of opposition movements. Hence the EU should focus on good governance reform even at the cost of leaving aside its support of wholesale democratic transition.

Such an approach is no easy task, as early experience with the EU's rule of law initiative suggests. The first annual seminar between Kazakh and EU academic and practicing lawyers on judicial and penal reform, which took place in Almaty at the end of June 2009, was widely considered a success by the participants. However, no member of the Kazakh government was present at the conference. The latter's record of undertaking only the minimum degree of reform needed to appease international actors does not inspire confidence that the government will take up any of the recommendations (Isaacs 2009). Such a scenario could be even truer for Uzbekistan, which only two weeks after the official launch of the EU's rule of law initiative, in late November 2008, issued a regulation that required all lawyers to requalify for their license to practice. It goes without saying that many lawyers who criticized the government were denied their new license (Isaacs 2009).

We know from international socialization literature that dialogue as a means of promoting human rights and democracy is more likely to yield results if educational practices are consistent and last for a reasonably long period of time and if the target elites have few ingrained beliefs inconsistent with the socializing agency's message (Gheciu 2005). Though the EU has significantly improved the institutional framework for dialogue with Central Asian elites, structural impediments to successful socialization remain. Regarding the socialization content, the EU advocates Western-style democracy. Its flexibility to incorporate regional sociocultural particularities is limited and unintended. From a democratization point of view, this is a faulty design. It is more likely that socialization will be successful if it is focused upon shared aspects of a Habermasian "common lifeworld" (Risse and Sikkink 1999).

Neopatrimonialism is a strong and resilient form of social organization in Central Asia. With the help of patron-client networks, Central Asian leaders consolidate power through the dispensing and withholding of political and material incentives. Strictly, this is corruption, but to some of those engaged in the process it is seen as necessary to serve the needs of their community. Such customs have been persistent in Central Asia and even permeated Soviet institutions due to the policy of *korenizatsiya*, the Soviet leadership's reliance on local cadre members and their adherence to traditionalism.

In a society in which the informal level matters enormously, the EU must avoid too narrow a focus on institutionalist theories of transition. Any dialogue that focuses on setting the Central Asian states on a democratic trajectory must systematically integrate informal organizations and informal politics. The EU must focus more resolutely on the basic principles of more open governance but through being flexible in working with local forms of representation.

NOTES

Research for this chapter was funded by the Fritz Thyssen Foundation.

1. A. Lobjakas, Central Asia: EU commissioner begins rare tour of region. Radio Free Europe/Radio Liberty Newsline, March 15, 2004.

2. Intercultural dialogue is also identified as a goal for EU–Central Asia relations (Council of the European Union 2007, 2).

3. See also Commission of the European Communities, news release, August 17, 2008.

4. The following figures build on project information provided by the EU delegation to Kazakhstan, Kyrgyzstan, and Tajikistan (http://delkaz.ec.europa.eu/joomla/index.php?option=com_content&task=view&id= 61&Itemid=122); and assistance information by the Europe House in Tashkent (http://tacis.uz/docs/Tacis_tables_EN.pdf).

5. Figures build on various EU National Indicative Programs.

6. EU official, interview with author, January 2009, Brussels.

7. A. Lobjakas, EU stresses "broad, deep" relationship with Uzbekistan, Radio Free Europe/Radio Liberty Newsline, September 15, 2009.

8. According to the German news magazine *Der Spiegel*, the base in Termez is staffed with 300 military staff, six transport aircraft, and seven helicopters.

9. This point was made by the German news report *Monitor* in a broadcast on May 19, 2005.

REFERENCES

Blank, S. 2004. Democratic prospects in Central Asia. *World Affairs* 166/3: 133–47.
Boonstra, J., and N. Melvin. 2008. The EU strategy for Central Asia at year one. EUCAM Policy Brief 1. Madrid: FRIDE.
British Petroleum. 2007. *Statistical Review of World Energy*. London.
Carothers, T. 2000. Struggling with semi-authoritarians. In *Democracy Assistance: International Cooperation for Democratization*, ed. P. Burnell. London: Frank Cass.
Collins, K. 2004. The logic of clan politics: Evidence from the Central Asian trajectories. *World Politics* 56/2: 224–61.
Commission of the European Communities. 2007. *Furthering Human Rights and Democracy around the Globe*. http://ec.europa.eu/external_relations/library/publications/2007_humanrights_en.pdf.
———. 2006. *Central Asia Indicative Program 2007–2010*.
———. 2004. *TACIS Central Asia Indicative Program 2005–2006*.
Council of the European Union. 2007. *The EU and Central Asia: Strategy for a New Partnership*. http://register.consilium.europa.eu/pdf/en/07/st10/st10113.en07.pdf.
———. 1998. Common position of 25 May 1998 concerning human rights, democratic principles, the rule of law, and good governance in Africa. *Official Journal of the European Union*. June 2.
Council of the European Union and Commission of the European Communities. 2008. *Joint Progress Report by the Council and the European Commission to the European Council on the Implementation of the EU Central Asia Strategy*. http://ec.europa.eu/external_relations/central_asia/docs/progress_report_0608_en.pdf.
Eder, F., and U. Halbach. 2005. *Regime Change in Kyrgyzstan and the Specter of Coups in the CIS*. Berlin: German Institute for International and Security Affairs.
European Community. 2006. Assistance to Central Asia for the period 2007–2013. Regional strategy paper.

Freedom House. 2009. *Nations in Transit.* Washington, D.C. www.freedomhouse.org/template.cfm?page=485.

Gheciu, A. 2005. Security institutions as agents of socialization: NATO and the "New Europe." *International Organization* 59/4: 973–1012.

International Crisis Group. 2006. Central Asia: What role for the European Union? *Asia Report* 113.

Isaacs, R. 2009. The EU's rule of law initiative in Central Asia. EUCAM Policy Brief 9. Madrid: FRIDE.

Laruelle, M. 2009. Russia in Central Asia: Old history, new challenges. EUCAM Working Paper 3. Madrid: FRIDE.

MacFarlane, N. 2003. European strategy toward Kazakhstan. In *Thinking Strategically: The Major Powers, Kazakhstan, and the Central Asian Nexus,* ed. R. Legvold. Cambridge: MIT Press.

Matveeva, A. 2006. EU stakes in Central Asia. Chaillot Paper 91. Paris: EU Institute for Security Studies.

Risse, T., and K. Sikkink. 1999. The socialization of international human rights norms into domestic practices. In *The Power of Human Rights: International Norms and Domestic Change,* ed. T. Risse, S. C. Ropp, and K. Sikkink. Cambridge: Cambridge University Press.

Swanström, N. 2004. The prospects for multilateral conflict prevention and regional cooperation in Central Asia. *Central Asian Survey* 23/1: 41–53.

Von Gumppenberg, M-C. 2002. *Usbekistan: FES-Studie zur länderbezogenen Konfliktanalyse.* Bonn. http://library.fes.de/pdf-files/iez/01934.pdf.

Warkotsch, A. 2008. Noncompliance and instrumental variation in EU democracy promotion. *Journal of European Public Policy* 15/2: 227–45.

———. 2006. The European Union and democracy promotion in bad neighborhoods: The case of Central Asia. *European Foreign Affairs Review* 11/4: 509–25.

CHAPTER SEVEN

Morocco
A Flawed Response

Kristina Kausch

Many regimes in the Middle East and North Africa (MENA) have moved from open repression to semiauthoritarianism. Partly in response to the changed features of the international environment outlined in the introduction to this volume, including international pressure for democratization, smarter forms of authoritarianism have emerged that combine formal democratic commitment with subtle, low-profile coercion via the strategic use of soft power, a process one scholar calls "upgrading authoritarianism" (Heydemann 2007).

Considering the case of Morocco, it becomes clear that this change of strategy among previously openly repressive authoritarian regimes in the MENA has not yet received a response through EU policies. Whether this shortcoming is due to an unrealistic perception of the increasingly complex political realities in the region or to a lukewarm, if not declining, EU commitment to democracy promotion in the neighborhood is hard to determine. The case of Morocco does show, however, how the EU's failure to adapt its policies to changing realities in the MENA is leading to a weakening of the potential effect expected from EU democracy support. The relative decline in the importance of democracy promotion in the face of competing strategic priorities, as outlined in the introduction, is also apparent in Morocco, where it is displayed less in financial terms than in conceptual ones. As in other cases in this volume, EU democracy discourse remains strong, but incoherent and occasionally toothless policies on the ground are leading to a de facto downgrading of EU democracy support. In the case of Morocco, both the EU's ineffective efforts to deal with a semiauthoritarian counterpart and its reluctance to exploit positive conditionality are likely to decrease policy coherence, to the detriment of democracy promotion.

While it is clearly ahead of other countries in the region in terms of human rights and liberalization, Morocco remains a centrally steered façade democracy that is far from the model of Arab democratization its leaders claim it to be. European member states, influenced by other policy priorities such as migration, antiterrorism cooperation, regional conflicts, and trade, are doing little bilaterally and actively to support democracy in Morocco. This task is largely left to the European Commission, which provides diplomatic cover and has the necessary policy structures in place through the European Neighborhood Policy (ENP). The ENP Action Plan for Morocco contains ambitious but selective reforms, which indirectly follow the Moroccan ruling elite's course of modernization. In October 2008 the new *statut avancé* singled out Morocco as the first ENP partner country to be granted an upgrading of bilateral relations with the EU (EU–Moroccan Association Council 2008). Though it fell short of designing a relationship that included "everything but the institutions," as claimed by EU leaders, the *statut* entailed a substantial intensification of diplomatic and trade relations. Above all, however, it constituted a long-awaited and well-advertised diplomatic coup for the Moroccan government. This became evident in the press releases of the Moroccan governmental news agency, which stated that the granting of the *statut avancé* constituted an "acknowledgement of Morocco's efforts in the consolidation of human rights" and of the "pertinence of the strategic choices made by His Majesty King Mohammed VI," in the opinion of EU Commissioner for External Relations Benita Ferrero-Waldner—who, according to the press release, was a "great admirer of the Moroccan model."[1]

As the EU's approach to democracy promotion is generally based on partnership, praise of achievements, and incentives, both the commission and member states have been reluctant to put significant pressure on Morocco to start implementing the system-level political reforms King Mohammed VI has pledged in countless speeches since his succession in 1999. Criticism is more freely voiced in closed bilateral committees. However, beyond the requirements of diplomatic tactics, tame official statements reflect how the favorable light of regional comparison has distorted Morocco's image in Europe into one of a shining model democratizer, when it is actually a smart strategic modernizer surrounded by police states.

European democracy funding to Morocco has increased in recent years but is still disproportionately low compared to overall official development assistance, which has increased sharply as Morocco's integration with the EU has advanced. Funding for NGO-channeled European Instrument for Democracy and Human Rights (EIDHR) projects is insufficient to counterbalance the top-down process of selective political reform currently undertaken by the Moroccan regime. The ENP Governance Facility, of which Morocco was one of the first two beneficiaries in 2007, is a step in the right direction but has extremely limited influence given the current funding levels and relatively opaque, closed allocation process.

Greater integration with the EU has been a personal aim of King Mohammed VI throughout the decade of his rule. On his first official visit to Europe as monarch in 2000, he stressed Morocco's aspiration to intensify bilateral relations with the EU in a way that was "deeper than association even if . . . it stops short of full accession" (King Mohammed VI 2000). Morocco's keen interest in greater integration with the EU and the EU's decision to grant Morocco an "advanced status" of partnership provide particularly favorable conditions for the EU to use its leverage to encourage Morocco to commit to deep, systemic political reform.

In a 2008 communication on the strengthening of bilateral relations with its Mediterranean partners, the commission stated that "formal upgrading would be based on the commitments to shared values and interests and when Action Plan implementation demonstrates the ambition of the partner to go further, notably as concerns democratic practices, respect of human rights and fundamental freedoms, and the rule of law" (Commission of the European Communities, 2008b). However, there are no indications that, during the negotiations of the details of the *statut avancé*, increased leverage was used to sharpen implementation mechanisms in the EU-Moroccan Action Plan or to move the Moroccan government to commit to a measurably deeper, more advanced level of democratization in the new contractual agreement. Arguably, the level of EU-Moroccan integration was already significant before the inception of the *statut avancé*, and the most powerful incentives of interest to Morocco—free movement of workers and full access to EU agricultural markets—have not been included in the new document (Martín 2009). Nevertheless, the EU's failure to employ existing leverage to achieve a deeper, more measurable democratic commitment from its Moroccan counterpart raises doubts regarding the seriousness of the EU's commitment to democracy as well as concerning the tame ENP's potential as an effective framework for democratization through integration, when EU membership is not an option.

The Myth of the Moroccan Model

Morocco is typically seen as a shining example of reform among Arab countries. Indeed, important reform measures has been undertaken during the last decade, leading to an unprecedented level of liberalism. Singular measures—such as the Equity and Reconciliation Commission (IER) to deal with past abuses of human rights under the current king's father's regime and the comparatively liberal personal status law (*moudawanna*)—have earned Morocco international attention and praise. The moderate Islamist Justice and Development Party (PJD), while failing to participate in the government following the 2007 legislative elections, has been widely held up as a positive example of the successful integration of an Islamist party into the political process. The level of liberalization in Moroccan society has been considerable and, in comparison to the rest of the region, outstanding. However, hopeful European talk of a regional model of democratization is misplaced. Political reforms, instead of being steps in a consistent, overarching process toward democracy, have been selective and often superficial. Most important, all meaningful power remains concentrated in the hands of the palace. With the support of the EU and other international partners, Morocco is modernizing and partly liberalizing but is far from, and might not even be heading toward, a genuine democracy.

Domestic structures—one of the three variables informing assessment of the cases in this volume—play a crucial role in Morocco. As in other semiauthoritarian countries, political life in Morocco is marked by a constant double reality. Democratic structures and institutions formally veil an informal shadow governance structure, commonly called the *makhzen*, a patronage network of the palace and its clients that dictates policy and acts to keep any kind of political reform at bay. By order of the constitution, King Mohammed VI has a combined religious and political supreme authority that provides his extensive executive powers with an untouchable justification that is singular in the region. There is neither separation nor balance of powers, with the palace-led executive exerting leading influence over legislature and judiciary. Government and Parliament execute the will of the *makhzen* rather than the will of the electorate. Political parties have so far been too weak to provide meaningful political alternatives. As the largely rubber-stamp Parliament is slowly gaining influence, the *makhzen* placed a palace confidant as an independent member of Parliament to found a new political party and gather all secular forces around him, with the ultimate aim of defending the *makhzen*'s control over the legislature, particularly against the increasing competition by the Islamist PJD.

The September 2007 legislative elections were hailed by international observers and political leaders as the most transparent in Moroccan history. Indeed, the admittance of the first-ever international electoral observer mission to Morocco and the involvement of an (EU-funded) domestic NGO electoral observer committee were markedly positive developments. However, the election results cemented the status quo, as four of the five parties that made up the previous coalition (Istiqlal, USFP, RNI, and PPS) remained in government. The political message of low voter turnout was largely swept aside. Moreover, contrary to a widespread European perception, the PJD's surprising failure to secure its participation in government was a setback for Moroccan political reform. While a government including the PJD would at least have meant a potential reshuffle of the terms of negotiation, the new Istiqlal-led government basically meant more of the same, changing the face but not the course of the political elite (Kausch 2008).

The apparent inability to have a meaningful effect on the course of political decision making has led to an increasing feeling of resignation among Moroccan voters. The shrinking voter turnout throughout a decade of political liberalization and modernization (official figures dropping sharply from 58 percent in 1997 to 52 percent in 2002 and 37 percent in 2007, with real participation estimated at closer to 20 percent) suggests not only that figures are less manipulated than before but also that reforms have failed to engender confidence that elections have any meaningful effect on daily lives. While the reforms that have taken place are valuable in and of themselves, they lose attraction to reform-minded citizens to the degree that they are instrumentalized to replace a genuine process of democratic transition. With the ruling elite of the *makhzen* (which is not monolithic but includes reformist factions and individuals) holding on to power and effectively controlling access to political decision making, EU policies do have a point in that political reform could only be systematically deepened *with* the palace, rather than *against* it.

The likelihood of a genuine democratic transition in Morocco and elsewhere in the region increases as the ruling elite sees giving up some powers as the only way of retaining or increasing others. As the space for maneuver available to Moroccan democracy activists in NGOs and parties widens, so does the likelihood of significant pressure from within being exerted on the palace. Moroccan civil society is known for being vibrant and (excluding the occupied territories of Western Sahara) largely free to develop its activities. While political taboos in general are softening, many who touch upon the few that remain (such as the monarchy, the distribution of powers, and independence for Western Sahara) are soon silenced, through either legal action or denial of a meaningful audience. The only television channels with nationwide coverage are effectively controlled by the state. Despite its limited outreach, the independent press shapes the agenda of political debate among Casablanca and Rabat intellectuals. Recent less-subtle clampdowns on regime-critical journalists and other opposition figures, and repeated violent dispersals of peaceful demonstrations, display the increasing nervousness of the *makhzen*. The ruling elite's vision for Morocco, as many Moroccans point out, appears to be prosperity via modernization, rather than via democracy.

Europe's Contrasting Interests

A common thread running through the cases assessed in this volume, and a key variable influencing the position occupied by democracy and human rights in EU policy makers' ranking of priorities, is the increasing weight of competing strategic interests, which seems to imply a return to the Mediterranean's traditional realist foreign policy approach. While the counterterrorism agenda in response to 9/11 changed priorities in the region toward democracy as a way to enhance security, a decreasing interest among European policy makers in actively promoting democracy in the Southern Mediterranean has been evident more recently. Among the main reasons for this, diplomats in Brussels list the greater importance of energy and other economic priorities, the dominance of the Arab-Israeli conflict, and the lack of personal commitment by key political figures both at the EU level and in member states. In addition, there is a generally low interest in North Africa (reflected by aid figures) as well as the policy dilemma that democracy promotion policies do not deliver the kind of quick results that can be presented to the electorate.

Migration is a crucial issue in EU-Moroccan relations. Management of border controls and the speedy finalization of negotiations on a readmission agreement are particularly pressing European interests, while Morocco would like the planned free trade area to include a pledge of full freedom of movement for Moroccan workers. Spain and France have been most affected by illegal migration from the South and have the largest Moroccan immigrant communities. Morocco, under increasing pressure as a transit country for migrants from the South, seeks enhanced European assistance for border controls and a lowering of the barrier for legal work migration. Harsh immigration laws, in France in particular, contrast with Moroccan interests.

Regional security often clashes with democracy policies. Against the background of regional conflict, transnational terrorist networks, human trafficking, and organized crime, Europeans value Morocco's stabilizing influence in the region and are reluctant to risk this for the sake of "optimizing" Moroccan democratic standards. By a similar token, European governments appreciate Morocco's moderating influence over the states in sub-Saharan Africa, whose demands it has been translating into softer terms more likely to be acceptable to European partners. The Arab-Israeli conflict draws attention and capacities away from an ostensibly stable country like Morocco. Morocco is also one of Europe's main partners in the fight against terrorism. A British diplomat noted that initial UK efforts to promote democracy in the region had given way to an increasing focus on activities "with a more discernable link to countering terrorism," with concerns for root causes having been largely sidelined.[2]

Security and trade concerns partly explain the strong European backing of Morocco within a UN-led solution to the Western Sahara conflict. France's clearly pro-Moroccan position has remained constant under Sarkozy.[3] Spain under Zapatero switched to a markedly uncritical posture. This earned the Spanish prime minister much criticism at home, including from some Spanish members of Parliament, who accused the government of "submission" to the Moroccan government and selling the interests of the Saharawi people for economic advantages.[4] However, the partly ambiguous stances of Europeans regarding Western Sahara did not entirely prevent Brussels institutions from criticizing Morocco's policies. Human rights violations, legal and practical restrictions to freedom of association and expression, and the use of disproportionate force by Moroccan authorities in Western Sahara have repeatedly been raised in EU official documents. In the EU-Moroccan *dialogue politique renforcé*, Western Sahara plays an important role, not least because the conflict directly damages other EU interests, including the establishment of a regional free trade zone.

Against the background of the rise of political Islam across the region, some European observers hope for positive regional spillovers from Morocco, as the Moroccan Justice and Development Party is seen as providing a far better model for an Islamist government than others in the region. In spite of this, Europeans have so far been rather ambiguous toward the PJD. Following predictions that the PJD might be part of the government after the September 2007 elections, many

European governments embarked on cautious engagement. However, the prospect of an Islamist-led government on the other side of the Strait of Gibraltar was still received with a certain awkwardness, and the PJD's failure to get into government provoked a sigh of relief on the northern shores of the Mediterranean.

The EU is Morocco's primary trading partner: EU member states account for nearly 60 percent of Morocco's trade volume, the bulk of which are textiles and agricultural goods (Commission of the European Communities 2009a). The creation of a Euro-Mediterranean free trade area by 2010 makes any potential obstacle to free trade in the region a priority concern for EU interests. The royal palace has large stakes in the Moroccan economy, and some European companies are reported to benefit from special privileges and toe the political line of the *makhzen* in order to retain them: for example, BMW reportedly withdrew advertisements from a popular regime-critical magazine. France is Morocco's biggest trade partner, accounting for 18 percent of imports and one-third of exports in 2005.[5] Nicolas Sarkozy has stayed true to the country's reputation as a stable and trade-oriented patron in the Maghreb. On his first visit to Morocco as president of France, he secured business contracts for French companies totaling €3 billion. French commentators cheered, "in Morocco it's raining contracts."[6]

In light of Europe's urgent need to diversify its energy supply against the background of high oil prices and deteriorating relations with Russia, Morocco is also gaining importance as an energy transit country, especially for gas from Algeria. A joint EU-Moroccan declaration on energy cooperation was signed in July 2007 as part of the EU's current regional efforts to promote the integration of MENA and EU energy markets, inter alia to open up additional energy supplies to Europe. The *statut avancé* foresees comprehensive EU investment in the improvement of Morocco's energy transit and producer infrastructure and capacities, with the explicit aim of improving security of supply.

Several bilateral disputes have interfered with smooth EU-Moroccan relations in recent years. France clashed with Morocco in October 2007 when a French judge issued international warrants against several senior Moroccan officials for their supposed connection to the disappearance of Moroccan dissident Mehdi Ben Barka in Paris in 1965. Spain's periodic rows with Morocco over Parsley Island and the Spanish enclaves of Ceuta and Melilla (seen in relation to the Spanish king's visit to the enclaves in late 2007) have led to temporary withdrawals of ambassadors. However, none of these disputes has substantially damaged relations in the long run.

European Democracy Policies

Democracy promotion as part of development programs in Morocco has been undertaken by the European Commission and, to a far lesser degree, by some member states. The commission's democracy efforts are seen by many member states as complementary to their own development policies, providing the necessary scale and diplomatic cover that member states are unable or unwilling to deploy bilaterally. Some diplomats in Brussels and Rabat argue that the commission's democracy activities make member states' bilateral efforts redundant, as the issue is "already taken care of." While many member states run regional programs aspiring to contribute to democratization in the Southern Mediterranean, democracy-related projects in Morocco are low key and aim at strengthening governance capacity, human rights, and social development.

As in other countries assessed in this volume, in Morocco the institutional architecture of the ENP provides a framework to promote democracy. Morocco was among the first countries to sign an ENP Action Plan with the EU (Commission of the European Communities 2004b). Priority objectives and measures identified under the headings "democracy and the rule of law" and "human rights and fundamental freedoms" include capacity building in public administration; decentralization; access to justice; modernization of courts, prisons, and legal procedures; support for IER recommendations; and adherence to and compliance with international conventions. Envisaged measures did not always clearly contribute to the declared objective, however. Moreover, some of the objectives that initially appeared more political ultimately turned out to be largely void of meaningful political content, mostly involving projects of modernization, equipment, capacity building, and exchange of experience. Crucially, the action plan failed to specify time frames, actors, implementation, and evaluation mechanisms that define how and when the envisaged objectives are to be achieved. The action plan has been widely criticized, including by the European Parliament (European Parliament 2007a) and several Moroccan human rights NGOs consulted by the commission in 2007 to evaluate implementation of the action plan. These NGOs demanded that the plan be "reformulated within a logical framework that will highlight better-defined goals as well as the actors, timelines, and financial, and human resources needed for each action" (Euro-Mediterranean Human Rights Network 2007, 6). In reflections on "successor documents to the current ENP Action Plans," the commission acknowledges the need for future ENP framework agreements to be "sufficiently precise for cooperation to go forward" and to identify, "wherever appropriate, the respective responsibilities of the different parties and provide an indication of the benchmarks to be applied in the pursuit of the document's objectives." Moreover, it recognizes the need for implementation to be monitored under existing bilateral institutional structures and encourages both ENP partner governments and EU delegations to consult local civil society before negotiation of the new agreement (Commission of the European Communities 2008c). However, the April 2009 ENP progress report on Morocco explicitly criticizes Morocco's reluctance to provide concrete timetables for the implementation of certain democracy and human rights reforms it had committed to (Commission of the European Communities 2009b).

In several in-house assessments since the inception of the ENP, the commission identifies substantial shortcomings in Morocco's democratic record, including fundamental structural deficits such as the lack of respect for the constitutional principle of the separation of powers, the limited powers of Parliament and government, the lack of independence of the judiciary, the weakness of political parties, and civil society's limited ability to influence major political decisions (Commission of the European Communities 2004a). Most of these deeper structural reform requirements got lost in the formulation of both the action plan and the *statut avancé*, leaving a collection of piecemeal political reform measures that are unlikely to contribute to genuine democratization, as most preconditions for many of the measures to take practical effect are left out, reflecting the scatter-gun approach that characterizes EU democracy policies in the region (Youngs 2006).

European diplomats point to the "irreversibility" of Moroccan democratization, the need for a "gradual" process, and the "accumulative" effect selective reforms will have in the long run. The EU's soft approach—of socialization via gradual reform—applies only partly to Morocco, however: the accumulation of more or less connected ad hoc reforms does not automatically add up to a gradual process, let alone to a transition to democracy. The priorities in the political chapters of the ENP Action Plan indirectly support this flawed logic by focusing on selective modernization measures rather than on a strategy that includes the more delicate aspects of systemic change, identified as crucial by the commission's own assessments (Baricani 2005).

European diplomats typically ascribe this gap to the requirements of consensus building in the process of negotiating an agreement with common ownership. At the same time, they point out the undeniable advantage of having a mutually agreed plan of reform priorities to which they can hold the Moroccan government accountable. Unlike most other contractual agreements, action plans, while not legally binding, allow closer monitoring via relatively specific legal, fiscal, and auditing measures that the partner government has committed to implement.

In a 2006 resolution on the ENP, the European Parliament underlined the "aim of not settling for the status quo but of committing the European Union to support the aspirations of the peoples of our neighboring countries to full political freedom" (European Parliament 2006). For the time being, however, both discourse and action suggest that European policies toward Morocco do not aspire to support full political freedom and genuine democracy. EU documents and statements about Morocco so far leave no doubt that reforms are expected within the boundaries of the current constitution and distribution of powers. Commission staff stress that in the relationship with their Moroccan interlocutors they can do little more than support Morocco in the gradual reform course it has committed itself to, while trying to concentrate on those areas in which change is likely to be achieved soon via incentives, dialogue, confidence building, and showing the cost of nonreform.

Reflecting its anticonfrontational approach, the commission has regularly praised positive Moroccan reform measures. While the EU's general reluctance to openly criticize takes into account the *makhzen*'s position as a gatekeeper for reforms, praise does not automatically equal incentive. Formulations are typically couched in a conspicuously relative language, emphasizing not Morocco's absolute achievements but its relative position compared to its neighbors. In addition, some EU statements and official documents praise highly flawed or incomplete reforms. This creates a distorted image of the reality of Moroccan political life, thereby indirectly bolstering the ruling elite.

However, recent commission statements do contain relatively strong criticism. The 2008 and 2009 ENP progress reports on Morocco address both achievements and shortcomings in an unusually systematic and explicit fashion. The April 2009 progress report treads less softly than usual, inter alia warning that the "dysfunctions of the judicial system risk emptying legal reforms of their effects" (Commission of the European Communities 2008c, 2009b).

EU reactions to the September 2007 legislative elections were conspicuously positive across the board. The Portuguese EU presidency expressed its "satisfaction" regarding the elections, saying that the "democratic conditions" in which they had taken place were "a testament to Morocco's commitment to the reform process" (European Council Presidency 2007). Nicolas Sarkozy wrote a letter to King Mohammed VI in which he expressed his "admiration for the democratic robustness your country has once again demonstrated."[7] High Representative Javier Solana classified the elections as proof of "Morocco's political maturity" (European Council Secretariat 2007). European reactions praised Morocco for the elections' transparency and for admitting the first-ever international election observer delegation, but the political message of low voter turnout was disregarded.

Conditionality and Incentive Power

Since the ENP's inception in 2004, the commission has stressed the framework's fundamental reliance on democratic conditionality (Commission of the European Communities 2004c). Against the background of deteriorating human rights records in the MENA, human rights NGOs across the Mediterranean have repeatedly asked the EU to apply its conditionality in ENP policy design to local aspirations for change and make any upgrading of bilateral relations conditional to prior progress in the area of human rights and democracy (Euro-Mediterranean Human Rights Network 2009). A focus on incentives is certainly more promising in the push for democratization in Morocco. However, the EU has so far failed to exploit the full margin of such positive leverage with Moroccan authorities.

In 2007 Morocco, along with Ukraine, was the first ENP partner country to receive additional allocations from the Governance Facility. It was hoped that the additional allocation of €28 million to Morocco would send a strong positive signal across the region and help the Moroccan government support the reform agenda. The commission argued that the possibility of using the funds for any of the agreed priorities, not necessarily governance projects, enhanced the attractiveness of the incentive. This was criticized by the European Parliament (Commission of the European Communities 2007). Morocco used the additional funds for the modernization of its public administration, poverty reduction, social services, and educational programs.

In a February 2008 outline of the principles for the implementation of the Governance Facility, the commission stressed its belief in rewarding relative progress rather than absolute levels of attainment and in recognizing achievements rather criticizing shortcomings. An earlier draft of the same document alluded to the allocation of funds to Morocco as a good example of the positive "signaling effect," with the measure having been "well advertised in the media and successfully presented by the government as justification and encouragement for its continued reform efforts" (Commission of the European Communities 2008a). The presumed signaling effect could be much stronger if funds for the Governance

Facility were substantially higher, if NGOs were involved in the process of allocation, and if allocations were granted as a reward for specific reforms rather than for unspecified "progress." Overall, the conditionality potential of the Governance Facility—or any other conditionality instrument—remains negligible as long as the sums and political incentives offered to the Moroccan ruling elite do not exceed the political cost of reform.

Assessment of relative rather than absolute progress has the advantage of facilitating regional and global comparison of the effect of EU policies. However, there is also the risk that the absolute shortcomings of better-performing countries like Morocco are neglected due to their being surrounded by full-fledged autocracies. The result of such a minimum-level approach to democratization appears barely sustainable against the background of migration, radicalization, and the growing discontent of a youthful population (McFaul and Wittes 2008).

In 2003 Morocco was the first ENP partner country to agree to the establishment of a "subcommittee on human rights, democratization and governance" within the EU-Moroccan Association Council. The annual subcommittee meeting provides the main institutional structure for EU-Moroccan dialogue in this domain. According to European diplomats, the subcommittee meetings are considerably more open and explicit than official discourse, with annual meetings increasing in frankness. The meetings have led to additional commitments on the Moroccan side, including lifting some reservations against international conventions and protocols, and have reportedly increased mutual trust among the parties, which diplomats judge just as important as concrete commitments. However, a "talking club" behind closed doors that fails to produce tangible results but provides both the EU and the Moroccan regime with a democratic gloss would undermine the very objective of the subcommittee.

Arguably, many of the points included in the advanced status document are not novelties and refer to political and economic integration mechanisms already in place (Martín 2009). Nevertheless, the Moroccan leadership's keen interest in greater integration with the EU via the *statut avancé* could enhance not only EU-Moroccan relations but also the ENP and EU-Mediterranean relations more broadly. The possibility of diplomatic upgrading accords the EU substantial leverage for integrating markets and diplomacy and for developing the Southern Mediterranean. It is no coincidence that Morocco's negotiations on a *statut avancé* have led three other Southern partner states (Israel, Egypt, and Tunisia) to demand a similar upgrade.

In Morocco, EU conditionality is particularly promising, beyond the incentive power of enhanced integration. The EU has stressed on numerous occasions that its approach to democracy support in Morocco is focused on holding the Moroccan government accountable with regard to the reforms it has committed to. With the explicit mandate of King Mohammed VI, the Moroccan ad hoc truth commission (IER) issued comprehensive recommendations for the reforms required to prevent a repetition of the serious human rights violations committed under King Hassan II's reign. These recommendations, personally endorsed by the king, also propose substantial systemic reforms, including changes in the constitution, reinforcement of the independence of the judiciary, ratification of the Rome Statute, and abolition of the death penalty. Set up on the initiative of King Mohammed VI himself, the recommendations of the IER provide the ideal framework for the EU to include these systemic reforms in action plans, bilateral agreements, and other conditionality instruments in a systematic and detailed way. While the recommendations of the IER are indeed mentioned in all EU documents, they are restricted to one or two sentences and do not go into detail regarding what they entail. Moreover, measures recommended by the IER—such as constitutional reform and the primacy of international conventions—are not explicitly included in the action plan or any other bilateral document. This shortcoming suggests that the EU is failing to exploit the IER recommendations for a deepening of political reform in Morocco.

The Moroccan regime's keen desire to keep up its international image as a model democratizer opens additional strategic opportunities for the EU. The Moroccan government will openly prevent or protest support for democratic forces and reforms only when it has a strong public stance to justify such action. The EU has failed to make use of Morocco's double discourse to push the boundaries of political reform.

European Political Aid

Democracy-relevant measures in Morocco have been funded largely by the MEDA (Mesures d'accompagnement) program and the European Neighborhood and Partnership Instrument (ENPI), the funds of which are negotiated with and channeled through governmental bodies. On a much lower scale, the European Instrument for Democracy and Human Rights (EIDHR) funds projects that are implemented directly by Moroccan NGOs or international organizations.[8] Between 2003 and 2006 the EIDHR funded €2 million worth of NGO microprojects in

Morocco. Annual EIDHR funding for microprojects increased from €1 million in 2004 to €1.23 million in 2007 but still remained relatively low, representing only 2 percent of commission funding to Morocco. Most of the microprojects financed via the EIDHR were funded with around €100,000. The beneficiaries are Moroccan NGOs, including many that are not fully independent from the government. EIDHR microprojects in Morocco for 2005–07 focused on participation and citizenship; good governance; human rights; reconciliation; media; and the rights of women, children, and the disabled.

The initiatives financed via the EIDHR proved their relevance especially in the run-up to the legislative elections of September 2007, before which several EIDHR-funded initiatives promoted citizenship and voter participation. Crucially, the EIDHR supported the first domestic NGO electoral observation commission both institutionally and through the training of some three thousand facilitators in electoral monitoring and reporting. The NGO commission published a well-publicized report that denounced irregularities in the electoral process and clearly linked low voter turnout with the need for deeper structural political reforms (Collectif Associatif 2007). While the direct channeling of funds through local NGOs makes the EIDHR a powerful tool to counterbalance the Moroccan regime's top-down reforms, low funding levels substantially weaken the instrument's potential.

MEDA and ENPI funds to Morocco have been substantially higher; however, a very low share of these are earmarked for governance and human rights (see table 7.1). With projects being channeled through government bodies, these are unlikely to contribute to bottom-up reform. Member states have also pursued efforts to promote democracy, governance, or human rights in Morocco.[9] While the commission and France alone provide two-thirds of official development assistance to Morocco (followed at some distance by Spain and Germany), the share of funds used to promote democracy and human rights has been strikingly low. This is especially so in the case of France, which provides one-third of assistance but dedicates hardly any of it to governance projects. Generally, bilateral funding from member states dedicated to specific democracy programs has been negligible. Southern EU member states, which traditionally have the closest political and economic links to Morocco, are also the most reluctant to engage in active, bilateral, democracy promotion.[10]

France is Morocco's largest trading partner and biggest aid donor, and Morocco is France's largest aid recipient.[11] Not surprisingly, King Mohammed VI's first visit abroad after succeeding to the throne in 2000 led him to Paris. Total French

Table 7.1. Allocations to Morocco, 2002–2010, Mesures d'accompagnement Program and the European Neighborhood and Partnership Instrument (MEDA and ENPI)

Time Period	Total Allocation (in millions of euros)	Allocation for Government and Human Rights Millions of Euros	% of Total
2002–2004	426	N.A.	N.A.
2005–2006	275	5	1.8
2007–2010	654	28	4.3

Source: European Neighborhood and Partnership Instrument 2007–10.

bilateral official development assistance to Morocco during the last decade remained relatively stable, averaging €188 million a year since 1999 (it was €159 million in 2005). As said, hardly any of this has been specifically dedicated to democracy. The few activities undertaken in Morocco under the heading of governance are not necessarily aimed at promoting democracy. These include programs on public administration modernization, decentralization, and modernization of justice but also more tenuously on land management and domestic security (Direction Générale de la Coopération 2007).

Spain's traditionally close relationship with Morocco became—after a rather frosty period under the Aznar government—decidedly friendly again under Zapatero. Spanish bilateral aid to Morocco increased from around €30 million in 2003 to €70 million in 2006, and total spending on the Development Assistance Committee's sector titled Government and Civil Society almost tripled from 2005 to 2006 (to €6.5 million). Under its own, narrower sectoral aid category, "democratic governance, citizen participation, and institutional development," however, Spain spent only 2 percent of official development assistance (Agency for International Cooperation 2006).

In summary, total EU funding to Morocco earmarked for democracy projects has increased during recent years but remains a small share of overall official development assistance. Commission NGO funding via the EIDHR is useful and relevant but also disproportionately low. This sits uneasily with the European Parliament's November 2007 assessment that civil society support is key to the success of the ENP, "regardless of the degree of willingness of partner countries' governments to cooperate" (European Parliament 2007b). MEDA/ENPI funds are substantially higher, but these are channeled through government bodies and programs aimed at modernization rather than democratization. Member states' bilateral commitments are negligible. The reluctance to commit significant amount of sensitive political aid is particularly striking in the cases of France and Spain, the member states most closely tied to Morocco by history, geography, migration, and trade.

Conclusion

As this and other chapters in this volume show, the EU and its member states' commitment to democracy promotion is above all determined by the position democracy support holds in the ranking of European governments' strategic priorities and interests regarding the country in question. In Morocco the mix of contrasting interests means that EU member states largely leave the active promotion of democracy to the European Commission and do not disguise the fact that democracy ranks far behind other priorities. The commission has made a valuable effort to assist the process of liberalization led by the Moroccan government in the ENP framework, including through increasingly explicit criticism in official documents, but systematic support to genuine democratization is yet to be introduced in EU policies toward Morocco.

Granting advanced status to a partner that demonstrates its maturity by committing to an advanced level of democratization could provide a strong boost for the currently tame potential of the ENP. Translating the *statut*'s general demands into a precise new action plan by 2011—a plan that allows for transparency and thorough monitoring—is important, given that that this will be the first of a new generation of ENP agreements. While the need for systemic reforms is raised in the new *statut avancé*, there is no evidence that these reforms are pressed for, leaving unclear the new agreement's value in the field of democracy and human rights in comparison with the 2004 European Neighbourhood Policy action plan. Critical commission statements do not appear meaningfully to inform EU strategic policy choices.

Some Moroccan civil society activists think their efforts for genuine democracy in Morocco are hampered by the fact that the country is internationally perceived as "one of the easy cases," which reduces international pressure on the government and casts all flaws as minor compared to those elsewhere in the region. Some even blame the EU for the discriminatory hypocrisy of having different understandings of democracy with regard to the Northern and Southern Mediterranean, implying Arab exceptionalism.

The palace's gatekeeper function within a carefully steered top-down approach to political reform implies that, in terms of external support for Moroccan democracy, intergovernmental cooperation must be accompanied by direct support to civil society. The total independence of NGOs and a substantial increase in funds directly channeled through them will be crucial if these measures are to help bring about genuine democratization.

The change of strategy in the Southern Mediterranean in recent years, and the increasing subtlety and sophistication of the North African political elite's strategies to preserve authoritarian rule in the face of increasing pressure for democratization, have not yet translated into a meaningful adaptation of EU policies. Compared to other MENA states, Morocco is no doubt an island of relative liberalism. Regardless, it remains a semiauthoritarian façade democracy, whose leaders are proficient in playing off Europe's naiveté to preserve their political and economic privileges. Aware of its strategic significance for many European interests, the Moroccan leadership successfully nurses the country's image as the leader of democratic reform and a center of stability in the region. So far the EU has failed to exploit the additional leverage it is given through this Moroccan strategic interest. Negotiations on the implementation of the *statut avancé* and the new ENP action plan provide an opportunity for the EU to adapt its policies to the requirements of dealing with the increasingly subtle and complex political reality of a semiauthoritarian partner. This includes a clearer understanding of Morocco's informal political economy and the way decisions are made outside formal rules and political institutions.

In contrast to the Ukrainian case, covered in this volume, an EU partnership short of membership does hold substantial potential in Morocco. While for Eastern European neighbors such as Ukraine any offer short of full membership will be perceived as a downgrade, the EU's Southern Mediterranean partners do not view EU membership as a realistic option and thus consider advanced status a significant incentive.[12] EU policies toward both its Eastern and Southern neighbors make use of incentive power to lock countries into a framework of integration. Advanced status, while unlikely to provide a framework for relations with Eastern and South Eastern Europe, does have the potential to become a model for incorporating Southern partner states into EU mechanisms and policy frameworks. As such, it is being tested in the Moroccan laboratory. It is still doubtful whether, by the time of implementation, the EU will succeed in taking advantage of its leverage potential to foster systemic political change in Morocco.

NOTES

1. Maghreb Arabe Presse, news release, December 5, 2008. Author's translation.
2. Joao Ridao, spokesman of the ERC in the Spanish Congress, December 15, 2009.
3. S. Blasse, Nicolas Sarkozy, Mohammed VI, Une amitié économique, October 25, 2007.
4. Hearing, Foreign Minister Miguel Angel Moratinos, before the Senate, 2007. Ministry of Foreign Affairs of Spain (www.maec.es).
5. Ministry of Foreign Affairs of France (www.diplomatie.gouv.fr/en/country-files_156/morocco_285/index.html).
6. D. Bennani, Le Sarko show, *Tel Quel*, October 2007.
7. M. Nicolas Sarkozy, President of the Republic, to His Majesty Mohammed VI, King of Morocco, September 9, 2007.
8. Formerly the European Instrument for Democracy and Human Rights (EIDHR), the only explicit EU democracy promotion instrument that allows for NGO funding without prior government clearance.
9. The range of aid categories and budget lines through which democracy is explicitly promoted by European donors makes a direct comparison of quantitative democracy assistance difficult. In some cases, democracy, human rights, gender, and other broad issues cut across funding themes and thus do not have a their own budget line.
10. Other donors active in Morocco include the United States, Japan, the World Bank, the Islamic Development Bank, the African Development Bank, and various UN agencies (UNICEF, UNDP, WFP, UNFPA, FAO, and WHO).
11. Official development assistance excluding debt reduction.
12. Morocco officially applied for EU membership in1987, but the request was turned down.

REFERENCES

Agency for International Cooperation. 2006. *Memoria de la Cooperación Española en Marruecos 2005–2006*. Madrid.
Baricani, E. 2005. *From the EMP to the ENP: A New European Pressure for Democratization? The Case of Morocco*. Beersheba: Centre for the Study of European Politics and Society.
Collectif Associatif pour l'Observation des Elections. 2007. *Rapport préliminaire d'observation des elections du 7 Septembre 2007*.
Commission of the European Communities. 2009a. *Directorate General for External Trade: Country Profile Morocco*. www.ec.europa.eu/trade/issues/bilateral/countries/morocco/index_en.htm.
———. 2009b. *Rapport de Suivi Maroc*.
———. 2008a. *Principles for the Implementation of a Governance Facility under ENPI*.
———. 2008b. *Communication from the Commission to the European Parliament and the Council: Strengthening of the EU's bilateral relations with its Mediterranean partners*.

———. 2008c. Successor documents to current ENP action plans, expanding on the proposals contained in the Communication to the European Parliament and the Council on Implementation of the European neighborhood policy in 2007.
———. 2007. Communication from the Commission: A strong European neighborhood policy.
———. 2004a. *European Neighborhood Policy Country Report: Morocco.*
———. 2004b. *EU-Morocco Action Plan.* http://ec.europa.eu/world/enp/pdf/action_plans/morocco_enp_ap_final_en.pdf.
———. 2004c. European neighborhood strategy paper Direction générale de la Coopération internationale et du Développement. 2007. *La Coopération de la France avec le Maroc. Evaluation Partenariale Maroc-Française, 1995–2005.*
EU-Moroccan Association Council. 2008. *Document conjoint UE-Maroc sur le renforcement des relations bilaterales/Statut Avancé.*
Euro-Mediterranean Human Rights Network. 2009. EMHRN position paper on the European Neighborhood Policy in view of the negotiation of new instruments between the EU and its Mediterranean partners.
———. 2007. *Human Rights in the EU-Morocco Action Plan under the European Neighborhood Policy.*
European Council Presidency. 2007. Presidency statement on the parliamentary elections in Morocco.
European Council Secretariat. 2007. Javier Solana, Haut représentant de l'UE pour la PESC, félicite le Maroc pour le bon déroulement des dernières élections legislatives.
European Neighborhood and Partnership Instrument. 2007–10. *National Indicative Program.*
European Parliament. 2007a. Resolution of 6 September 2007 on the functioning of the human rights dialogues and consultations on human rights with third countries.
———. 2007b. *Strengthening the European Neighborhood Policy.*
———. 2006. European Parliament Resolution on the European Neighborhood Policy.
Heydemann, S. 2007. *Upgrading Authoritarianism.* Washington, D.C.: Brookings Institution Press.
Kausch, K. 2008. Elections 2007: The most transparent status quo in Moroccan history. *Mediterranean Politics* 13/1.
King Mohammed VI of Morocco. 2000. Speech. Paris.
Martín, I. 2009. EU-Moroccan relations: How advanced is "advanced status"? *Mediterranean Politics* 14/2.
McFaul, M., and T. Cofman Wittes. 2008. Morocco's elections: The limits of limited reforms. *Journal of Democracy* 19/1.
Youngs, R. 2006. *Europe's Flawed Approach to Arab Democracy.* London: Centre for European Reform.

CHAPTER EIGHT

The Gulf Cooperation Council
The Challenges of Security

Ana Echagüe

Despite increased European foreign policy coordination and presence in most areas of the world, the Gulf region, and more specifically the countries of the Gulf Cooperation Council (GCC)—Bahrain, Kuwait, Oman, Qatar, Saudi Arabia, and the United Arab Emirates—continues to be an area of neglect. One need only compare policies toward the Gulf with policies toward the North African and Middle Eastern states included within the Euro-Mediterranean Partnership (EMP) to witness this deficit. Despite the shortcomings of the EMP, this initiative represents a coordinated and embedded European strategy toward the Southern Mediterranean that has not been extended to GCC countries. This is all the more surprising given the fact several pivotal issues of international concern are concentrated in the Arabian Peninsula, including energy security, Middle Eastern regional security, counterterrorism, and Arab democratic reform. European weight in this region remains negligible, and the European Union as a collective entity has failed to develop a comprehensive and coherent policy toward this crucial part of the Middle East.

This neglect reflects two European judgments. First, that the Gulf does not present the kind of acute geopolitical urgency that would merit the costs associated with a greater engagement in the region; and second, that the EU has limited capacity to affect social, economic, or political change in the Gulf and that its interests are thus best served by stability-oriented caution. The current financial crises and volatility in the energy markets can only be expected to exacerbate the primacy of stability and to entrench the traditional realist framework that governs relations with the Gulf. This is a case in which the three explanatory variables outlined in chapter 1 can be seen at work militating against an effective EU policy. Shallow institutional links preclude any leverage, domestic political structures explain the lack of access points for EU involvement, and strategic calculations sideline committed democracy promotion.

European Involvement

Historically, European involvement in the Gulf was precluded by the perception that the region was a U.S. sphere of influence. European states, except for the United Kingdom, do not have a history in the region, which they disregarded until the first oil crisis of 1973 revealed Europe's vulnerability, through its dependence on oil and its geopolitical exposure, to the negative spillover of the Middle East conflict (Khader 2005, 10).

Perhaps because the region was seen as an American area of influence, Europe has not shown the will to adopt an independent policy. European foreign policy toward the Gulf has maintained a low profile, focusing on economic negotiations to the detriment of political concerns (Youngs 2006, 171). Initially relations were conducted on a bilateral basis, by individual European countries involved in military sales, infrastructure projects, and trade, with collective EU relations emerging only more recently.

In 1989 the European Economic Community (EEC) and the GCC signed the Partnership and Cooperation Agreement, under which they committed to enter into negotiations on a free trade agreement. From the beginning, the agreement was neither ambitious in scope nor pursued with urgency. The EU's decision to pursue the relationship on an interregional basis would prove to be crucial in the shaping of relations, which remained much shallower than would otherwise have been the case (Youngs 2006, 172). A regional approach was favored due to, on the one hand, the pragmatic realization of the lack of capacity to hold simultaneous bilateral negotiations with the various countries and, on the other, an effort inherent in the EU's external relations approach to encourage regional development. One EU official has observed that it was not in the interest of the EU to open up to smaller states like the United Arab Emirates, its main interest being Saudi Arabia.

Not until after September 11, 2001, were real attempts made to inject greater momentum into EU relations with the region. The decision announced in 2002 to open a European Commission delegation in Riyadh, the first and only one in the region, seemed to signal a further commitment (although the office did not actually open until 2004). In December 2003 the commission and the Office of the High Representative for the Common Foreign and Security Policy (CFSP) issued a policy document that stressed the need to broaden and deepen the EU-GCC dialogue and to link the EU-GCC and EU-Mediterranean frameworks (Solana, Patten, and Prodi 2003). That same month a new policy document made reference to the need for a broader engagement with the Arab world. This was followed in June 2004 by the adoption of an EU strategic partnership with the Mediterranean and the Middle East (Commission of the European Communities 2004). This document incorporated the Gulf region into an overall Mediterranean and Middle Eastern framework and committed the EU to advance a partnership with Gulf countries. It noted how EU relations with countries east of Jordan were less developed and how the economic and social characteristics of these countries called for instruments different from those of the Barcelona process. It also suggested that the EU would consider "bilateral political engagement" with individual Gulf states wishing to cooperate on reform issues—a shift of emphasis from the regional foundations upon which EU efforts had long been predicated; this shift did not, however, materialize to any significant extent. In this new document, the EU also committed itself to investing more resources to support reform efforts in the Gulf. This cautious attempt to support political reform was partly a reflection of new security thinking and partly a response to the beginnings of political change in some countries in the region (Youngs 2006, 177).

The partnership was presented as a strategic framework, circumventing what was judged by some governments to have been the ineffectual and low-profile technical approach led by the commission. It was based on an initial Franco-German proposal, forwarded as a response to the U.S. proposal for a greater Middle East initiative. However, there was no consensus within the EU over what the strategic partnership should seek in practice. Skeptical states were reluctant to adopt any strategy that could be associated with the U.S. vision of a regional security framework. Others were eager to protect the supremacy of the Mediterranean within the EU's ranking of priorities and to avoid burdening the EMP with the complexities inherent to the Gulf.

Reflecting most states' lack of enthusiasm, the strategic partnership has achieved little in practice, remaining, in the words of one diplomat, an essentially "hollow framework." In familiar fashion, in its policies toward the Gulf the EU has attempted to walk a fine line between a modicum of transatlantic cooperation, on the one hand, and (what it judged to be) a different approach to that of the United States, one that emphasized participation, cooperation, and consultation with the governments involved, on the other hand. It has also frequently made the point of recognizing the importance of addressing the Arab-Israeli conflict as an inseparable part of the overall framework of relations with the region (El-Ghoul 2005, 19). While the Obama administration is, at least formally, much more aligned with the EU approach in terms of an emphasis on "mutual respect and mutual interest," its first year in office suggests that differences remain and that deep transatlantic cooperation in the Gulf is unlikely.

The fact that the U.S. push for political reform in the region has abated will probably further limit the little political leverage the EU might have had. At the same time, China, India, and Japan are demonstrating increased interest in the region, with trade between the GCC and Asia having nearly tripled in the last five years. The GCC is becoming an increasingly important source of energy for the growing Asian economies, while countries such as India and China are becoming key investment markets for Gulf petrodollars.[1] The added attraction of these countries as business partners is their lack of interference in domestic politics, with discussions focusing on economics instead. As noted by one analyst, "The proactive and tightly coordinated Chinese approach stands in marked contrast to the dispersed and reactive policy of the EU towards the GCC states" (Hertog 2006, 9). Japan is also stepping up its engagement in the region, through involvement in oil-related projects and increased investment.

Lack of European Involvement

Despite the pretence, at least formally, of a Europeanized policy toward the Gulf states, a heavy dose of bilateralism persists. Some EU member states allude to their lack of historical presence in the region as a reason for not wishing the EU to adopt too high a profile. The member states that do have a historical legacy, principally the UK, want greater support from EU cooperation but without relinquishing their bilateral, national room for maneuver. Where states (the UK, France, and Germany) have developed commercial links, they are keen to protect them, despite any push for broader collective relations. Countries with fewer links, such as Italy, have seen the region's lack of transparency as an obstacle to upgrading relations (Aliboni 2005, 10).

Within the council, officials suggest that the Gulf has not generated sufficient high-profile or dramatic challenges to move EU policy into a higher gear. Commission officials claim concerns over more pressing issues, such as enlargement, in explaining a disregard for the region. In short, a lack of political will, differing interests, and structural difficulties have all militated against a deeper European involvement in the Gulf. In the last few years, policymakers have frequently suggested that the time is right to grant greater priority to the region. Saudi Arabia's increasingly assertive role in relation to the Arab-Israeli conflict and other regional issues (Lebanon, Iran, and Iraq, among others) has increased the premium on a more structured and strategic European engagement with the kingdom. But for many senior officials and ministers, the Gulf still fails to register as a priority. One political activist from the Gulf complained that for Javier Solana, for instance, the region continued to be a black hole.

Aside from broader historical questions and national interests, the lack of progress can also be attributed to institutional obstacles on the part of both the EU and the GCC. In the EU, overlapping competencies between the EU Council and European Commission and a lack of specific instruments or leverage that can be deployed effectively in the region undermines progress. Part of the difficulty in strengthening relations on this regional basis stems from the historical pursuit of relations along bilateral lines. GCC countries have difficulties moving away from this pattern to a framework of dealing with the EU as a whole. GCC states prefer dealing with states on an individual basis for specific issues, especially since several member states have better diplomatic representation in the region than the commission. Gulf States have not been "socialized" into a familiarity with the EU as such in the same way that other Arab states have with the EMP. Having technical negotiations on the commission-led FTA while the council and presidency lead on political aspects (such as nonproliferation and human rights clauses) has led to confusion.

Moreover, some EU member states remain suspicious of the commission, accusing it of wanting to extend its power beyond its technical and financial remit. The Gulf region remains the area of the Middle East where the EU has the least leverage and where standard EU forms of cooperation are less applicable. Economic and civil society structures do not lend themselves to standard forms of cooperation, and the lack of economic interpenetration militates against European leverage (Youngs 2006, 193). The region does not qualify for development aid and is not included in the ENP, reducing the scope for the use of conditionality. Overall, the EU's adoption of a regional approach neglects the social, political, and economic differences among the six countries and ignores how these condition the EU's scope of action. Indeed, the GCC secretariat has no independent negotiating competence comparable to the commission's responsibility to negotiate EU external trade agreements; deep-seated differences and mistrust persist among GCC members (Nonneman 2007, 22).

Due to all these difficulties, and despite a clear rationale for strengthened relations, both parties use the failure to conclude the FTA as justification for delaying any intensification of relations. The GCC saw the signing of the FTA as a basic test of the EU's willingness to commit to the region, and with talks collapsing in early 2009 the prognosis is bleak. As of late 2009 the talks have not been resuscitated. The oil-rich states of the Gulf do not receive the large amounts of development assistance that accord the EU some leverage in other parts of the world, although the GCC benefits from a small commission budget line that supports cooperation in energy, education, science and technology, and the environment in high-income countries (Council of the European Union 2006). There is talk of allocating part of this budget to a dialogue among the civil societies of the Gulf and Europe, and a higher education exchange program is under way. Yet the lack of mainstream development aid makes progress on trade more important as a basis for political engagement, despite calls by some member states not to make free trade the foundation upon which to build a deeper geopolitical presence. Calls for political engagement to be pursued more directly through the council remain unheeded for the time being.

Avoiding a Direct Approach

The EU's direct support for political reform and human rights issues in the Gulf has been circumspect. In all states in the region, debate over democratic reform has surfaced, and most regimes have allowed at least modest liberalization. GCC governments' main concern is regime security. So far, political liberalization has been led from above, often in response to underlying domestic pressures such as unemployment and unsustainable rentier state dynamics. The EU and national European governments offer rhetorical support for such reform, and a modest set of governance, women's rights, media, and parliamentary training programs have been supported by the UK, the Netherlands, and Germany in Kuwait, Oman, and Bahrain. But in private, EU officials at both the commission and the council still fret about the possibility of political opening leading to genuine democratization, one that might allow Islamists to assume power. Therefore, GCC states have blocked the creation of a formal human rights dialogue with the European Union, EU civil society initiatives have been discontinued, and governance projects have often been rejected.

Gulf States have resisted offering an opening for the EU to cooperate on or to prompt political reform, their interest in a broader strategic partnership excluding any scrutiny of their domestic political situation. The EU has by its own admission struggled to find access points to support low-key civic projects in the same way as in other regions. There has been little European criticism of reversals to tentative processes of reform. In practice, the promised move away from the regional approach as a means of "rewarding" more reformist states has not materialized, perhaps because the EU has little to reward them with. As one diplomat explained, for the EU the unity and stability of the GCC are seen as more important in security terms than the prospect of increasing leverage over reforms in individual states. Until recently EU officials were still likely to argue (whether correctly or not) that the United States was pushing coercively for regime change in the Gulf, while the EU would at most provide "advice" at the request of incumbent regimes (rather than democratic reformers, apparently), while asserting that economic development would eventually lead to political reform. With the return of a more pragmatic approach toward the Gulf under Obama, the EU might rest easy, but it is unlikely that underlying tensions will be resolved.

The EU could also be accused of a lack of nuance in its understanding of the different pressures that beset each country. While Bahrain is a relatively brittle regime under much social pressure and Kuwait is more democratic than any of its neighbors, there is little domestic pressure and few participatory structures in the remaining four cases. Therefore, there might be some scope for bottom-up engagement in Bahrain and Kuwait, while external assistance in the other cases would not accomplish much. In these other states, corporatist initiatives have led to the creation of state-licensed "interest groups," which could be cautiously engaged while carefully avoiding legitimizing cosmetic political openings and taking care not to crowd out real bottom-up movements that are not formally organized (Echagüe 2006).

Many policymakers lament that it is hard to press for political reform in the absence of a broad political relationship. An EU-GCC political dialogue does take place at the Joint Council meetings, but the meeting excludes domestic reform questions, focusing instead on regional issues, nonproliferation, and the issue of weapons of mass destruction. Eventually this forum, as well as the yearly regional directors' meeting, may provide a framework within which to broach reform issues, but for the moment it is up to the heads of mission and local ambassadors, in their more regular meetings, to raise human rights issues at their discretion. In fact, any discussion of these issues has come from individual member states, often in private rather than public (Nonneman 2007, 23). Arguably, public pressure could be counterproductive at the current stage, with coordination of informal pressure perhaps being more useful.

Member states' bilateral aid has amounted to a few ad hoc projects. Many civil society programs, such as education exchanges, had to be prematurely stopped, with support for government-led educational reform becoming the best alternative. The British government provided support for a project on "participatory democracy" in Bahrain, which included training for prospective female parliamentary candidates and the drafting of a more liberal law governing the creation of civil society organizations. In Kuwait improved campaigning techniques for women activists were supported, and a program for Arab women parliamentarians was run in Kuwait, Oman, and Bahrain. Other measures included public sector training and capacity building for the attorney general's office in Oman, transparency in accounting standards in the Omani civil service, work in the Gulf States under the OECD-UNDP good governance initiative, and strengthening the role of women in local councils across the region. The German development ministry embarked on a wide-ranging program in the region, addressing the following: technical support for elections, women's role in development, combating female genital mutilation, social care housing for women, social development funds; training television journalists; and technical advice and support to anti-corruption and auditing committees. Sweden invested €300,000 in a parliamentary training program for women, bringing Gulf women into programs coordinated from Cairo, in order to circumvent restrictions on directly funding relatively rich GCC states with development aid (Youngs 2006, 178).

The difficulty in justifying aid resources going to relatively rich GCC countries is part of the problem, such that any project would have to be cofinanced and thus require the recipient governments' participation. Bahrain and Saudi Arabia have been included as states eligible for European Instrument for Democracy and Human Rights (EIDHR) funding. Early attempts to begin EIDHR microprojects were unsuccessful due to a lack of local civil society capacity and the fact that European NGOs themselves found it virtually impossible to work in the region. The inclusion of GCC states for eligibility under the commission-managed Instrument for Cooperation with Industrialized and other High Income Countries is unlikely to have much effect, as the allocation is small (€2 million a year) and is focused on the Mundus Erasmus program and on promoting awareness of the EU.

On the other hand, some pressure can also derive from nonpolitical factors such as the economic reforms required to comply with WTO membership and with free trade agreements with both the United States and EU members. These factors require greater transparency, which could eventually temper regimes' absolute power. The opening of Gulf economies will make it difficult to resist pressure to reduce subsidies, and this could eventually lead to demands for political reform (Nonneman 2007, 24).

Free Trade Agreement

It is not surprising that EU-GCC relations have for a very long time focused on the conclusion of a free trade agreement, as in this area the EU enjoys the clearest supranational mandate to negotiate on behalf of its member countries.

From an EU perspective, the major benefits of such an agreement would be equal access to the GCC service sector and the opening up of the GCC's lucrative public procurement contracts with EU companies. But most of all, the FTA would be a positive step toward a rule-based framework, which would improve the perception of certainty in trading conditions and potentially lead to increased foreign direct investment in the region. More generally, the EU's stated aim is to consolidate the GCC's own regional economic integration process in order to foster peace, stability, and prosperity in the region (Rutledge 2005, 15). In this sense, overall levels of intra- and interregional trade in the Gulf and its neighbors are already significant enough that governments will be averse to any politically motivated interruption of commerce. In addition, increasing cross-border investment creates a strong interest in stability and cooperation in the private sectors of the countries of origin and among the governments of recipient countries. The private sector plays an increasing role and is more independent from state contracts than before. Increased business and administration exchanges also lead to the creation of cooperation networks and lobbies for intergovernmental coordination. Capital investment in neighboring countries contributes to service and capital markets integration (Rutledge 2005, 15). The EU also has an incentive to integrate Gulf countries into the global economy by encouraging and supporting their economic diversification so as to reduce incentives to maximize oil revenue.

In the nineteen years since the EC-GCC's Partnership and Cooperation Agreement came into force, trade between the two blocs has grown steadily, and the EU currently maintains a significant trade surplus with the GCC: the GCC is the EU's fifth-largest export market and its seventh-largest source of imports. The EU is the GCC's major trade partner. Around 12 percent of GCC exports are destined for the EU, making it its second-biggest export market after Japan. Recent foreign direct investment levels are still modest compared to investment flows to other regions, but they have increased rapidly since 2000. Recent years have witnessed heightened international interest in the Gulf economies, as institutional investors and industrial players slowly moved into markets that have seen a progressive erosion of national privileges and investment restrictions since the late 1990s. Although there seemed to be an increased level of confidence that GCC countries managed the recent oil boom better than during the 1970s price hike, there is still uncertainty regarding the extent to which the region will be affected by the current financial crisis (Hertog 2006, 10). Gulf states' surpluses, which had increasingly been redirected from the United States to Europe, are expected to shrink substantially. Europe had benefited from the changing pattern of overseas asset allocation of GCC public and private sectors post-9/11, as significant funds were invested in European stocks, real estate, and European heavy industry (especially refinery, oil, and petrochemical deals by SABIC and IPIC).

In contrast to the U.S. approach of seeking cooperation with individual states, the EU decided to pursue trade enhancement and liberalization on an interregional basis. As stated by a commission trade officer: "Concluding a Free Trade Agreement with the Gulf countries will be a significant step in deepening the relationship between the two regions, in the economic and trade fields but more generally in setting up solid, preferential links. Depending on when, and if, it is eventually concluded, it could be the first 'region to region' Free Trade Agreement" (Genand 2005, 11). This decision is judged to have been mistaken by many analysts, who point to the inherent difficulties in reaching an agreement with Saudi Arabia. The decision meant that until the GCC itself established a full customs union it was hard to proceed with significant economic cooperation and liberalization. In the late 1990s the GCC stated that it would set up a customs union by 2005, the date later being brought forward to 2003, with a transitional period of three years. Negotiations for the free trade agreement were thus relaunched in 2002, and the council issued its new negotiation directives for what was now to be a comprehensive free trade agreement, including services, investment, and public procurement rather than simply goods. Nevertheless, by the end of 2009 talks were moribund.

GCC officials claimed undue interference in their affairs through the democracy and human rights clause, while Europeans pointed to unresolved technical issues.

From a GCC perspective, negotiations were always somewhat unbalanced, given the bloc's limited size relative to the EU. The EU insisted that concessions be reciprocal, despite the fact that—aside from oil—there are only a small number of GCC products, such as aluminum and petrochemicals, that could be exported in significant quantities to the EU, compared to the thousands of European products that the agreement will make more competitive in GCC markets (Aluwaisheg 2005, 8). While the EU requires the GCC to comply with its governance regulations on transparency and openness, these are delicate issues for the GCC countries to the extent that they touch on the core structure of their political systems and societies. In the GCC states, contracts are not usually allocated through open tenders but rather through a consensual, informal process often related to the patronage-based distribution of resources. In this sense, GCC regimes' caution on some specifics of the FTA talks is related to their strategies for holding political reform at bay within their own societies. Bilateral free trade agreements signed by Bahrain and Oman with the United States have also not helped negotiations, both because these agreements have undermined cooperation within the GCC itself and because the EU refuses to accept any conditions that do not match those offered to the United States.

Although several moments of optimism have come and gone in recent years, when the agreement's conclusion was said to be imminent, negotiations seemed to have reached a dead end. It appeared that the more specific stumbling blocks toward the conclusion had been resolved. These included the Gulf states' differential pricing of gas exports, European companies' access to the GCC services sector, the lack of transparency in GCC government procurement regulations, and rules of origin provisions for goods coming through the Gulf region. But at the end of 2008 the GCC unilaterally terminated talks. From the European side there is talk of disagreement over export duties, while the GCC claims that despite finally having reached an agreement on all technical issues, talks have been suspended due to disagreements over the EU's standard democracy and human rights clause. As stated by Abdulmalik Al Hina, undersecretary at Oman's Ministry of National Economy, "It is suspended because we reached a roadblock on political issues."[2] There was already tension in 2005 when the requirement was added to sign human rights and migration clauses, as Gulf states perceive the EU's insistence on raising governance and human rights issues as a distraction, despite these clauses being an obligatory part of all EU comprehensive agreements with third parties. The GCC states see these issues as irrelevant to economic negotiations. As Al Hina also states in the news release, "The European side is trying to impose political issues on human rights and democracy that overstep and do not consider local regulations." As of late 2009 the two sides were consulting, but formal negotiations had not been resumed.

Energy Issues

The policy area that would seem most firmly to place the Gulf on the EU's geopolitical map is that of energy security. Increases in oil prices after 2003, combined with Russia's growing assertiveness in the use of its energy-based power, placed energy security at the top of the EU's foreign policy agenda. Despite this changing context, it is not clear what impact new EU energy security concerns will have on its policies in the Gulf. The EU papers published on energy since late 2005 focus overwhelmingly either on domestic energy policy (such as completion of the internal market in energy and development of renewable energy sources) or on the question of how to deal with Russia (Koch 2006, 88). The external relations element of EU energy policy is not well defined, and in the area of energy policy the EU does not enjoy strong competence over member states. After some internal debate, the EU decided not to reduce its free trade demands in order to progress on energy cooperation, a decision lamented by diplomats charged with an energy remit, who had insufficient sway to ensure priority for a broader geostrategic focus on energy security.

Nevertheless, the EU-GCC "energy dialogue" has gathered pace, and small-scale cooperation projects have begun, including the commission's initiative for a technical energy center in Saudi Arabia. The EU's incipient approach to energy security appears heavily based on incorporating regulatory cooperation within formal contractual agreements. Hence, the commission has proposed that the EU work toward an energy treaty between the EU and members of the ENP that could subsequently be extended to the Gulf and Central Asia. Some officials raise the possibility of moving to bilateral energy agreements with individual GCC member states. However, GCC states are not interested in the kind of formal energy cooperation that the EU has offered elsewhere.

The EU currently sources 22 percent of its oil imports from the Gulf, and predictions are that Europe's dependence on Gulf oil will deepen during the next two decades. As oil production from the GCC increases in importance, its potential as a source of energy for the EU will increase (Koch 2006, 83). Gas supplies from the Gulf could also become more important as the objective of diversifying gas supplies away from Russia gains urgency.

Some EU officials suggest that the Gulf region has not to date been a priority for energy policy mainly because the relationship has been unproblematic. The willingness of Gulf suppliers to support stable markets and prices and their eschewal of supply disruptions have, according to many policymakers, rendered unnecessary any more formalized or geopolitical approach to energy cooperation with the GCC. Any deeper EU energy relations have been left to ad hoc bilateral or company-to-company arrangements. Furthermore, the GCC itself has limited competence on energy matters and exhibits significant internal differences on this question among member states. Broader multilateral forums such as the International Energy Forum are judged to provide the necessary interaction, with skeptical voices in Europe arguing that more targeted energy initiatives at the EU level would be of little value.

GCC states complain that they are treated by the EU only as sources of energy, when the GCC seeks a broader strategic partnership to offset U.S. power, especially in relation to the Arab-Israel conflict (Nonneman 2007, 15). Some European officials complain, conversely, that dialogue is already far too dominated by efforts to coordinate positions on Palestine and that this issue invariably displaces all debate and cooperation on energy. Senior officials admit that so far there has been no debate on how the EU's new energy strategy would affect European relations with the Gulf monarchies. The energy imperative is invariably cited as the major factor militating against support for democratic reform. Some analysts, however, argue that the oil/democracy relationship is more complex than commonly assumed. Those who question the standard line that the rentier states of the Gulf are robustly protected from democratic dynamics suggest that in fact the wealth brought by oil and gas has made the region's population more confident in pushing for change (Nonneman 2006, 20). The implication is that the stalling of reform, rather than reform itself, could be the trigger for the kind of instability that could threaten European energy interests.

The EU needs to recognize that the long-term security of oil and gas exports and markets is of crucial importance for Gulf regimes. This has foreign policy implications in terms of their foreign economic policy and in terms of maintaining Gulf security and outside powers' good will (Baabood 2005, 152). However, if such complexity requires careful and detailed deliberation on long-term approaches to energy security, there has been little such strategizing guiding EU policy. One well-placed senior official observes that only the UK and France are interested in domestic political developments within the Gulf, other states being "happy to just keep buying the oil." And the UK's decision not to investigate kickback allegations related to its Al Yamamah defense deal hardly increases the credibility of EU strictures on governance standards. Remarkably, there has so far been no CFSP discussion on the foreign policy effect of energy challenges related to the Gulf. One critic argues that EU policy sees energy in too compartmentalized a way, separate from broader Gulf security issues and detached from any effort to understand the way in which Gulf states and societies are changing (Koch 2006, 86).

Security Challenges

The United States has acted as security guarantor in the Gulf since the 1970s, a role that Europe cannot and would not provide. The EU could do more in the field of confidence building (especially with regard to Iran) and the facilitation of dialogue frameworks. The EU still enjoys certain civilian power credibility, which the United States lacks. After 9/11 new proposals were forthcoming in the security domain. The European security strategy and other initiatives, such as NATO's Istanbul cooperation initiative seemed to signal the beginning of a European attempt to define a security role in the Gulf. A new mandate was agreed to negotiate a counterterrorism agreement with the GCC, an EU-GCC workshop was convened on terrorism, and the notion of supporting a Gulf regional security forum gained currency.

Bilaterally, France and the UK have defense agreements in place with several GCC countries, and in 2008 France established a permanent military base in Abu Dhabi. Germany conducts training for Iraqi security personnel with the support and cooperation of the United Arab Emirates. France and Qatar recently signed an accord to cooperate in the areas of judicial cooperation, crisis management, drug smuggling, money laundering, and terrorism and have regularly engaged in large-scale military exercises. Some EU member states are also major defense equipment exporters to the region. Since the 1990s arms sales to the region from the UK, France, Italy, and Germany have significantly increased in part thanks to the U.S. pro-Israeli lobby successfully restricting American arms sales to the region.[3]

In December 2005 Britain signed an agreement with Saudi Arabia to supply seventy-two Eurofighter Typhoon combat aircraft to replace Tornado planes and others currently in service with the Saudi air force. The deal is said to be worth €60 billion and includes training, spare parts, and refurbishment follow-on contracts. The deal follows the controversial UK-Saudi Al Yamamah II deal (Davis and Mayhew 2005, 1). In July 2004 Britain's Serious Fraud Office began an investigation into British Aerospace concerning payments made in relation to the Al Yamamah deal to recipients in Saudi Arabia. The investigation was discontinued for "public interest" reasons—namely, its effect on security relations between the UK and Saudi Arabia—but most probably because it would have put the new deal in jeopardy.

Against this background, the EU has failed to move beyond the ad hoc bilateral activities of its member states and map out a coherent strategic plan commensurate with the Gulf's geopolitical importance. One Brussels diplomat acknowledged that, despite the post-9/11 efforts, there was "still no EU policy" in the Gulf.

The Istanbul cooperation initiative, agreed on at the June 2004 Istanbul summit meeting, calls for NATO's cooperation with the GCC countries in twelve areas, including counterterrorism, border security, disaster preparedness, civil emergency planning, training, and education. Excluded from NATO's Mediterranean dialogue during the 1990s, the GCC is for the first time to be offered a separate security initiative. This initiative was pushed in particular by the UK, but its scope was reined in by southern EU states, which insisted on NATO retaining a preferential and more institutionalized Mediterranean dialogue, with French and Spanish post-Iraq ambivalence toward NATO also cutting across the effort to deepen security cooperation in the Gulf. The Istanbul initiative includes a commitment to improve "security governance" in the Gulf that would involve cooperation on defense reform and civilian oversight of security forces, albeit without the formal acceptance by all partners of the principle of democratic control of armed forces as applied in the Partnership for Peace (PfP) framework in Eastern Europe (Youngs 2006, 178). Four out of six GCC countries have so far adhered to the initiative.

The initiative is designed to follow the PfP model, which was aimed at former members of the Warsaw Pact and implemented in the 1990s. Nevertheless, it is highly doubtful that NATO's experience in Eastern Europe will be useful in building a partnership with GCC countries. The approach assumes that partner countries are in favor of modernizing their security apparatuses along Western lines. However, the rulers of the GCC states favor an extremely gradual model of reform that is domestically driven. It is problematic to believe that this can be supported from outside (Legrenzi 2007, 6). A significant gap between policy commitment and actual implementation besets the Istanbul initiative.

The security sector is seen as a key aspect of sovereignty and is unlikely to be reformed fundamentally. The separation between the regular army and the National Guard and other separate units, such as tribal levies, exists for important domestic political reasons. A careful management of the security sector has allowed Gulf States to be among the few Middle East countries that have not had a revolution in the last seventy years. Monarchical regimes have many reasons to fear professional armies. Procurement in GCC states is as much a foreign policy tool as an instrument of defense policy. The security services in these countries are set up like they are (separation between national guard and military) for a reason, namely to maintain the domestic balance of power. There are also good reasons that defense budgeting, the transparency of which is one of the objectives of the Istanbul initiative, is opaque: it provides one of the main sources of patronage for influential members of the royal families (Legrenzi 2007, 6).

Incompatible expectations and agendas among the actors on each side are likely to prevent the initiative from succeeding. GCC regimes are happy to cooperate as long as they are not required to make significant reforms. NATO acknowledges the limited military value of the initiative while expecting it to have more of a political reform potential than is feasible. GCC countries have also expressed uneasiness at being lumped together with Mediterranean countries—as expressed in the idea that the NATO training cooperation initiative, launched at the Riga summit in 2006, may include the development of a common training facility for both Mediterranean dialogue and Istanbul initiative countries. The prize of eventual NATO membership is explicitly not available to GCC states (Legrenzi 2007, 8–19).

Conclusion

European foreign policies toward the countries of the Arabian Peninsula have been narrowly focused. For nearly two decades sectoral trade concerns (on both sides) have prevented the signing of a free trade accord that all states acknowledge would provide the essential first step toward a broader partnership between the EU and GCC. This region illustrates how domestic structural factors and geopolitical specificities can account for divergence from a purported common normative orientation in EU foreign policy. The nature of Gulf polities has allowed little scope for the kind of economic and social bottom-up engagement that is the EU's trademark in international relations. Despite a change in rhetoric and a handful of new reform projects, since 9/11 the EU has struggled to gain meaningful traction on economic and political change in the Gulf. Indeed, the Gulf is the part of the

Middle East in which EU policy has changed least from alliance building with autocratic regimes still seen as bulwarks against radical Islam.

While a strategic rationale in terms of energy, economics, and security converges with a normative case for supporting tightly controlled and limited political reform, in the absence of a major crisis the GCC looks likely to continue to be an area of EU neglect, lacking a comprehensive and coherent European policy. The lack of European leverage to effect change limits its role to the low-level technical approach favored by the European Commission, and the strategic partnership is unlikely to be imbued with significance in the foreseeable future. Nevertheless, more can be done in the area of technocratic capacity building, and a concerted effort to promote economic integration could lead to the deepening of a relationship for which a framework for political interaction is already in place.

Europe has greater credibility and economic influence in the region than any other economic bloc, and its expertise in coordinating regulatory reforms in different states is well recognized. There is room for technical cooperation in the implementation of the customs union, and cooperation with the European Central Bank on Gulf monetary union could be a good precedent. EU institutions have considerable experience in legal and regulatory reform and could help in building standards and capacities. For this purpose, the EU needs to build up a cadre of people with expertise in the region. Mutual secondments to administrative bodies could help, as could twinning programs between national and supranational European institutions, on the one hand, and Gulf institutions, on the other. Europe could also play a role in terms of technical cooperation and capacity building in the area of cross-border projects and could emphasize the benefits of regional economic integration. In this context, targeted bureaucratic reform and standardization would be a priority. The scope of current foreign direct investment, which has grown despite administrative obstacles, indicates how large the gains in a more liberalized regional environment could be. In working toward regulatory reform, it will however be important not to apply an EU-centric model. Procedures need to be adjusted to level of development, and often limited regulatory convergence will suffice (Hertog 2006, 15). The conclusion of a free trade agreement would be a useful foundation for further institutional cooperation.

The informal nature of politics in the Gulf will make it difficult for the EU to assist with anything but technical issues in areas such as education, health, and welfare, and even judicial training and penal reform. In an effort to assist indigenous efforts at political liberalization, the EU could also offer to share European experience in terms of electoral principles or procedures and constitutional reform with governments embarking on such processes (Luciani and Neugart 2005, 25). EU electoral observer missions could also help to limit, or at the very least record, irregularities.[4]

While such practical steps forward can be envisaged, these still depend on greater European political will. In contrast to emerging international actors like China, the EU's focus on the Gulf has been negligible. The Gulf is a key geoeconomic region in which the EU has been hardly present as a collective actor. Member states and EU institutions still harbor serious misgivings about investing significant effort in the Gulf, despite all the reasons that point to the need for stronger engagement. This is a curious judgment given events in recent years. EU relations with the Gulf seemed for many years to run according to the maxim, If it is not broken, do not fix it. In light of post-9/11 strategic developments, the deterioration of the post-Iraq Middle Eastern security environment, tightening energy markets, the harsh effect of the 2008–09 financial crisis, pressure for political reform, and increased competition in the Gulf from rising powers, this logic must now be recognized as insufficient.

NOTES

1. N. Janardhan, Convert East-East opportunity into strategy," *Arab News*, March 12, 2007.
2. Political row stalled Gulf-EU trade talks, says official, Reuters, December 29, 2008.
3. D. S. Cloud and H. Cooper, Israel's protests are said to stall Gulf arms sale, *New York Times*, April 5, 2007.
4. Opposition candidates in the recent parliamentary elections in Bahrain (November 2006) stated in interviews that they would have welcomed an EU observer mission, as irregularities were rampant.

REFERENCES

Aliboni, R. 2005. An Italian perspective on future EU-GCC relations. *GCC-EU Research Bulletin* 1: 10–11.
Aluwaisheg, A. A. A. H. 2005. The EU-GCC free trade area negotiations: The home stretch or first base? *GCC-EU Research Bulletin* 2: 7–9.
Baabood, A. 2005. Dynamics and determinants of the GCC states' foreign policy, with special reference to the EU. In *Analyzing Middle East Foreign Policies*, ed. Gerd Nonneman. New York: Routledge.

Commission of the European Communities. 2004. Interim report on an EU strategic partnership with the Mediterranean and the Middle East. *Euromed Report* 73: 1–11.
Council of the European Union. 2006. Establishing a financing instrument for cooperation with industrialised and other high-income countries and territories. Council Regulation 1934/2006.
Davis, I., and E. Mayhew. 2005. What happens when a white elephant meets a paper tiger? The prospective sale of eurofighter typhoon aircraft to Saudi Arabia and the EU code of conduct on arms exports. Occasional Papers on International Security Policy 49: 1–12. British-American Security Information Council
Echagüe, A. 2006. Political change in the Gulf States: Beyond cosmetic reform. *Democracy Backgrounder* 5: 1–16. Madrid: FRIDE.
El-Ghoul, B. 2005. Towards a new political partnership between the EU and the GCC: The challenges of the new European Commission. *GCC-EU Research Bulletin* 1: 17–19.
Genand, L. 2005. A view of the FTA from an EU perspective. *GCC-EU Research Bulletin* 2: 10–11.
Hertog, S. 2006. Perspectives of economic integration in the Arab countries. Study for the Committee of Foreign Affairs of the European Parliament, September.
Khader, B. 2005. Is there a role for Europe in Gulf security? *GCC-EU Research Bulletin* 3: 10–12.
Koch, C. 2006. European energy and Gulf security. *European View* 4: 81–88.
Legrenzi, M. 2007. NATO in the Gulf: Who is doing a favor for whom? *Middle East Policy* 14/1.
Luciani, G., and F. Neugart, ed. 2005. *The EU and the GCC. A New Partnership.* Florence: Bertelsmann Stiftung.
Nonneman, G. 2007. EU-GGC relations: Dynamics, perspectives, and the issue of political reform. *Journal of Social Affairs* 23/92: 13–33.
———. 2006. Political reform in the Gulf monarchies: From liberalisation to democratisation? A comparative perspective. Sir William Luce Fellowship Paper 6. Middle East Papers, University of Durham.
Rutledge, E. 2005. Quantifying the GCC's expected economic gains. *GCC-EU Research Bulletin* 2: 14–15.
Solana, J., C. Patten, and R. Prodi. 2003. *Strengthening the EU's Partnership with the Arab World.* Brussels: Council of the European Union and European Commission.
Youngs, R. 2006. *Europe and the Middle East: In the Shadow of 11 September.* Boulder: Lynne Reinner.

CHAPTER NINE

Iraq

A New European Engagement

Edward Burke

The strategic interests of the European Union in Iraq are clear: Iraq lies at the heart of the troubled Middle Eastern region, bordering Saudi Arabia, Kuwait, Iran, Syria, Jordan, and a prospective EU member state, Turkey. A regional conflict over Iraq would have disastrous consequences for European security. In recent years Iraq has topped the list of countries of origin for asylum requests within the EU, straining the capacity of member states to cope with such an influx (United Nations High Commission for Refugees 2008). The sectarian conflict in Iraq has also had a radicalizing effect upon sections of Europe's Muslim communities, a reality driven home in 2008 when al-Qaeda's second in command in Iraq was discovered to be a Swedish citizen.[1] For a Europe short of reliable energy partners, Iraq presents a significant opportunity to ease the strain on supply, possessing the third-largest oil reserves in the world and largely unfulfilled potential as a major gas exporter. The prospect of an increase in Iraqi energy revenues also presents a significant investment opportunity for European countries in a time of a global economic downturn (Energy Information Administration 2008). Stabilizing Iraq is therefore vital to Europe's interests.

A specificity relative to the other cases in this volume is that EU democracy promotion in Iraq cannot be separated from state building. The implosion of Iraq after the 2003 invasion meant that a divided international community had to try and contain mounting sectarian violence while simultaneously attempting to establish an institutional framework that would foster the emergence of a capable and accountable democratic state. The rhetorical commitment of all EU member states to the latter was not matched by a coherent plan to leverage the full potential of the EU's state-building capacity. EU officials admit that the EU's High Representative for the Common Foreign and Security Policy (CFSP), Javier Solana, neglected Iraq in favor of concentrating on other threats in the region, including Iran's nuclear program and Europe's commitment to Afghanistan.[2]

Given Iraq's proximity to Europe and the economic potential of a strong bilateral relationship, it is perhaps surprising that the EU has yet to consolidate strong ties with Baghdad. This is despite the considerable funds provided by the EU to the United Nations' and the World Bank's reconstruction efforts in the country, a commitment that is now approaching €1 billion from the European Commission alone. In the case of Iraq, in terms of funds, EU support for democracy promotion has clearly proliferated at a rate far greater than that of the other countries analyzed in this book. Yet this should not obscure the fact that the EU has preferred to act as a donor to the UN's efforts to consolidate Iraqi democracy rather than assuming its own role in the country. Due to the acrimony that poisoned European Council discussions on Iraq in 2003, the deep misgivings of some member states over the U.S.-led occupation, and the rapid deterioration of security, Iraq presents unique circumstances that set it apart from other case studies. Iraq clearly demonstrates how the specificities of EU policies result from the interaction between "local" domestic complexities, available European policy instruments, and limits to the degree of potential leverage.

Although 2008 and 2009 have seen a significant reduction of violence in Iraq and the emergence of a more capable, democratically elected government under Prime Minister Nouri al-Maliki, the EU has not moved decisively to take advantage of the changed situation on the ground to realize its ideals and its interests. There is a small European Commission delegation in Baghdad and a limited bilateral training program aimed at improving Iraq's justice system, but relations to date have been obstructed by a residual caution and lack of unified purpose among EU member states. According to one Iraqi diplomat, interviewed in October 2008, "Iraqis do not know what the EU does, they don't see the EU. I myself don't know what they do." While EU officials stress that they have been engaged in Iraq since the introduction of an Iraq strategy paper in 2004, the perception prevails among member states that the EU has largely absented itself from a meaningful role on the ground in the country. Indeed, in November 2008 the French presidency of the EU circulated a paper on Iraq to EU foreign ministers recommending that the time was now finally right for the EU to "re-engage in the country without delay."[3] Swedish UN special representative of the secretary-general to Iraq, Staffan de Mistura, referred to the lapse in violence in Iraq as the "magic moment" to facilitate reconciliation and build institutions, an opportunity that will either be seized or squandered (European Parliament 2008b). Following the signing of a status of forces agreement with the United States restricting the role of its military in Iraq and mandating its withdrawal, the Iraqi government also removed an important obstacle to European engagement. But as of late 2009 the EU had taken few concrete steps in response.

Peace and prospects for democracy in Iraq hinge upon the resolution of the following six potential drivers of conflict: (1) division of power between the federal and regional; (2) sharing of oil revenues; (3) redressing de-Baathification; (4) disarmament, demobilization, and reintegration of militia; (5) minority rights; and (6) the status of Kirkuk and disputed areas. Although there has been a major downturn in violence in Iraq since 2007, it is still too early to assert that Iraq has definitively "turned the corner."[4] Despite significant improvements, levels of unemployment, disease, and hunger are still alarmingly high.[5] In summer 2008 a report by the House of Commons Defense Committee of the United Kingdom noted that economic progress would be the crucial difference between support either for the government or for opposition militia, for which "unemployment and poverty are among their greatest recruiting sergeants" (UK House of Commons 2008).

Obstructing Iraq's economic recovery is the delicate system of co-option and patronage woven by the government, which, combined with years of weak state capacity, has seen Iraq become one of the world's most corrupt countries.[6] Although Iraq's energy revenues, from which over 90 percent of the national budget is drawn, approached €50 billon for 2008, government capacity to invest this capital remains limited despite a generally accepted improvement in the performance of Iraq's ministries (Said 2008).[7] The standoff between the Kurdish regional government over the sharing of oil revenues and the status of disputed territories such as Kirkuk could escalate into outright conflict and the dismemberment of the country. Meanwhile, the successes enjoyed by Prime Minister Nouri al-Maliki's government in co-opting the predominantly Sunni Majlis al-Sahwa (Awakening Councils) and the 2008 victory of the Iraqi Security Forces over elements of the

Jaish al-Mahdi are easily reversible. These outstanding obstacles to peace mean that Iraq's future continues to hang in the balance in 2009 and should act as a warning against European complacency.

Member States: Withdrawal and Neglect

EU member states' commitments to Iraq have ranged from the deployment of 46,000 troops by the UK in 2003 and expenditure of approximately €6.5 billion in military/civilian operations to the resolute nonengagement of France (Ministry of UK Defense 2008). Since 2009 significant military deployment by EU member states as part of the multinational force–Iraq (MNF-I) has effectively ended following the withdrawal of the UK's 4,100 troops together with the 500-strong Romanian contingent.[8] Of the twenty-seven provincial reconstruction teams in Iraq, Italy and the UK initially assumed responsibility for two: Dhi Qar and Basra. The Dhi Qar team is Italian-led but has relied upon support from the United States, the UK, and Romania, while the UK-led team in Basra drew upon U.S. and Danish assistance (Katzman 2008, 38).

The UK and Italian governments have increasingly outsourced much of their provincial reconstruction team activities to hired consultants: the number of UK civilian officials assigned to the Basra team was always comparatively much lower than, for example, the UK's commitment of fifty personnel to the Lashkar Gah team in Afghanistan. As the insurgency intensified during 2006 and 2007, the UK-led team failed to make the transition from a primarily civilian entity to one that took a more military approach to stability operations. During this period Basra Palace was being hit daily by up to forty rocket and mortar attacks, often bringing the reconstruction team's work to a virtual standstill. Reconstruction efforts were also hampered by internal conflicts between senior team personnel and the military, arising principally from "a lack of clear guidelines" as to its role and objectives. The fact that British and Danish civil-military structures in Basra "ran along parallel tracks and were not integrated" only served to add to the confusion (Hoffmann 2009, 56).

Poor coordination and restrictions of movement had a severe effect upon the monitoring of UK reconstruction and democracy projects in Iraq. In the case of the Southern Iraq Employment Program, lack of oversight over the local authorities who received a grant of €4.6 million meant that fraudulent reporting went unnoticed for over a year until it was eventually concluded that only €1.1 million could be accounted for (UK Department for International Development 2008, 22).

As the violence escalated, the Department for International Development was reduced to trying to monitor projects through the use of aerial photography (UK Department for International Development 2008, 25). The improvement of security following "the charge of knights" (a U.S.-Iraqi operation in Basra in 2008) allowed the reconstruction team greatly to increase its effectiveness. In 2008 the UK team moved away from infrastructure assistance to putting in place innovative projects aimed at improving local governance capacity and establishing the Basra Investment Commission to encourage economic growth. The aim, as one official noted, "was to salvage our reputation," after Basra's descent into chaos during 2006 and 2007. The abrupt end of the UK command of the Basra team in April 2009 was seen as premature by some UK officials, given that conditions had only just changed sufficiently to permit an effective civilian approach in the province.[9]

The Italian-led reconstruction team, Dhi Qar, relies heavily upon the security company Aegis Defense Services for local political analysis, due to a lack of Italian diplomats on the ground (Ministry of Foreign Affairs of Italy 2008). Italy has maintained a commitment to Dhi Qar since 2003 (the Italian troop contribution to MNF-I was withdrawn in 2006), although it is perhaps no coincidence that the Italian oil company ENI was in the running for lucrative oil contracts in the province. Rome has led team Dhi Qar with a hands-off approach, which allows the team leader, the Italian diplomat Anna Prouse, to make decisions based on her own evaluation of the political and security situation. Prouse's leadership, combined with the presence of security and intelligence personnel from Aegis Defense Service, has allowed Italy to gain unique political knowledge, experience of best practices, and a consistency of approach. The Dhi Qar team is civilian heavy, preferring not to travel or to integrate too closely with the U.S. military, agreeing on a careful division of labor in order to seize upon the relative security of the south to transfer out of a military approach. The Dhi Qar team has generally shied away from the heavy infrastructure projects of their U.S. counterparts, focusing instead on skills training for local Iraqi officials and businessmen.

Despite the withdrawal of troops, the UK remains the most conspicuous EU member state on the ground in Iraq. Following the withdrawal of British troops from Iraq in 2009, the emphasis of the UK's assistance to Iraq has moved from the provincial to the federal level. Both the Foreign and Commonwealth Office and the Department for International Development provide capacity-building programs for Iraqi ministries, including the previously dysfunctional Interior Ministry, and have trained more than 3,700 health sector staff. The UK has also attempted to ease tensions between the Kurdistan regional government and the federal government, facilitating a visit of Kurdish political leaders to Belfast to discuss frameworks for regional autonomy with Northern Irish political leaders.[10] Worryingly, given the widespread corruption in Iraq, the UK significantly reduced its judicial training initiative in Iraq due to lack of results.[11]

The UK has maintained a police-training mission in Iraq since 2003, investing more than €105 million to train approximately 13,000 Iraqi police officers, 1,000 prison staff, and 213 judges and lawyers. Indeed, the current head of the EU's police and justice sector reform mission (EUJUST LEX), Stephen White, was formerly a senior police adviser to the Coalition Provisional Authority in Basra during 2003–04. UK police advisers not only provided training within MNF-I bases but also mentored Iraqi trainees in the streets of Baghdad and Basra, where in 2008 eight and seven advisers, respectively, were based. The UK Police Mission has switched from a Basra-focused initiative to working with the Iraqi Police Service (IPS) and the Ministry for the Interior on a new strategic framework for Iraqi policing. The mission has also expanded its operations to focus on providing mechanisms to deal with corruption in the IPS and designing training modules at the Shaibah Police College (UK Foreign and Commonwealth Office 2008). Toward the end of 2009 the UK Police Mission was set to wind down, to be replaced largely by the UK's commitment to EUJUST-LEX.

Although the UK has now wound up most of its projects, in 2009 it initiated a €3.2 million local governance program in Basra Province. Less positively, the majority of these funds will go to private security companies contracted to guard consultants, due to the continuing threat of violence in the region. At the national level the UK aims to implement almost €21 million of projects over 2009–12 aimed at improving public financial management, developing international partnerships with Iraqi third-level institutions, and improving the climate for private sector investment (UK Department for International Development 2008).

If France has made a rhetorical commitment to engage in Iraq, it still has to take practical steps to deliver on these statements. In an article published in the *International Herald Tribune* in summer 2007, Foreign Minister Bernard Kouchner appeared to draw a line under the rancor and division caused by the 2003 invasion, admitting that France had "ignored the country politically" and could not now "turn a deaf ear to the Iraqis because they were—over our objections—liberated and then controlled by our American and British allies. Iraq's troubles lie at the heart of the world's problems—the hostility between communities, religious fanaticism, and conflicts of civilization that are being played out against a backdrop of terrorism, nuclear proliferation, and globalization."[12] Kouchner has also frequently emphasized the urgent self-interest of both France and the EU in stabilizing Iraq.[13]

It is obvious that the French government has not allocated sufficient resources to prioritize a new relationship with Iraq; there is currently only one permanent Iraq desk officer at the Ministry of Foreign Affairs in Paris. Some European diplomats also suspect that "there is an ingrained caution in the French system about Iraq."[14] Such irresolution was evident in an interview given by a French diplomat to the Lebanese *Daily Star* shortly after France recommended that the EU "re-engage" in Iraq. "At the moment, the country is probably still too insecure. But we're starting the discussion now. The better things get, the more we can do."[15]

In 2007 Bernard Kouchner expressed his desire for France to move quickly to provide technical expertise on health.[16] To date no major project has been launched to this effect, and France lacks any signature bilateral capacity-building project with Iraq, preferring to provide limited assistance to Iraq through EU, UN, and NATO programs. While France was initially hesitant in agreeing to launch EUJUST LEX, the Foreign Ministry in Paris is now one of its most vocal supporters and has expressed an interest in further expanding EU capacity-building initiatives on the ground in Iraq.[17] Given France's opposition to the invasion of Iraq in 2003, its leadership in embarking upon a new phase of EU-Iraq relations is highly desirable and would help establish a more cohesive relationship between Europe and the United States in the region.[18] In doing so, France can draw upon diplomats with profound experience in Iraq and the region, including leading negotiations in Damascus and Tehran.[19]

Italy has provided more than €270 million for reconstruction projects since 2003 and has dispatched eighty-three consultants to Iraq to conduct capacity-building exercises in Iraqi institutions (including at the Ministry for Oil, with the cooperation of the Italian energy firm Eni), training more than 2,200 Iraqi police and civilian officials. Uniquely among EU member states, Italy has also undertaken a project to build awareness of European institutions among Iraqi parliamentarians and has established workshops on federal- and local-level democratic institutions. In early 2007 Italy signed the Treaty of Friendship, Partnership, and Cooperation with Iraq. The agreement established an annual meeting between the heads of government and another between the ministers of foreign affairs of the two countries. It further specified that the Italian government would respond positively to Iraqi requests for technical assistance, appointed a joint high-level commission to implement the treaty, and made €400 million available in soft loans to the Iraqi government. In sum, the agreement places Italy-Iraq relations at a more advanced level than most other EU member states (Ministry of Foreign Affairs of Italy 2007).

Poland sent 2,500 troops to Iraq in 2003 but did not combine this considerable force with any development assistance. In 2005, despite Iraq being designated a priority country for Polish aid, Warsaw allocated only €250,000 in development assistance to Iraq, a tiny proportion of its development budget. After the election of the government of Prime Minister Donald Tusk in 2007 and the withdrawal of its military from Iraq in 2008, Poland's bilateral relations with Iraq diminished considerably. Iraq is no longer listed as a priority country for assistance, and Poland's aid to Iraq is now predominantly channeled through its contribution to EU assistance, including hosting EUJUST LEX training (Baginski 2007).

Following the departure of the Polish contingent in 2008, the timetable was unclear for the withdrawal of Romania's contingent, the last significant non-UK member state contingent in the MNF-I. In November 2008 Defense Minister Teodor Melescanu pledged to withdraw its 500 troops from Iraq by the end of the year, only for that statement to be contradicted by President Traian Basescu, who claimed that Romania had been requested by the Iraqi government to keep their troops there until the end of 2011.[20] The Romanian contingent eventually left Iraq in June 2009. Romania's nonmilitary assistance to Iraq, like that of its neighbor Bulgaria, which withdrew its 155 troops in December 2008, has predominantly been channeled through the EU.

The Czech Republic did not make Iraq a priority during its EU presidency in the first half of 2009. Prague has further decreased its already small presence in Iraq, withdrawing Czech force protection and police training teams at the beginning of 2009. The bilateral assistance provided by the Czech Republic to Iraq, which amounted to almost €60 million during 2003–05, has dwindled considerably and is now predominantly directed through the EU and NATO.[21]

Sweden, which took over the presidency of the EU from the Czech Republic in the second half of 2009, provides the highest level of democracy support as a percentage of its assistance to Iraq, which amounted to approximately €50 million during 2004–07 (Ministry of Foreign Affairs of Sweden 2008a). The majority of Sweden's democracy promotion activities take place under the direction of the Olof Palme International Centre, and to date more than 6,000 Iraqi civil society representatives have participated in workshops on democracy and human rights organized by the center. Sweden has also provided funding to the United Nations Development Fund for Women to organize training workshops for women parliamentarians. In addition, the Swedish government has initiated a training program with the Iraqi central bank, and in 2008 the Swedish international development cooperation agency began a program in cooperation with the Jordanian National Electricity Company to provide training for Iraqi engineers from the Ministry of Electricity (Ministry of Foreign Affairs of Sweden 2008a).

Due to its liberal asylum system, Sweden claims to host more Iraqi refugees than the United States and other EU member states combined but, since a controversial ruling by the Swedish courts in 2008 that defined Iraq as no longer being in a state of "armed conflict," has begun repatriating asylum seekers (United Nations High Commissioner for Refugees 2008). Yet despite this clear vested interest in a stable Iraq, the Swedish government did not make Iraq an important issue of their presidency of the EU in 2009 and has not devised any major new strategic objectives for the country. In May 2008 Sweden hosted a meeting of the International Compact with Iraq, an initiative that aimed to consolidate donor efforts to improve Iraq's economy and governance but that did not mark a new departure in European-Iraqi relations. Sweden reopened an embassy in Baghdad in 2009, although there are no plans for a significant expansion of bilateral assistance.[22]

Denmark has played a prominent role in Iraq since 2003, maintaining a battalion of troops until 2007 and contributing a consistent and large amount to reconstruction and humanitarian efforts. During 2003–10, Denmark will have allocated €128 million in reconstruction and humanitarian assistance to Iraq, an amount that, relative to Denmark's size, rivals the commitment of the UK. Like the UK, Danish assistance was hampered by a lack of civil-military coordination as violence escalated during 2006 and 2007. Following the withdrawal of the Danish battalion from Basra in 2007, the Danish government directed €13 million toward increasing their capacity-building initiatives in Baghdad, while reducing their local commitment to the Basra province (Ministry of Foreign Affairs of Denmark 2007). In 2007, Denmark was the third-highest humanitarian donor in absolute terms to Iraq, granting over €26 million in assistance to Iraqi internally displaced persons and refugees (Ministry of Foreign Affairs of Sweden 2008b). In 2008 Denmark completed a €4 million technical assistance project with the Basra local authorities on agricultural irrigation, complementing a broader UK initiative to improve water supply for the region (Danida 2008).

Some traditional EU donor member states such as Germany and the Netherlands are notable for their low level of engagement in bilateral assistance projects in Iraq. Germany has supported German foundations and nongovernmental organizations in providing training programs on democracy and human rights as well as promoting an awareness campaign with regard to the Iraqi constitution, providing funds of just under €2 million in 2005 and 2006. Berlin also funded the Friedrich Ebert Foundation's training program for electoral observers in advance of the 2009 provincial elections and recently announced an initiative to twin the German Institute for Human Rights with the Ministry for Human Rights in Baghdad in 2009 (Ministry of Foreign Affairs of Germany 2008). However, Germany's bilateral engagement in Iraq has generally not been proportional to the challenge that Iraq poses to European security. Meanwhile the Netherlands, a contributor to the MNF-I until 2005, is now remarkably unengaged in Iraq, maintaining a minimal diplomatic presence and preferring to focus on providing assistance to refugees in Syria and Jordan and working through the EU and NATO to provide capacity-building opportunities to the Iraqi Security Forces (Council of the European Union 2008a).

In Spain the internal and external divisions wrought by Socialist Prime Minister José Luis Zapatero's decision rapidly to withdraw Spanish troops from Iraq in 2004 led to a rethinking of policy that honored Spain's extensive commitment of €160 million to reconstruction. This commitment was made at the Madrid donors conference in late 2003 under the government of the former Partido Popular leader José María Aznar but did not extend to bilateral programs of assistance. This reticence to engage bilaterally appears to be slowly evolving toward a more positive role; in 2007 the Spanish government convened a human rights training program for 160 Iraqi civil servants in Madrid and is expected to review its bilateral engagement in 2009 (Ministry of Foreign Affairs of Spain 2008). In late 2009, however, the overall neglect of relations with Iraq by Madrid, reflected by the almost complete absence of any reference to Iraq during preparations for its EU presidency in the first half of 2010, appeared to negatively affect Spanish energy bids.[23]

More than six years after the invasion of Iraq, bilateral assistance to the country from traditional donor member states can still be divided into two categories, those who supported the war and those who did not. While member states such as the UK and Italy, which were committed to bilateral assistance, backed up their contribution to the European Commission with significant bilateral support to Iraq, those member states opposed to the invasion in 2003 tended not to follow suit. In 2005, 94 percent of humanitarian assistance was provided by those donors that had been part of the invading coalition (Oxfam International 2007, 27). Those countries resolutely against the war in 2003 have still not demonstrated a bilateral commitment, beyond that of debt relief, to help consolidate the recent security gains made by the Iraqi government, despite it being in their interests to do so.

Europe-Iraq Relations: Subcontracting Engagement

The European Commission 2004 strategy paper that informs current EU policy in Iraq emphasizes the importance of a stable Iraq for Europe, not least as continued violence risks embroiling an EU candidate country, Turkey, in a regional conflict. It also recognized the need to "prioritize EU assistance for elections, good governance, the development of Iraqi civil society and the protection and promotion of human rights" (Commission of the European Communities 2004, 5). The paper was not intended to set an ambitious agenda for developing relations but rather represents the practical sum of what could be achieved considering the disharmony at the council level.

The funding of the UN in Iraq offered a means for the EU to subcontract its engagement in Iraq due to misgivings over security and disagreement over the international presence there. Those member states that opposed the war were able to pay for an enhanced role for the UN, confident that the most workable solution toward building a stable Iraq would come from a return to the multilateral institutions that the United States and its allies had rashly ignored. For countries such as France and Germany channeling money through the EU would also be a means to show solidarity with the Iraqi people while avoiding dealing with a transitional government whose legitimacy was regarded as questionable. In sum the 2004 Iraq strategy allowed the commission to attempt to consolidate democracy in Iraq through the UN and other multilateral agencies (Youngs 2004, 3). From 2003 until 2009, EU humanitarian and reconstruction assistance to Iraq amounted to more than €933 million, of which approximately €265 million was spent on governance and democracy programs (Serwer and Chabalowski 2008, 285; Commission of the European Communities 2008a). The EU has been a leading donor in funding the UN Assistance Mission for Iraq.[24] To date the commission has provided 42 percent of overall funding for the International Reconstruction Fund for Iraq (IRFFI), which finances the activities of UN agencies and the World Bank (Commission of the European Communities 2008a, 1). For 2009–10 the EU plans to reduce its overall development cooperation budget to €65.8 million—€42.0 million in 2009 and €23.8 million in 2010—in addition to a humanitarian assistance budget of €20 million foreseen for 2009 alone (Commission of the European Communities 2009, 3).

The strategy suggested that Iraq be included in the EU's Strategic Partnership for the Mediterranean and the Middle East as part of its "east of Jordan" engagement. But this initiative floundered and offered little in the way of specific benefits to Iraq. In June 2005, during the UK presidency of the EU, the High Representative for CFSP Javier Solana visited Baghdad, together with the UK Foreign Secretary Jack Straw, and pledged to open an EC delegation in Iraq, a specific objective of the 2004 strategy. This was accomplished later that year, and a head of delegation, Ilkka Uusitalo, the former head of the EC delegation in Islamabad, was appointed in July 2006 to lead the European Council's presence in Baghdad. The council has not yet mandated a strong representation in Baghdad, with the bulk of its Iraq team remaining in Jordan due to security concerns. In 2009 some commission staff began to move from Amman to Baghdad, with plans to establish a separate delegation building and a more visible presence away from its previous location within the UK embassy.[25]

The policy of not deploying commission personnel to Iraq because of security concerns and the subcontracting of reconstruction assistance to UN agencies is not without its critics. The movements of UN personnel are greatly restricted, impacting prejudicially on decision making and aid efficiency. Although the EU was able to select which projects it wanted to fund, it found it difficult to evaluate their performance. During 2007 and 2008 some European Parliament members began to complain of poor reporting practices by the UN and the concern that, despite the expenditure of significant funds in Iraq, "there prevails in the Iraqi population the impression of a complete absence of the EU in the solution of the political, social, and economic problems of their country" (European Parliament 2007a). On several occasions, the Foreign Affairs Committee of the European Parliament registered its unease that IRFFI was not providing a comprehensive and verifiable account of the spending of EC funds (Brie 2005). This frustration with the performance of IRFFI led the European Parliament's Committee on Budgetary Control to recommend that the EC withhold 20 percent of that year's contribution to IRFFI pending receipt of "an exhaustive overview of the use of funds in Iraq in 2006, 2007, and planned for 2008" (European Parliament 2007b). Portuguese Socialist member Ana Gomes, in a report on Iraq submitted to Parliament on March 13, 2008, concluded that "Europe can do much more and much better, namely by engaging more intensively with Iraqi institutions and civil society actors by considerably expanding its presence on the ground" (European Parliament 2008c). Such views are representative of a growing awareness among members that Europe's interests are being jeopardized by the absence of a strong EU presence in Iraq.

The major exception to the EU's largely detached relationship is EUJUST LEX, an initiative that was established as a mission under the European Security and

Defense Policy to provide training to senior Iraqi police and prison officers and magistrates. The mission has thirty full-time members of staff, mostly based in Brussels with a liaison team in Baghdad. It has been led since its inception in 2005 by a highly experienced former assistant chief constable of the Policing Service of Northern Ireland, Stephen White, and to date more than 1,800 Iraqi officials have been trained by the program, on a budget of €30 million. Training programs have been hosted in eighteen member states, and in October 2008 EUJUST LEX received one of the most prestigious awards for international policing. While EUJUST LEX has been rightly praised for its achievements, some Iraqi officials suggest that resources would be better spent in Iraq: "For every judge you train in Europe, you could train five to ten in Iraq."[26] A significant breakthrough was made in November 2008 when the council extended the mandate of EUJUST LEX beyond June 2009 and permitted the mission to conduct "progressive and experimental pilot activities, where security conditions permit, in the area of the rule of law on Iraqi territory" (Council of the European Union 2008b). EUJUST-LEX trainers are finally able to review some of the results of their program on the ground in Iraq and to plan future initiatives there. However, highly restrictive security regulations on the movements of EUJUST-LEX personnel further limit the scope of the already short one- or two-week training courses they undertake in Iraq. The bulk of EUJUST-LEX personnel will continue to be based in Brussels rather than Baghdad along a 4:1 ratio. One EU official describes the new arrangements for EUJUST-LEX's activities in Iraq as a diplomatic compromise.[27]

Strengthening Europe's Role in Iraq

In a meeting with Javier Solana in April 2008, Prime Minister Nouri al-Maliki was unambiguous in stating what he wanted from a strengthened bilateral relationship with the EU: "We are a rich country, we don't need funds; we need technical expertise" (European Parliament 2008a). The EU has already allocated considerable funding to political development and election management (€138 million), capacity building (€50 million), and assistance to Iraqi civil society organizations and human rights groups (€45 million). It has also targeted symbolic reconstruction projects such as the rebuilding of al-Askari mosque in Samarra, the bombing of which was blamed for an escalation in sectarian killings in 2006 (Commission of the European Communities 2008b). After four years of funding programs principally through the IRFFI, commission contributions to the fund are gradually being phased out. Iraq's own budget for 2008 far exceeded the €32 billion originally forecast. The commission is increasingly focusing on capacity-building programs within the Council of Representatives and various Iraqi ministries (including finance, interior, and planning) to be implemented primarily by the World Bank and UN agencies. In 2009–10 the European Commission will dedicate €22 million toward democratic governance programs as part of its overall development support.

In May 2008 the council expressed its desire to strengthen EU presence in Iraq in response to the downturn of violence in the country. Consequently, a series of visits were undertaken by EU officials to evaluate whether bilateral ties could be strengthened further (included were Tomás Dupla del Moral, director for the Middle East and Southern Mediterranean at the Directorate-General for External Relations, and Kees Klompenhouwer, EU civilian operations commander). Nonetheless, it is still uncertain to what extent EU officials will work on the ground in Iraq rather than continue to subcontract activities to other actors. In 2009 the EU sent two electoral experts to assist and monitor preparations for the Provincial Council elections and those for the Kurdish National Assembly and appeared set to send a slightly expanded electoral mission in advance of the national parliamentary elections scheduled for early 2010. Despite sending an electoral observation mission to Afghanistan in 2009, the EU did not plan to do so in the case of Iraq in either 2009 or 2010, citing security concerns as the main factor in its decision. Nevertheless, such a small number of election experts seemed to be only a token gesture rather than a commitment to consolidate the democratic process in Iraq. The subcontracting of EU assistance denies Iraq the considerable governance and development expertise accumulated by European institutions.[28] The EU has also not yet moved toward multiyear planning for Iraq, as it has for Afghanistan.

As a first step toward engaging on the ground in Iraq, the council might consider appointing an EU special representative to Iraq to coincide with the opening of an expanded EC delegation office in Baghdad. As of late 2009 there were eleven EU special representatives in the world's trouble spots: appointing a representative to Iraq would send a clear message and enhance EU coherence in the country. This representative should preferably be French, underlining France's recent commitment to engaging in Iraq. A new EU special representative to Iraq would do well to take the advice offered to the EC by the UK government: "Given the scale and dominance of US activity in the rule of law and justice sector in Iraq, it is of vital importance to the success of any future EU activity in these fields that the Secretariat/Commission report on Iraq develops a comprehensive understanding of US current and planned activity in this field" (UK Foreign and Commonwealth Office 2008). In recent years, the Foreign and Commonwealth Office's stabilization adviser has assisted the U.S. Inter-Agency Rule of Law Coordination Center, and the UK has advised that the EC develop a similar liaison capacity. Regardless of previous disagreements, such advice is realistic and reflects a need to address EU-U.S. coherence in Iraq. It remains to be seen if old fears of legitimizing Washington's policy in Iraq can now be put aside in favor of cooperation with the Obama administration.

Trade Relations

Iraq has once again become a significant trading partner of the EU; even during the intensely disruptive violence of 2007, bilateral trade reached €8.2 billion. The EU is the second-biggest importer of Iraqi oil as well as being the third-largest source of exports to Iraq (Commission of the European Communities 2008a). In 2008 and 2009 the EU negotiated a Trade and Cooperation Agreement that will regulate its economic relationship with Iraq with regard to public procurement, intellectual property rights, statistical cooperation, and other areas designed to enhance confidence in the Iraqi market.

The agreement has prepared the Iraqi government well for further international trade negotiations, including for membership in the World Trade Organization. However, European officials generally acknowledge that the agreement does not offer significantly improved access to the European market.[29] Some of the rhetoric surrounding the initial phases of the negotiation of the agreement has led Iraqis to believe that they might secure a favored trading status with the EU in the near future. In fact, Iraq currently has no prospect of attaining a privileged trade relationship with the EU such as that enjoyed by its neighbor Jordan. This is bitterly disappointing for those Iraqis who favor strong EU-Iraq relations. To date the EU has given Iraq observer status at meetings related to the Barcelona Process: Union for the Mediterranean, but this offers little in the way of securing privileged access or practical advantage.

Energy dialogue between the EU and Iraq has also been infrequent and low level. In January 2008, Commissioners Benita Ferrero-Waldner (external relations) and Andris Piebalgs (energy) spoke of a new "EU-Iraq energy partnership," noting that the EU was "keen to see Iraq play a full role in the Arab gas pipeline which will supply the EU including through the Nabucco."[30] These encouraging statements have not been followed up by regular high-level political and energy dialogue with Iraq. The intrinsic self-interest of the EU in securing a strong energy partnership with Iraq has not been translated into a coherent bilateral dialogue to realize this aim.

As a "first entry" into the Iraqi energy sector, in 2007 the EC undertook a feasibility study into exporting Iraqi gas through Syria (Commission of the European Communities 2007, 2). It has since signed a memorandum of understanding on energy with Iraq. The EU is also now beginning to explore ways of upgrading Iraq's creaking energy infrastructure and ensuring access to the country's vast hydrocarbon reserves for a European market short of reliable energy partners on its southern and eastern borders.[31] The question over the management of energy resources and supply for the domestic market is inseparably linked to the development of democracy in Iraq. In 2009 the EC proposed undertaking projects to address the inability of the government to supply domestic demand, although these projects would be limited in scale (Commission of the European Communities 2008a). In early 2010 a new memorandum of understanding established the EU's Strategic Energy Partnership with Iraq. However, the text is generally a reiteration of previous statements on enhancing energy cooperation, and it remains to be seen whether the resources and political priority will be allocated by both sides for this agreement to enable a major improvement in EU-Iraq energy relations.[32] To the irritation of Iraqi officials, the EU has yet to take measures to prevent European energy companies from signing energy contracts with the Kurdistan regional government against the wishes of the federal government until a consensus on revenue management emerges.[33]

Democracy and Human Rights

The EC has contributed substantially to democracy projects carried out by UN agencies through the IRFFI. During 2005–06 all UN activities undertaken in relation to the constitutional process were enabled by EC funding (Commission of the European Communities 2007). In 2007 the EC allocated €20 million to preparations for holding provincial elections on January 31, 2009, and national elections twelve months later, again mostly channeled through UN agencies. A twinning capacity-building exercise is now under way by the European Parliament and the Iraqi Council of Representatives. In 2009 the EC announced its intention to create a program that would focus on the development of a national NGO network and support the drafting of a new NGO law to regulate and promote freedom of association (Commission of the European Communities 2009, 4).

Within the field of human rights, the commission, through the EIDHR, provided €2.6 million during 2006–07 toward a project run by the United Nations Office for Project Services that trained seventy Iraqi human rights organizations and helped establish rehabilitation centers for victims of torture (Commission of the European Communities 2007). As the absorption capacity of Iraqi NGOs grows, the EU has said it will consider increasing EIDHR funding, including the resumption of country-specific calls for proposals, which were discontinued in 2005. The EU is currently designing a program of technical assistance to the newly established Independent High Commission for Human Rights. There are also growing calls from Iraqis to strengthen educational ties as a means of spreading cultural awareness and building capacities within Iraq. The twinning of educational institutes and increased funding for the Erasmus Mondus program from the current budget of €3 million divided among Iraq, Iran, and Yemen are obvious means of reaching this goal. Meanwhile, the EC has announced its intention to provide technical assistance for strengthening law faculties in Iraq's universities during 2009 and 2010, a welcome initiative aimed at reversing the long-term decline of education in Iraq (Commission of the European Communities 2009, 4). However, considering the rapid downscaling of bilateral assistance from member states, the EC allocation of approximately €20 million represents a drop in the ocean compared to the true scale of capacity building that Iraq's institutions still require. The limited nature of the EU's commitment to Iraq becomes glaringly obvious when compared to spending on governance assistance by the United States in Iraq: for the same period of 2009–10 one U.S. government agency, USAID, has allocated €89 million to its local governance program, which is only one of its major capacity-building initiatives in Iraq.[34]

Conclusion

The end of the military contribution of EU member states to the MNF-I presence in Iraq has helped reduce tensions that precipitated a cautious approach to EU engagement by those member states opposed to the 2003 invasion. This divergence has resulted in a lack of harmonization among European institutions, individual member states, and NATO in relation to capacity building and democratization in Iraq. The downscaling of the EU member state presence in Iraq now presents an opportunity to structure European engagement in Iraq within an overall EU strategy.[35] However, an anticipated move by the EU to engage robustly in Iraq during 2009 did not transpire. Following the election of President Barack Obama, Europe is rapidly running out of excuses for its lack of focus on Iraq. In 2009 the opening of bidding for Iraqi oil contracts prompted a flurry of statements advocating an enhancement of ties, especially from France and Spain, whose major international oil companies, TOTAL and Repsol, were interested in securing contracts with Baghdad. However, this interest in hydrocarbons did not translate into the type of investment in capacity-building programs and democracy assistance that Iraq so badly needs. It is perhaps not a coincidence that, despite Italy's best efforts, Japanese international oil company, Nippon, is set to win lucrative oil contracts, following the announcement of a bilateral aid package by Tokyo, worth €2.4 billion in 2008.[36]

In responding positively to requests for assistance from the Iraqi government, the EU can prove its capabilities and develop relations in a region in which it is scarcely represented or understood. It is by no means certain, however, that member states will choose to deploy such a mission to Iraq, preferring to focus efforts on the war in Afghanistan. European interests in Iraq—regional stability, energy security, migration, and combating terrorism—imply that opting out of a significant role in Iraq lends credence to the contention that the EU is unable to act robustly to protect its external interests and to follow through on political openings to build democratic institutions. The EU has yet to apply the full potential of its own instruments to make a serious contribution to the consolidation of Iraq's brittle democracy. The EU's institutional capacity to assist reform in Iraq is precisely what is required to win a viable peace for Iraq following the tentative "truce" that emerged between the main factions in 2008. Europe should not miss such an opportunity.

NOTES

1. D. Haynes, Abu Qaswarah, al-Qaeda no. 2, killed in Mosul, was Swedish national, *Times*, October 16, 2008.

2. EU official, interview with author, Brussels, June 2009.

3. EU aims to re-engage in Iraq after Obama administration takes office, *Daily Star*, November 7, 2008.

4. D. Browne, July 10, 2008, Brookings Institution, Washington, D.C.

5. Exacerbating the problem faced by the Iraqi government and international donors is the severe brain drain that has taken place in recent years. The International Committee of the Red Cross (2008) estimates that, of the 34,000 doctors registered in Iraq in 1990, at least 20,000 have left the country. Also see U.S. Department of Defense (2008), 17.

6. Iraq ranks 178th of 180 countries surveyed in Transparency International's Corruption Perceptions Index. This is below Haiti, which ranks 177th and above only Myanmar and Somalia.

7. Also see Iraq 08 oil revenues about $60 bn., Associated Press, January 8, 2009.
8. Iraq and UK agree to let troops stay until July, Reuters, December 30, 2008.
9. UK officials, interviews with author, March and April 2009, Basra.
10. Speaker of Kurdistan's parliament meets UK Minister Bill Rammell, Iraq Updates, December 11, 2008.
11. The UK has, however, made considerable progress in developing the use of forensic evidence by the Iraqi Police Service and the judiciary. UK Foreign and Commonwealth Office 2008; UK diplomat, interview with author, October 13, 2008, London.
12. B. Kouchner, What France can do in Iraq, *International Herald Tribune*, August 26, 2007.
13. Again on November 12, 2008, Kouchner reassured United States policymakers that he "would continue . . . making the case in Europe, and in France" for a greatly enhanced European role in Iraq. Brookings Institution, Washington, D.C.
14. European diplomat, interview with author, October 9, 2008, Brussels.
15. F. Schmid, EU aims to re-engage in Iraq after Obama administration takes office, *Daily Star*, November 7, 2008.
16. Ministry of Foreign Affairs of France, news release, October 17, 2007. Statements made by M. Bernard Kouchner, Minister of Foreign and European Affairs, and Jalal Talabani, President of Iraq, October 17, Paris.
17. French diplomat, interview with author, October 10, 2008, Paris.
18. Another interesting role for France to play could be that of facilitator of talks among the Iraqi parties. Bernard Kouchner's offer in 2008 to host a round of "château diplomacy" in Paris to address the challenges of reconciliation, away from the political pressures of Baghdad, may be a means of diffusing tensions.
19. One such diplomat is Jean Claude Cousseran, who led French efforts to engage Syria over its role in Lebanon during 2007 and 2008, which resulted in a tentative warming of EU-Syrian relations. International Crisis Group, briefing, January 15, 2009.
20. President: Romanian troops to remain in Iraq until 2011, Xinhua, December 1, 2008.
21. Czech diplomat, interview with author, October 9, 2008, Brussels.
22. Swedish diplomat, interview with author, October 7, 2008, Brussels.
23. S. Webb and A. Rashid, Repsol out of Iraq Nassiriyah oil-field race, Reuters, June 24, 2009.
24. Resolutions 1770 and 1830 expanded the mandate of the mission to address issues regarding internal borders, internationally displaced persons, and national reconciliation as well as facilitating regional dialogue.
25. European diplomat, interview with author, October 8, 2008, Brussels.
26. Iraqi diplomat, interview with author, October 2008.
27. EU official, interview with author, June 2009, Brussels.
28. UN SRSG Staffan de Mistura has requested that the EU engage in bilateral programs on the ground in Iraq. De Mistura specifically suggests that the EU lead a disarmament, demobilization, and reintegration program in Iraq with regard to the Majalis al-Sahwa. This echoed a proposal made by the commission to the council in 2006 (European Parliament 2008b; Commission of the European Communities 2006).

29. European diplomat, interview with author, October 9, 2008, Brussels.
30. Commission of the European Communities, news release, EU and Iraq discuss ways of enhancing energy cooperation, 2008.
31. One such precedent for upgrading energy infrastructure is the assistance provided by the European Investment Bank to Algeria to improve pipelines to Spain.
32. Commission of the European Communities, news release, EU and Iraq sign a strategic energy partnership memorandum of understanding, 2010.
33. These European companies include OMV (Austria), Perenco (France), Gulf Keystone Petroleum (UK), and Kalegran/MOL (Hungary). International Crisis Group 2008, 25.
34. USAID (www.usaid.gov/iraq/accomplishments/locgov.html).
35. An example of such duplication is the tendency of several member states to propose technical assistance programs for the same Iraqi ministry that the EC has also suggested working.
36. Japanese Bank for International Cooperation, Overview of activities for 2008 (www.jbic.go.jp/en/).

REFERENCES

Baginski, P. 2007. Polish aid program. Paper prepared for UNDP regional workshop, Budapest, March 5–6.
Brie, A. 2005. Speech to the European Parliament: Opinion of the Committee on Foreign Affairs for the Committee of Budgets. Brussels, September 14.
Commission of the European Communities. 2009. Capacity Building Programme for Iraq 2009–2010.
——. 2008a. Information note on EC assistance activities foreseen for Iraq in 2008.
——. 2008b. EU-Iraq: State of play.
——. 2007. Information note on EC assistance activities foreseen for Iraq in 2007.
——. 2006. Communication from the Commission to the Council and the European Parliament: Recommendations for renewed European Union engagement with Iraq.
——. 2004. Communication from the Commission to the Council and the European Parliament—the European Union and Iraq: A framework for engagement.
Council of the European Union. 2008a. Council conclusions on the reception of Iraqi refugees.
——. 2008b. Council conclusions on Iraq.
Danida. 2008. *Danish Agricultural Support for Iraq: Irrigation, Rehabilitation in the Basra Area Finalized.* Copenhagen.
Energy Information Administration. 2008. *Iraq Energy Data Statistics and Analysis: Oil, Gas, Electricity, and Coal.* Washington, D.C.
European Parliament. 2008a. Iraqi Prime Minister Nouri al-Maliki paints upbeat picture to MEPs.
——. 2008b. Minutes. Meeting of the ad hoc delegation for relations with Iraq.
——. 2008c. Report by Ana Gomes MEP to the Foreign Affairs Committee with a

proposal for a European Parliament recommendation to the Council on the European Union's role in Iraq.
———. 2007a. Financial assistance by the EU and its member states to Iraq since 2003. Parliamentary question P-4260/07.
———. 2007b. Opinion of the Committee on Budgetary Control for the Committee on Budgets on the draft general budget of the European Union for the financial year 2008.
International Committee of the Red Cross. 2008. *Iraq: No Let Up in Humanitarian Crisis*. Geneva.
Hoffman, K. 2009. *The Danish Experience in Iraq, 2003–2007*. Copenhagen: Danish Institute for International Studies.
International Crisis Group. 2008. Turkey and Iraqui Kurds: Conflict or cooperation. Middle East Report 81.
Katzman, K. 2008. *Iraq: Post-Saddam Government and Security*. Washington, D.C.: Congressional Research Service.
Ministry of Foreign Affairs of Denmark. 2007. Denmark's involvement in Iraq. Copenhagen.
Ministry of Foreign Affairs of Germany. 2008. German assistance in stabilizing and reconstructing Iraq. Berlin.
Ministry of Foreign Affairs of Italy. 2008. Italy-Iraq information. Rome.
———. 2007. Treaty of Friendship, Partnership, and Cooperation between the Italian Republic and the Republic of Iraq. Rome.
Ministry of Foreign Affairs of Spain. 2008. Monografía: Iraq. Madrid.
Ministry of Foreign Affairs of Sweden. 2008a. What does Swedish development assistance to Iraq entail? Stockholm.
———. 2008b. Minister for Development of Denmark, address to Iraq Compact Annual Review Conference, May 29. Stockholm.
Oxfam International. 2007. *Rising to the Humanitarian Challenge in Iraq*. London.
Said, Y. 2008. Political dynamics in Iraq within the context of the surge. Submission to the U.S. Senate Foreign Relations Committee, April 2.
Serwer, D., and M. Chabalowski. 2008. Scenarios for the future of Iraq and the role of Europe: How will Europe engage. In *Bound to Cooperate: Europe and the Middle East II*, ed. C. P. Hanelt and A. Möller. Gutersloh: Bertelsmann.
UK Department for International Development. 2008. Operating in Insecure Environments. October 16.
UK Foreign and Commonwealth Office. 2008. UK information note to the Council Secretariat and the Commission: Current activity in the rule of law and justice sectors, 2008–2009. London.
UK House of Commons. 2008. *UK Operations in the Iraq and the Gulf*. London: Defense Committee, Fifteenth Report of Session 2007–08.
United Nations High Commission for Refugees. 2008. Asylum levels and trends in industrialized countries: First half of 2008. Geneva, October 17.
U.S. Department of Defense. 2008. *Measuring Stability and Security in Iraq*. Report to Congress, September.
Youngs, R. 2004. Europe and Iraq: From stand-off to engagement. Madrid: FRIDE.

CHAPTER TEN

Nigeria
Conflict, Energy, and Bad Governance

Anna Khakee

In recent years, the European Union (EU) and its member states have paid allegiance to the goal of democracy and good governance in Nigeria. As elsewhere in Africa, this pursuit has met with limited success, as testified to by, for example, the fundamentally flawed 2007 Nigerian presidential, parliamentary, and state elections and continuing severe problems with corruption. Addressing the questions delineated in chapter 1, this chapter examines how European democracy promotion has played out in the Nigerian case. To what extent has democracy been important for EU-Nigerian relations? How have EU countries and institutions worked on the ground to promote good governance and democratic practices? How united are EU countries in their pursuit of democracy in Nigeria? How is European democracy promotion perceived by Nigerian actors?

Nigeria is an obvious target for efforts aiming to eradicate the ills of inadequate governance in Africa. It is infamous for its corruption, which has been fuelled by the massive income derived from oil. Corruption in Nigeria is not, as most observers agree, an aspect of how the state bureaucracy works: it is in many cases the main activity of the state. Corruption and sleaze often leave the, in-principle, oil-rich Nigerians without even basic education and health care.[1] Aside from corruption and electoral malpractices, other governance-related problems include a poorly administered justice system, a lack of state transparency, and widespread human rights abuses. Underlying all of this is a state with shallow roots in a society marred by interethnic, economic, political, and religious conflict.

The EU, traditionally an important player in Africa and its largest donor, increasingly stresses governance in its relations with African countries. As a result, governance and democracy held a prominent place in the common vision to guide future development actions presented for the first time in 2006 by the EU Parliament, the EU Council, the EU Commission, and EU member states. This common vision underlines that "progress in the protection of human rights, good governance and democratisation is fundamental for poverty reduction and sustainable development" and that, as a consequence, these issues will become standard in all EU development activities (European Union 2006, paragraphs 86 and 101). The 2000 Cotonou Agreement, the most recent partnership agreement between the EU and the members of the African, Caribbean, and Pacific (ACP) group of states, contains a similar provision (European Union/ACP 2000). The EU Strategy for Africa of 2005, which provides a "comprehensive, integrated, and long-term framework" for EU-African relations, also stresses "good and effective governance" as a "central prerequisite for sustainable development" (European Union 2005). The subsequent Africa-EU joint strategy did likewise. Most recently, good governance and democracy were stressed in a 2009 political framework, the Nigeria-EU Joint Way Forward (European Union 2009).

What has been the effect of EU and EU member states' policies with regard to democracy in Nigeria? Put simply, the main obstacles have been oil and other economic interests, political concerns over issues such as migration, Nigeria's status as Africa's great power, the country's fragile internal balance, lack of leverage, and lengthy assistance procedures. Economic and political interests have weakened European resolve over Nigerian democracy. Although the EU issued scathing criticism of the fraudulent 2007 elections, the European Commission, the EU Council, and EU member states quickly returned to "business as usual," to quote the disillusioned words of the European Parliament, avoiding any talk of suspending aid or using other measures permitted by the Cotonou Agreement. In general, individual EU countries rarely make public statements on democracy-related issues in Nigeria, and common EU pronouncements are few.

With economic and political interests in mind, EU countries have also sometimes adopted policies that have worked contrary to what a democratization agenda would prescribe. Most prominent is their promotion and protection of European oil companies, which largely continue to feed into the downward spiral of environmental degradation, loss of livelihood, and civil strife in Nigeria. An illustration of this came in mid-2008 when French President Nicolas Sarkozy and British Prime Minister Gordon Brown offered to send military personnel to the Niger Delta to train and advise Nigerian troops so that they could restore law and order and oil output.[2] Other "governance insensitive" policies include military and security cooperation in which security sector reform and governance issues have lagged behind; some EU countries' failure to return proceeds of looting and corruption stashed in their banks; and European treatment of migrants from Nigeria, which at times has failed to live up to EU human rights standards.

To this problem of economic and political interests taking the upper hand is added another: lack of leverage. Nigeria is Africa's most populous country, and its dependency on aid is low. Governance problems are massive and entrenched, although the situation is arguably improving slowly. Unless the EU decides to upgrade its relationship with Nigeria in a very significant way—Nigerian interviewees talked longingly of a pre-accession status for the country—expectations of visible results must be scaled down accordingly.

At program level, there are also problems. European Commission funding mechanisms are slow and hence cannot be responsive to unforeseen political developments on the ground. Even when funds have been granted, disbursement is at times delayed, which means that the Nigerian partners are left stranded. The cumbersome processes sometimes have the paradoxical effect of forcing administrators to spend the allocated money fast, which does not always mean spending it well. The piecemeal approach, with many small projects on various governance-related issues, is also seen as problematic, including by some inside the European Commission. It also remains to be seen whether the programming of the Commission and the British Department for International Development(DFID) has struck the right balance with its emphasis on state institutions over nongovernmental organizations.[3]

This does not mean that despair is ubiquitous. EU democracy promotion has not been without effect. The lack of postelection actions notwithstanding, the EU decision to send an election observation mission to Nigeria in 2007 and the findings of the mission have received widespread support in Nigeria. Its work was considered important to support would-be democratizers in Nigeria in one of their darker moments, and there has been a significant demand for more of the same. The EU's moral and financial support of the Economic and Financial Crimes Commission (EFCC) has also, at least until recently, been important for an institution that has for a long time been a thorn in the side of many corrupt Nigerian leaders. After encouragement from several European governments, Nigeria was also the first country to sign the Extractive Industries Transparency Initiative (EITI). On the program level, there are also no signs that European commitment to democracy in Nigeria is weakening: if anything, the opposite seems to be true.

In a longer-term perspective, European policies have also evolved considerably since Nigerian independence in 1960. Western states have reduced reckless lending to ill-governed kleptocracies such as Nigeria. The thinking of the European Commission and some EU governments on governance has evolved. There now seems to be agreement, for example, that service provision and other "technical" projects and programs must henceforth be governance-sensitive to be effective in the medium and long term. Since the September 11, 2001, terrorist attacks in the United States, EU countries (among others) have started to crack down on proceeds from looting and corruption ending up in the banks of European states. Although progress is somewhat uneven, formerly important havens such as the United Kingdom have been considered "extremely helpful" by people inside the EFCC.

Whether EU policies are evolving quickly and radically enough remains to be seen, however. The situation in the Niger Delta is still very fragile, and due to President Umaru Yar'Adua's ill health and hands-off governing style, his would-be successors are already vying for power in what could become an ugly struggle. Today, international democracy promotion is not viewed with the same skepticism in Nigeria as in the oil-rich Middle East or Russia. The EU and EU states can hence hope to make an (albeit modest) impact, both with its assistance projects and at the political level. However, European governments' balancing act between realpolitik and idealism is a risky one, and prospects for democracy promotion could quickly decrease.

Two Unequal Giants

Democracy promotion is not a top priority in EU-Nigerian relations. Oil is widely regarded as paramount, followed by trade relations more generally, concerns over migration, Nigeria's role as a regional power, its fragile internal balance, and attainment of the millennium development goals.[4] However, all of these concerns are in fact related to, and affect, governance and democracy in varied ways.

Since its independence from Britain in 1960, Nigeria's relations with the EU have at times been complicated. In 1993 the results of the Nigerian presidential elections (which were supposed to reintroduce democracy) were annulled. As a consequence, the EU suspended military cooperation, introduced travel restrictions for members of the security forces, and restricted high-level visits (European Union 1995). In the aftermath of the execution of Ken Saro-Wiwa and other Ogoni leaders in late 1995 for their protests against Shell operations in the Niger Delta, political relations came to an almost complete standstill. The EU reinforced travel restrictions, imposed an arms embargo, and suspended most development cooperation with Nigeria (European Union 1995).[5] The Shell connection notwithstanding, there was no oil embargo and no freezing of Nigerian leaders' assets in Europe, including those of the military dictator Sani Abacha. EU businesses, including oil companies such as Shell and Total, also continued their operations.

With the return to democracy, political and aid relations between the EU and Nigeria were resumed, and the new, charismatic president, Olusegun Obasanjo, quickly became something of a Western darling. The 1999–2000 quick-start assistance package of €100 million was followed by Nigeria's signature of the Cotonou Agreement in 2000 and an EU-Nigeria country support strategy worth approximately €600 million in 2002.[6] This was the largest sum available to any ACP country during the 2001–07 period but was among the smallest on a per capita basis. Debt relief was one of Obasanjo's priorities, and in 2005 the Paris Club granted Africa's biggest-ever debt relief package to Nigeria.[7] The EU's commitment has remained more or less constant: for 2008–13, €580 million has been allotted to Nigeria. Democracy assistance was among the top priorities of development aid. The quick-start package included €18.6 million in support of the 2003 elections, national and state assemblies, and democracy and human rights generally. The focus on governance and democracy has been strengthened in subsequent assistance packages.

It must be stressed, however, that Nigerian aid dependency is low: official development assistance as a share of gross national income in 2007 stood at 1.7 percent, much less than most African countries.[8] This means that donors cannot set policy priorities in Nigeria but instead must follow the government's lead and reinforce whatever positive policies the Nigerian federal and state governments decide upon. Apart from the European Commission and DFID, other donors have not been quick to move in. One reason is perhaps the lack of leverage. A second reason is probably oil wealth: Nigeria was until recently classified as a "blend" rather than an "ODA-only" country, which meant that it was not considered among the poorest, or "worthiest," of the developing countries (World Bank/Department for International Development 2005, 4). A third reason is that many EU countries are wary of Nigeria, with its reputation as corrupt and "impossible."

In the military domain, cooperation resumed quickly. Arms exports to Nigeria restarted within a couple of years of the end of dictatorship, and the UK rapidly became the leading exporter, followed by Italy and Germany. In 2006 EU countries licensed exports of military equipment to Nigeria, including ground vehicles, aircraft, and large-caliber firearms, worth €98 million in total. The latest official EU statistic available is €165 million in 2007, with the Czech Republic the top exporter for the first time (European Union 2008, 176; 2007a, 160). Military cooperation has also resumed, although the United States is a crucial Western player in this respect (Lubeck, Watts, and Lipschutz 2007, 10–20). The UK has provided funds and expertise for military training and training facilities through its African Peacekeeping Training Support Programme (Malan 2006). For the first time in history, France and Nigeria have established military collaboration, including through RECAMP (Reinforcement of African Peacekeeping Capacities). Other EU countries, including Germany, have also been active in this area (Embassy of the Federal Republic of Germany 2007).

This security cooperation stems from the European view that Nigeria is crucial to peace and security in West Africa and beyond. As manifested by the EU-funded African Peace Facility (which helps fund African peacekeeping operations), Europeans would like to see more African-dominated peacekeeping on the continent. Nigeria's peacekeeping forces have, ever since independence, been among the largest and most active in the Economic Community of West African States Monitoring Group (ECOMOG), in African Union peacekeeping missions, and under the auspices of the UN—it ranked fourth among the top UN contingencies worldwide during 2008 (United Nations Department of Peacekeeping Operations 2009). Security cooperation is also motivated by Western interests in ensuring a steady oil supply. Security sector reform has lagged behind European countries' efforts to boost Nigerian military capacity, however. To date, no European security sector reform programs or programs to improve democratic control of the armed forces exist in Nigeria, its military-dominated past notwithstanding. However, the inclusion of a security sector reform component in the Tenth European Development Fund has been discussed.

Nigeria is the largest African country in terms of population. Hardly surprisingly, it is also the sub-Saharan African country from which the largest number of migrants leaves each year. A number of these, especially women and children, are trafficked for sexual exploitation and end up in countries such as Italy, Spain,

Belgium, and the Netherlands (Carling 2006; European Union 2002, 21; Ijeoma Nwogu 2006). The flow of migrants has led the EU and individual EU states to conclude readmission agreements with Nigeria. The Cotonou Agreement includes a provision stating that "each of the ACP States shall accept the return of and readmission of any of its nationals who are illegally present on the territory of a Member State of the European Union, at that Member State's request and without further formalities" (European Union/ACP 2000, article 13). Critics claim that, with the focus so squarely on repatriation, EU states and Nigeria have overlooked ensuring better conditions of admittance and residence for migrant laborers. EU countries are regularly criticized by UN bodies, the Council of Europe, and non-governmental organizations for their lack of respect for human rights—such as the prohibition of inhuman or degrading treatment, right to due process, right of access to a lawyer, and the principle of nonrefoulement—in their handling of Nigerian and other African migrants.

Many EU countries have strong and long-standing commercial and economic ties to Nigeria. Oil and gas extraction form the backbone of this relationship, but other industries, such as infrastructure and services, are also important. The UK is one of the largest investors. For more than half a century Shell has invested several billion euros in the Nigerian oil and gas sector. British firms are also active in travel and transport, pharmaceuticals, and consumer products. Similarly, the French presence is strong: French investment in Nigeria is equal to the sum of its investment in all other West African countries, which is especially noteworthy given France's traditionally strong ties to francophone West Africa. Again, the oil and gas sector dominates (Total, Technip), but other sectors such as manufacturing, services, and infrastructure are also well represented. Italy has been involved in the Nigerian petroleum industry since 1965, through Nigeria Agip Oil Company of the Eni group. Italian presence in construction and shipping is also strong: Italian firms handle more than 30 percent of Nigerian maritime traffic. About fifty German companies operate in Nigeria, with offices or production facilities. The largest construction company in Nigeria, Julius Berger, is partly German owned and directed.

As the eleventh largest producer in the world, the Nigerian economy is dominated by oil. Oil accounted for 85 percent of government revenue and 99 percent of its exports in 2007 (World Bank 2008). Oil exports are set to grow, as the rate of new discoveries is high and production is technically easy. It is not surprising that energy accounts for the bulk of EU-Nigerian merchandise trade: in 2008 more than 95 percent of EU imports from Nigeria derived from the energy sector.

However, EU dependency on Nigerian oil and natural gas is limited. In 2008 Nigeria accounted for 3.6 percent of its oil and 4.8 percent of its gas imports (European Commission 2009). The EU is also not the main purchaser of Nigerian energy: the United States is Nigeria's largest customer by far.

Europe plays a key role, nevertheless, as European energy companies are active in oil and gas extraction in Nigeria. As noted above, Shell, Total, and Agip, together with U.S.-based Exxon Mobil and Chevron, dominate the Nigerian energy industry. Although technically easy, oil production in Nigeria has become increasingly difficult at the societal and political levels. Oil revenues have helped fuel massive corruption, while ordinary Nigerians continue living in the deepest misery. The Nigerian government's efforts to return some of the oil money to the Delta region (where it is extracted) have been generally unsuccessful and often even counterproductive: very little money has reached the poor, and corruption at the state level has remained as widespread as ever. The same is true for the so-called community outreach activities of the multilateral oil companies (Stakeholder Democracy Network 2006, 10). According to World Bank sources, approximately 80 percent of oil revenues are in the hands of 1 percent of the population (Lubeck, Watts, and Lipschutz 2007, 7).

Such corruption has created deep resentment and a breeding ground for both political contestation and violence, in the Niger Delta in particular. As political protest has been unsuccessful and violence often has proved effective, the insurgency (often targeting oil installations) has escalated in recent years.[9] Inequalities, environmental degradation (due to oil spills, massive flaring of gas when extracting oil, and so on), political alienation, and the destruction of the social fabric encourage small-scale oil thefts, arms dealing, protection rackets, and kidnappings. Large-scale oil thefts, in contrast, are undertaken with the help of high-ranking military officials, politicians, and businessmen. Insecurity has led to important disruptions of production. Unrest in the Niger Delta in 2006–07 reduced oil output by about 17 percent, and an estimated €3.6 billion worth was lost to oil theft and vandalism between January and September 2008.[10]

The response of federal politicians has often been to send in security forces. Local politicians have turned to armed gangs—which are often involved in criminal activities—for protection. In 2009 a mix of strategies was pursued: the Nigerian government launched a new military offensive in the Delta, before offering a peace deal to rebels and promising to allocate an increased share of oil revenues to the region. Hence, as in many other countries living off extractive industries, oil has drastically worsened governance problems in Nigeria.[11]

Although the links between (bad) governance and extractive industries have been clear for a number of years, the policy community has only begun to address the issue in earnest relatively recently. Hence an EC official said that it was not until 2004 that they "discovered" that it is impossible to separate the Delta communities and the oil companies and that no solution can be found without the involvement of all stakeholders. The issue of policy coherence has also become more prominent in the last half decade, although until now it seems to have led to more concrete results in the financial sector (see below) than in the energy sector.

While analysts and those within the donor community stress the importance of addressing the developmental and political woes of the Delta region, European politicians have often taken a security approach. This has, at least up until recently, been the case with the Gulf of Guinea Energy Security Strategy (GGESS), set up in 2005 by Nigeria, the United States, and the UK to secure the Delta for oil production by coordinating efforts to stamp out oil theft, illegal small-arms dealing, and money laundering. Since then Canada, France, the Netherlands, Norway, and Switzerland have joined the GGESS (Ministry of Foreign Affairs, Netherlands 2007). For Nigeria this has meant that it now receives assistance to equip and upgrade its amphibious capacity and that a tagging mechanism, preventing stolen oil from being easily sold internationally, has been developed. Although the GGESS now has a working group on sustainable development, there is no governance dimension to this initiative. With its strong focus on energy security, the GGESS has attracted strong criticism from NGOs, analysts, and practitioners alike. As one European Commission official put it, "This is not the right way forward." Reactions to the Sarkozy/Brown offer of sending military trainers to the Niger Delta in summer 2008 were similar in nature.

More promising from a governance perspective is the EITI, whose main goal is the verification and full publication of company payments and government revenues from extractive industries such as oil and gas. Nigeria was the first country to sign up and is also at the forefront in implementation, with the publication of a fully audited and reconciled EITI report. However, the picture is not perfect: at first, Obasanjo handpicked the civil society representatives on the stakeholders' committee overseeing the process, and this committee has met irregularly, stimulating perceptions that civil society is being marginalized (Publish What You Pay 2006). Moreover, some companies were "extremely slow" in providing information necessary for the report (Publish What You Pay 2006, 24). EITI was perceived positively by most people interviewed, although some inherent weaknesses were pinpointed: it focuses only on government income, leaving aside both issues arising before companies' payments to governments, like the distribution of rights of exploration and contracting, and issues following these payments, like budgeting and spending according to budgets (Human Rights Watch 2007, 103). It also leaves out whatever oil companies pay to security providers and other nongovernment entities.

The issue of corruption is ubiquitous in Nigeria and is, as noted, closely linked to oil extraction. Sani Abacha looted approximately $3 billion to $5 billion from the Nigerian people during his years in power (Africa All Party Parliamentary Group 2006, 45). After the return to civilian rule, the new government asked the international community for assistance in returning the funds. Swiss banks eventually returned $458 million in 2005.[12] Abacha also stashed money in banks in the UK, Jersey, Lichtenstein, and Luxembourg, but due to lengthy litigation processes, so far none of these countries have returned funds, which remain frozen. The UK Financial Services Authority refrained from publicizing the names of the British banks involved, despite the fact that Swiss authorities did so for the implicated Swiss banks (Africa All Party Parliamentary Group 2006, 45). Given the poor treatment of the Swiss during the return process and the bad publicity they received, other EU states will want to ensure that any return of funds from their countries is done discreetly, according to a diplomatic source in Abuja.

Illicitly gained money has continued flowing from Nigeria following the return to civilian rule. According to World Bank sources, 70 percent of Nigerian private wealth is held abroad (Lubeck, Watts, and Lipschutz 2007, 7). Before the 2007 elections, foreign exchange outflows reportedly increased dramatically. Analysts believed that part of this increase was due to so-called politically exposed persons sending illicit money abroad.[13] Banks in Great Britain, Isle of Man, Jersey, Lichtenstein, Switzerland, and to a lesser extent the United States are important recipients of such funds. Non-Western destinations include Dubai, Malaysia, Singapore, and China. While in the past not many Western states were supportive, countries such as the UK, Switzerland, and the United States are seen as having become more cooperative, although some loopholes in legislation remain. The watershed was not the Sani Abacha scandal but rather the 9/11 terrorist attacks and the subsequent efforts to curb terrorist financing networks. The Metropolitan Police restrained €48 million in 2004–07, and money is sent back to Nigeria regularly. However, not all EU countries are equally quick to assist Nigeria: cooperation with France, for example, has been slow and subject to technical and communication problems.

The EU and individual EU states also recognize the importance of the issue through their substantial support for the EFCC, an independent Nigerian state institution that investigates and prosecutes cases of corruption and other types of financial crimes. The EFCC collaborates with financial intelligence units internationally. European support has been not only financial but also moral. In 2007 the government wanted to restrain the prosecuting powers of the EFCC but reversed its stance in the face of strong criticism, including from the EU. In the wake of the removal of the EFCC head, Nuhu Ribadu, in December 2007 on procedural grounds and the subsequent harassment he has endured from Nigerian authorities, it seems as if European clout has weakened.

It is worth stressing that interviewees for this study from the donor community generally showed little knowledge of EU and EU states' efforts to combat money laundering. This is somewhat surprising, given its centrality to anticorruption strategies.

Observation Missions and Nigerian Elections

By far the most visible EU activities to promote democracy in Nigeria are election observation missions. The EU sent its first such mission to Nigeria for the 2003 elections. The EU assessment of those elections was severely critical of almost all aspects of the voting process (European Union 2003). Early on in the following electoral cycle it became evident that the 2007 elections were likely to be marred by similar problems. Interviewees for this study cited factors such as early mismanagement by the Independent National Electoral Commission (INEC), the arming of militias, and President Obasanjo's attempts to tinker with the constitution so as to be able to stand for a third term. However, EU governments were not active in trying to change the course of events. According to one EU official, "In practice, beyond attending briefing sessions that were INEC led, EU member states did not exert political influence that was strong enough to change the direction in which the elections preparation went." There were discussions as to whether the EU should indeed monitor the 2007 elections. The chief observer, Max van den Berg, would not want to call it hesitation but stressed that "it was a serious question to be researched."

Many within and outside of Africa saw the 2007 Nigerian elections as a test for democracy across the whole of sub-Saharan Africa. It was the first time in Nigerian history that power would be transferred from one democratically elected president to another. The dismay—although not the surprise—was great when most observers, including the Domestic Election Observation Group (with 50,000 Nigerian observers on the ground), the normally very discreet Economic Community of West African States, and the EU mission declared that the elections had obviously been rigged (Chukwuma 2007; European Union Election Observation Mission Federal Republic of Nigeria 2007). The immediate EU reaction was severely critical. The EU declared itself "disappointed" and "deeply concerned that these elections were marred by many irregularities and by violent incidents resulting in a high toll of victims." The EU stressed attempts at vote rigging, "serious organisational problems" in many states, and distortion of results (European Union 2007b). These views were echoed in the capitals of some EU member states: London stated that it was "deeply concerned."[14]

At the same time, the EU declaration outlined a cooperative way forward: it stressed the EU's willingness to engage in dialogue with Nigeria in order to "support Nigeria to overcome post elections difficulties and to take into account lessons learnt in view of the next elections" (European Union 2007b). Albeit with some delay, EU member states also mostly chose to congratulate Yar'Adua before his swearing-in ceremony on May 29.[15] Such developments made the European Parliament fear that "the current 'business as usual' policy is damaging and defeats the credibility of EU Election Observation Missions." It demanded that EU aid to federal and state structures be withheld until new, credible elections had been held (European Parliament 2007, points 15, 16). The EU governments did not agree on any such freeze; hence article 96 of the Cotonou Agreement, whereby the EU could have asked for special consultations or even unilaterally decided on "appropriate measures," was not invoked.[16]

The treatment that former President Olusegun Obasanjo (ultimately responsible for the fraud) has received from the international community has been lenient. He is—along with such leaders as Kofi Annan, Tony Blair, Bob Geldof, and Muhammad Yunus—part of the Africa Progress Panel, which focuses on good governance among other issues. His inclusion hardly signals that undemocratic behavior is penalized.

Among NGO interviewees, the EU decision to send an election observation mission in 2007 receives unanimous support. As one interviewee put it, "I am proud of the European Union because it did not compromise." The mission gave credence and moral support to Nigerians fighting for democracy. The report on the elections was, in their view, complete and credible. However, some Nigerian and international NGO representatives consulted felt that the mission should have started its work earlier and that the omission of Delta, Bayelsa, and Rivers states (for security reasons) was unwarranted. There were also regrets that the EU did not monitor subsequent elections for local government councillors, perceived as crucial for strengthening grass-roots democracy.

Many within the Nigerian establishment will admit, at least in private, that the elections were flawed. Some also did so in public. Senate President Ken Nnamani said widespread irregularities would leave a "legacy of hatred and a crisis of legitimacy for the winner."[17] In his inaugural speech, Yar'Adua acknowledged that "our elections had some shortcomings" and set up a twenty-two-member panel to examine and reform the electoral process. The panel, partly funded by DFID, the European Commission, and the UNDP, submitted its final report in December 2008. The report concluded that INEC and the state independent electoral commissions were not sufficiently independent to perform their duties. The panel recommended inter alia that additional agencies take over some of INEC's current functions (International Foundation for Electoral Systems 2009). The election results were also challenged in court by opposition leaders. However, in late 2008 the Nigerian Supreme Court upheld the results, calling the challengers' evidence insufficient. The INEC strongly criticized the EU final report, claiming that the mission had acted contrary to the EU's own codes of conduct.[18]

The EU's activities relating to the Nigerian elections extend beyond voting. A €40 million project for the 2006–11 period aims to strengthen the capacity of INEC through advisory and technical assistance and to support civil society involvement in the electoral process (European Union 2007c). The EU also contributed to INEC, as well as to NGOs (for voter education, gender monitoring and mainstreaming, domestic electoral observation, and media monitoring), through the UNDP-managed joint donor basket supporting the 2007 elections. Unsurprisingly, given that INEC was severely criticized for its incompetence, lack of preparation, and partisanship (Chukwuma 2007), EU support for this institution is regarded with skepticism. "Why invest in structures known to be flawed?" a source in the international NGO community asks. The EU delegation was aware of the problem and spent only part of the money allotted. One diplomat reports: "It was very clear from the outset . . . that we were dealing with an 'introverted' elections management body, which, though keen for international endorsement of the electoral process, was not interested in sharing information that was critical to elections preparation and management." The reason for pursuing the project was strategic: "The timing between one election and the next provides ample opportunity for the election administration body and other stakeholders to absorb lessons learned and focus on building capacity to better prepare for the next elections." This, opines another official, has to be done "early, within the two years following the election; after that the situation heats up too much." The EU has reportedly since resumed cooperation with INEC, which was halted after the elections, albeit with some tacit conditionalities. UNDP's management of the joint donor basket was also widely and severely criticized as hasty, wasteful, and undercutting of the work of other international bodies by lax spending and supervision. "Waste" and "money badly spent" are recurrent criticisms raised in interviews with international and Nigerian NGOs. Most interviewees find it important to continue supporting the electoral process but, arguably, with a larger share going to grassroots NGOs, political party development, the media, and the police.

Governance Assistance Projects

Resources from the European Instrument on Democracy and Human Rights (EIDHR) allotted to Nigeria during 2003–09 were approximately €18.3 million.[19] Projects focused on gender issues (including women in politics and gender-sensitive budgeting), citizen participation and civil society capacity building, budget transparency, strengthening of the media in budget monitoring, and human rights monitoring and promotion. EU officials stress the success of the media budget-monitoring project in particular.

The quite modest EIDHR contribution—€18.3 million for a country the size of Germany and France combined—is only one part of recent EU support for Nigerian democracy and good governance. In fact a number of other EU projects have a governance focus, such as assistance in the form of training and infrastructure to the federal parliament and state assemblies, a program to improve management of public finances, and support for the EFCC and the judiciary in their fight against economic and financial crimes.

A governance aspect is also often built into the more service-oriented projects. This follows the Nigerian government's own poverty reduction strategy, NEEDS (SEEDS at state level), which is founded on the pillars of empowering people, building a social contract, and changing the way government works. Hence EU service provision projects work not only with the local governments but also with civil society actors, whose capacity to monitor civil servants is thereby strengthened. Thus a participatory approach was built into microproject programs in Niger Delta states that focus on water supply and sanitation, village transport, health centers, schools, and income generation. However, an NGO representative active in the region feels that, although the project was one of the most successful he had encountered, the governance aspect was minimal. A DFID representative close to the project echoes this, stressing that the project was "governance blind" in that it bypassed local and state governments entirely. While it had an effect on community cohesion and set an example for governments of how little projects that are financially transparent actually can cost, it did not alter community-state relations.

Among officials there seems to be unanimous support for combining governance and service provision, in particular as many governance problems cannot be dealt with in an abstract way but only in conjunction with actual public policies. SEEDS benchmarking, in which the performances of states are compared regarding policy setting, budgeting, service delivery, and transparency, is often cited as among the best projects. Peer pressure, many interviewees agree, works comparatively well in Nigeria. Such bottom-up projects, with a focus on state and local levels, are as a rule more challenging, as governance problems are even more severe than at the federal level, and patronage networks are dense. However, there is agreement among EU institutions, bilateral donors, and NGOs that, in the future, democracy assistance should target the more cooperative states and local governments.

Goodwill generated by EU election monitoring seems to spill over into its assistance projects; generally speaking, Nigerian civil society actors seem to call for increased, rather than reduced, EU engagement in this area. The fact that the EU is a multilateral donor also makes it less threatening to those fearful of political interference. However, some criticisms are recurrent. EU funding mechanisms are slow, which means that it cannot be responsive to political developments on the ground, beyond withholding funds, as it did before the 2007 elections. According to one interviewee, it often proves difficult for an organization even to change the order in which it conducts certain activities. When money has been granted to a project, its disbursement can sometimes be delayed, which means that the Nigerian partners are left stranded and cannot keep promises at their end. As previously mentioned, these lengthy processes can force administrators to spend allocated funds quickly and perhaps unwisely. The piecemeal approach, with many small projects focusing on various governance-related issues, is also at times seen as problematic, including by some inside the European Commission.

Only a handful of EU member states have bilateral development cooperation programs in Nigeria. Of these, only the United Kingdom has a substantial governance program with presence on the ground. However, although the German development agency is focusing on other issues in Nigeria, three of Germany's political party foundations are working on democracy-related issues: the Friedrich

Ebert Foundation (FES), the Heinrich Böll Foundation (HBF), and the Konrad Adenauer Foundation (KAS).[20]

UK development assistance is by far the largest of the EU countries, at a projected €400 million for 2008–11. The work of DFID is, at least in theory, squarely focused on governance issues. Of the three key objectives that govern all British assistance to Nigeria, two are governance related: improving public expenditure management and service delivery (62 percent of the program budget) and empowering people to demand reform and building a social contract (19 percent of budget). The third objective is to promote sustainable growth to aid the poor (Department for International Development 2004, 20).[21] For 2005–09, DFID and the World Bank have developed a joint country-partnership strategy, and some programs are implemented jointly (World Bank/Department for International Development 2005).

On the program level, this is translated into a number of governance-related projects. Some are focused on corruption. Assistance to EITI and the so-called coalitions for change (aiming to empower elements within the media, civil society, government, and the private sector to confront patronage and corruption) fall into this category. Others center on federal and state administrations, helping to strengthen national audit institutions and to improve state governments' use of public resources. Yet other projects focus on reform in the justice sector or on involving select Delta communities in issues such as service delivery, training, and empowerment vis-à-vis the government. Moreover, DFID was one of the partners in the UNDP-managed joint donor basket for the 2007 elections; it also ran a separate program to support the elections. Its focus is expected to shift somewhat from government effectiveness to issues of accountability and responsiveness. The work on elections will be put into the wider context, with broader projects focused on deepening democracy. Whether this will lead to a shift in beneficiaries (NGOs versus government) is not yet clear.

The DFID does not have the same administrative problems as the EU. Its programs are often viewed positively: interviewees mentioned the DFID Security, Justice, and Growth Program as successful and its program called Supporting Transparency and Accountability in the Niger Delta as promising. However, DFID's close collaboration with the World Bank is not always perceived in a positive light. The British alliance with the United States in the war on terrorism and the latter's quest for alternative sources of oil has led to a certain apprehension regarding British motives for democracy assistance among interviewees from Nigerian NGOs.

The FES, HBF, and KAS all have permanent offices in Nigeria and have worked on governance issues in the country for several decades. FES's main activities have been trade union cooperation and budget transparency. It works principally through training, capacity building, dialogue forums, and study trips.[22] The HBF focuses on human (and in particular women's) rights, civil society participation in politics, and conflict prevention. Specific projects include attempting to improve knowledge and understanding of Sharia, with the aim of fostering Nigerian national cohesion, "Abacha loot monitoring" (that is, supporting NGO monitoring of the way the Abacha funds returned from Switzerland were used), and training courses for women and men to prevent discriminatory practices toward women.[23] The KAS concentrates on four states (Cross River, Imo, Kano, and Plateau) with a focus on political education. Concrete activities include training of candidates and members of the state assemblies, campaigns to raise political awareness, and media training.[24] The main problem for the three German foundations is size: with yearly budgets of approximately €1 million each, activities are restricted, and many of those interviewed for this study did not know much about them.

Conclusion

European democracy promotion in Nigeria has been at least as timid as in the other countries discussed in this volume. For Europe, oil and other economic interests, Nigeria's role in Africa, Nigerian migration, and reaching the UN's millennium development goals are all more important than democracy. At the same time, Europeans would like to see a stable democracy in Nigeria. This relates to the point raised in the volume's opening chapter: that democracy and self-interest are neither mutually exclusive nor straightforwardly in harmony. The complex relationship between interests and ideals is well illustrated by the European attitude toward the "oil curse" and the Niger Delta. On the one hand, the EU and Britain are stepping up their development work in the Delta, implicitly and explicitly acknowledging that there is no military solution to the problem and that the military is actually part of the problem. They are encouraging EITI and helping the Nigerians recover looted funds. On the other hand, they are involved in military cooperation of various kinds and fail to hold European companies accountable for what they do in the Delta region and beyond. The 2007 Nigerian elections offer another illustration. Before, during, and after these elections, the EU mixed a hands-off, business-as-usual approach with extensive support for the electoral process, with a one-off criticism of the way the elections were handled.

This pragmatic approach, with glimmers of idealism, perhaps represents the art of the possible in the complex relationship between the European power bloc and the African giant. However, it is a delicate balance to maintain. Today international democracy promotion is not viewed with the same skepticism in Nigeria as in parts of the Middle East or Russia, as is testified to by positive civil society reactions to the 2007 EU election monitoring, the de facto acceptance at the highest political levels of the EU's severe assessment of these elections, and the eagerness for deeper EU engagement on governance issues. The EU can hence hope to make an (albeit modest) impact, both with assistance projects and at the political level. If European governments pursue their security and economic interests—including the interests of European oil giants active in the volatile Niger Delta—too persistently and without regard for social and environmental concerns, this could change. As governance, peace and security, environmental degradation, poverty, migration, and energy security are all intertwined, the price to pay for tilting the balance too heavily in favor of the short term could be high.

INTERVIEWS

Hafsat Abiola, President, KIND, September 18, 2007
Priscilla Ankut, Program Officer, Good Governance and Institutional Reform, EC Delegation, Abuja, July 16, 2007 (via e-mail)
Thierry Barbé, Desk Officer, West Africa, EuropeAid Co-operation Office, September 20, 2007
Max van den Berg, Chief Observer, European Union Election Observation Mission, July 30, 2007 (via e-mail)
Richard Butterworth, Governance Adviser, DFID, Nigeria, August 31, 2007
Stefan Crammer, Director, Böll, Nigeria, July 4, 2007
Joseph Hurst Croft, Stakeholder Democracy Network, July 2, 2007
Marc Fiedrich, former Governance Adviser, EC Delegation, Abuja, June 29, 2007
Graham Gass, Social Policy Adviser, DFID, Nigeria, November 24, 2008 (via e-mail), and September 4, 2007
Annabel Gerry, Senior Governance Adviser, DFID, Nigeria, December 5, 2008
Jens U. Hettmann, Resident Representative, FES, July 16, 2007
John Ikupaje, Senior Program Officer, Center for Democracy and Development, September 28, 2007
Chibuike Mgbeahuruike, Program Officer, Transition Monitoring Group, September 27, 2007
Dapo Olorunyomi, Chief of Staff, EFCC, September 28, 2007
Attilio Pacifici, Desk Officer Nigeria, EC Directorate-General for Development, September 20, 2007

Klaus Paehler, Resident Representative to Nigeria, Konrad-Adenauer-Stiftung, July 17, 2007
Ismaila Zango, Center for Democratic Research and Training, Kano, September 25, 2007

NOTES

The author wishes to thank the interviewees, who gave of their time to answer my many questions. Many thanks also to Richard Youngs and Gareth Williams for comments on early drafts. The responsibility for any errors remains with the author.

1. Regarding the effects of corruption in Rivers State, see Human Rights Watch (2007). The 2009 UNDP human development indicators also provide glum reading, with Nigeria ranking 158th of 177 states. In 2007 almost 30 percent of young Nigerian children were underweight, more than half of the population lacked access to clean water, and life expectancy was just 47.7 years (United Nations Development Program 2009).

2. Wasteful Wars, Foreign Friends, *Africa Confidential*, August 22, 2008.

3. As is further explained below, the European Commission and DFID are the two main donors active in the areas of governance and democracy in Nigeria.

4. EU officials, European diplomats and aid agencies, international and national NGOs, interviews with author.

5. Exceptions were made for Nigerian participation in regional projects and funding for democracy, human rights and decentralized poverty alleviation activities (European Union 2002).

6. This sum includes uncommitted balances of earlier EDFs (European Union 2002, 31).

7. Paris Club, news release, October 20, 2005, www.clubdeparis.org.

8. Organization for Economic Cooperation and Development, Nigeria Recipient Aid Chart (www.oecd.org/dataoecd/23/55/1882649.gif).

9. Little reliable data exist on the number of conflict-related deaths in the Niger Delta. One report claims that "political conflict" deaths numbered 200–400 annually between 2006 and 2008 (Nigeria Watch 2008, 8).)

10. International Crisis Group, Nigeria: Ending unrest in the Niger Delta, *Africa Report*, December 5, 2007, 10; Niger Delta Committee proposes 25% derivation, *This Day*, December 2, 2008.

11. The political situation in the Niger Delta is well described in a number of reports. See for example Lubeck, Watts, and Lipschutz 2007; International Crisis Group, Nigeria: Ending unrest in the Niger Delta, *Africa Report*, December 5, 2007; International Crisis Group, Fuelling the Niger Delta crisis, *Africa Report*, September 28, 2006.

12. For further information on how this money was used by the Nigerian government, see World Bank 2006; Ugolor, Nwafor, and Nardine 2006.

13. Huge outflow of forex pre-election period, *Business Day*, June 21, 2007.

14. C. Albin-Lackey, Nigerian debacle a threat to Africa, *Business Day*, May 15, 2007.

15. The German government, for example, sent a message wishing him well rather than formally congratulating him.

16. Sanctions under this article have to date been used mainly against small states of little strategic importance. Between 2000 and 2006, article 96 was used on ten occasions, against Haiti, Fiji, Ivory Coast, Liberia, Zimbabwe, Central Africa Republic, Guinea-Bissau, Togo, the Republic of Guinea, and Mauritania (Laakso, Kivimäki, and Seppänen 2007).

17. O. Quist-Arcton, Nigerian election results hotly disputed, April 23, 2007 (www.iri.org/newsarchive/2007/2007-04-23-News-NPR-Nigeria.asp).

18. *BBC News*, April 23, 2007.

19. European Commission Nigeria, Project timeplan (www.delnga.ec.europa.eu/projects/Project%20TimePlan1.xls).

20. These foundations are linked to three of the main German political parties: the Christian Democrats, the Social Democrats, and the Green Party.

21. Priorities for the upcoming program cycle had not been finalized at the time of writing but were expected to be similar. A. Gerry, interview with author, December 5, 2008.

22. See www.fes-nigeria.org/priority_areas.php.

23. See www.boellnigeria.org/projects.html.

24. See www.kas.de/proj/home/home/33/2/about_us-1/index.html.

REFERENCES

Africa All Party Parliamentary Group. 2006. The other side of the coin: The UK and corruption in Africa. March.

Carling, J. 2006. *Migration, Human Smuggling, and Trafficking from Nigeria to Europe.* Geneva: International Organization for Migration.

Chukwuma, I. 2007. An election programmed to fail: Preliminary report on the presidential and National Assembly elections. April 21. Domestic Election Observation Group.

Department for International Development. 2004. Nigeria: Country assistance plan 2004–08. London. www.dfid.gov.uk/pubs/files/nigeria-cap.asp.

Embassy of the Federal Republic of Germany. 2007. Partnership and cooperation: An overview of German development cooperation with Nigeria. May. Abuja.

European Commission. 2009. Directorate-General for Transport and Energy, EU energy and transport in figures. In *Statistical Pocketbook 2009*. Luxembourg: Office for Official Publications of the European Communities.

European Parliament. 2007. European Parliament resolution on the recent elections in Nigeria.

European Union. 2009. Joint communiqué. Nigeria-EU ministerial troika meeting. June 9. Prague.

———. 2008. *Tenth Annual Report According to Operative Provision 8 of the European Union Code of Conduct on Arms Exports.*

———. 2007a. *Ninth Annual Report According to Operative Provision 8 of the European Union Code of Conduct on Arms Exports.*

———. 2007b. Declaration by the presidency on behalf of the EU on the elections in Nigeria. www.eu2007.de/en/News/CFSP_Statements/April/0427Nigeria.html.
———. 2007c. *Support to Nigerian Electoral Cycle 2006–11*. European Union–Nigeria project sheet.
———. 2006. The European consensus on development. Joint statement by the council and the representatives of the governments of the member states meeting within the council, the European Parliament, and the Commission on European Union Development Policy.
———. 2005. *EU Strategy for Africa: Towards a Euro-African Pact to Accelerate Africa's Development*.
———. 2003. *Election Observation Mission Final Report*. Nigeria National Assembly elections, April 12, 2003; presidential and gubernatorial elections, April 19, 2003; State Houses of Assembly elections, May 3, 2003.
———. 2002. *Nigeria–European Community Country Support Strategy and Indicative Program for the Period 2001–07*. http://www.delnga.ec.europa.eu/docs/Country Strategy.pdf.
———. 1995. Common position of 20 November 1995, defined by the council on the basis of article J.2 of the Treaty on European Union on Nigeria.
European Union/ACP. 2000. *Partnership Agreement between the Members of the African, Caribbean, and Pacific Group of States, of the One Part, and the European Community and Its Member States, of the Other Part*.
European Union Election Observation Mission Federal Republic of Nigeria. 2007. *Statement of Preliminary Findings and Conclusions: Elections Fail to Meet Hopes and Expectations of the Nigerian People and Fall Far Short of Basic International Standards*.
Human Rights Watch. 2007. *Chop Fine: The Human Rights Impact of Local Government Corruption and Mismanagement in Rivers State, Nigeria*. New York.
Ijeoma Nwogu, V. 2006. Nigeria: Human trafficking and migration. *Forced Migration Review* 25.
International Foundation for Electoral Systems. 2009. *Spotlight on Nigeria's Electoral Reform Process*. Washington, D.C.
Laakso, L., T. Kivimäki, and M. Seppänen. 2007. *Evaluation of Coordination and Coherence in the Application of Article 96 of the Cotonou Partnership Agreement*. Copenhagen: Conflict Transformation Service.
Lubeck, P. M., M. J. Watts, and R. Lipschutz. 2007. *Convergent Interests: U.S. Energy Security and the "Securing" of Nigerian Democracy*. Washington, D.C.: Center for International Policy.
Malan, M. 2006. The European Union and the African Union as strategic partners in peace operations: Not grasping the planning and management nettle. Paper 13. Accra: Kofi Annan International Peace Keeping Training Center.
Ministry of Foreign Affairs, Netherlands. 2007. Niger Delta conference. August 2.
Nigeria Watch. 2008. *Second Annual Report on Public Violence, 2007–08*. www.nigeriawatch.org/media/html/NGA-Watch-Report08.pdf.
Publish What You Pay. 2006. *Eye on EITI: Civil Society Perspectives and Recommendations on the Extractive Industries Transparency Initiative*. New York: Revenue Watch Institute.
Stakeholder Democracy Network. 2006. *The Triple Threat: Growing Violence in the Niger Delta Poses Risks to a Broad Range of Stakeholders in the Region*.

Ugolor, D., A. Nwafor, and J. Nardine. 2006. *Shadow Report on the PEMFAR Monitoring Exercise*. Nigerian Network on Stolen Assets.

United Nations Department of Peacekeeping Operations. 2009. *Monthly Summary of Contributors of Military and Civilian Police Personnel.* New York, www.un.org/Depts/dpko/dpko/contributors/.

United Nations Development Program. 2009. *Human Development Report 2009*. New York.

World Bank. 2008. *Nigeria Country Brief.* Washington, D.C.

———. 2006. Nigeria—Utilization of repatriated Abacha loot: Results of the field monitoring exercise. Working Paper 39390. Washington, D.C.

World Bank/Department for International Development. 2005. Country partnership strategy for the Federal Republic of Nigeria, 2005–2009. Report 32412-NG. Washington, D.C.

Contributors

Jos Boonstra is a senior researcher at FRIDE and co-chair of the EU–Central Asia Monitoring project (EUCAM). Before 2006 he worked as a program manager and head of research at the Center for European Security Studies (CESS) in the Netherlands.

Edward Burke is a researcher at FRIDE, concentrating on political and security trends in the Middle East. He previously worked at the Club of Madrid.

Ana Echagüe is researcher at FRIDE, focusing on the Gulf region. Before joining FRIDE she was deputy director at the University of the Middle East project in Madrid.

Kristina Kausch is a researcher at FRIDE. Previously she worked for the German Technical Cooperation (GTZ) on programs of democratic governance and institution building. She is the author of numerous publications on EU relations and co-editor of *Islamist Radicalisation: The Challenge for EU-Mediterranean Relations* (FRIDE/CEPS, 2009).

Anna Khakee is an associate researcher at FRIDE. She has previously been a consultant to, among others, the Policy Practice, the Euro-Mediterranean Study Commission (EuroMeSCo), the UNDP, Amnesty International, the UN University for Peace, and the Swedish Ministry of Justice.

Geoffrey Pridham is emeritus professor and senior research fellow at Bristol University, UK. He has published widely on problems of democratic transition and consolidation, including *Designing Democracy: EU Enlargement and Regime Change in Post-Communist Europe*. He recently held an ESRC fellowship to work on the topic "Europeanising Democratisation? EU Accession and Post-Communist Politics in Slovakia, Latvia, and Romania."

Sofia Sebastian is a researcher at FRIDE. She holds a doctorate from the London School of Economics. She has published in peer-reviewed journals on the role of the EU in conflict management and on state building and constitution making in Bosnia.

Natalia Shapovalova is a researcher at FRIDE. Previously she worked for the International Center for Policy Studies in Kyiv on Ukraine's democratization and EU integration policies.

Alexander Warkotsch is associate researcher at the University of Wuerzburg, Germany. Previously he was a postdoctoral researcher at the University of Western Australia, Perth, and a lecturer on European studies at King's College London.

Richard Youngs is director of FRIDE and an associate professor at the University of Warwick, UK. He is the author of four books on elements of European foreign policy and of, more recently, *The European Union's Role in Global Politics: A Retreat from Liberal Internationalism* (Routledge, forthcoming).

Index

Page numbers in *italics* indicate tables.

AA (Association Agreement) with Ukraine, 59, 66, 67–75
Abacha, Sani, 179, 184
Abazovic, Dino, 46
absorption capacity of EU, 48
Abu Dhabi, 148
accession process. *See* enlargement of EU
Aegis Defense Services, 158
African Peace Facility, 180
African Peacekeeping Training Support Programme, 180
Africa Progress Panel, 186
aid dependency in Nigeria, 179–80
Albania, 92
Al Hina, Abdulmalik, 145, 146
Almatov, Zokirjon, 109
Al Yamamah defense deal, 148, 149
Arab-Israeli conflict, 138, 139, 147
Armenia, 59, 90
Association Agreement (AA) with Ukraine, 59, 66, 67–75
authoritarianism, 115
Azerbaijan, 59, 80, 90
Aznar, José María, 163

Bahrain, 141, 142, 145, 152n4
Balkans: CEE as model for approach to, 39–40; Croatia, 38–39, 41; democracy promotion in, 40, 51–52; EU fatigue over, 50; failure of inducements in, 47–50; interethnic divisions in, 50–51, 52–53; OSCE and, 85; policy toward, 44–47; Republika Srpska, 39, 54; stabilization and association process in, 38, 39, 40–44, 47, 53–55; wait and see policy in, 54–55. *See also* Bosnia and Herzegovina; Macedonia; Serbia
banks and Nigeria, 184
Barroso Commission, 19
Basescu, Traian, 32, 161
Basra reconstruction team, 157–58
Batt, Judy, 54
Belarus, 59, 80, 92, 93
Belfrage, Frank, 107
Belgium, 62, 67, 88
benchmarking, 46
BiH. *See* Bosnia and Herzegovina
bilateral programs: in Gulf region, 138–40; in Iraq, 157–63; in Nigeria, 189–90; with Ukraine, 64
Bonn powers, 44
Bosnia and Herzegovina (BiH): civil society programs in, 52–53; constitutional reform in, 45–46; OSCE field mission in, 92; reform process in, 48; refugee return in, 51–52; stabilization and association agreement and, 39, 42–43
Brammertz, Serge, 43
Brown, Gordon, 177
Bulgaria, 16–17, 19–20, 161
Bush administration, 3, 83
Butmir talks, 42–43, 46

CARDS (Community Assistance for Reconstruction, Democratization, and Stabilization), 40, 51–52, 53
Carnogursky, Jan, 22
case studies: limitations of foreign policy and, 3–4, 8; variations among, 8–11

Central and Eastern Europe (CEE): corruption and, 34; democracy promotion in, 9, 16–17; enlargement process in, 46, 48, 60; foreign policy toward, 9; as model for approach to Balkans, 39–40; political conditionality and, 18–21. *See also* Bulgaria; Romania

Central Asia: democracy promotion in, 99, 101–3, 104–5, 112; democratic rights in, 99; elections in, 107; energy security and, 109; foreign policy toward, 10; governance of, 99–100; judicial reform in, 101, 102, 110, 111–12; OSCE and, 92, 93, 94; Partnership and Cooperation Agreements with, 100, 103–4, 107; and policy instruments, 102–8; refocusing strategy in, 110–12; rhetoric-reality gap in, 108–10. *See also specific countries*

CFSP (Common Foreign and Security Policy): GCC and, 137, 148; Ukraine and, 59. *See also* Solana, Javier

Chechnya, 85, 91

China and Gulf region, 138

CIS (Commonwealth of Independent States), 79, 85, 108

civil society: in BiH, 52–53; in Central Asia, 102, 104, 105–6, 110–11; in Gulf region, 142; in Morocco, 119–20, 128–31, 132; in Nigeria, 188–89; in Ukraine, 72. *See also* nongovernmental organizations

Common Foreign and Security Policy (CFSP): GCC and, 137, 148; Ukraine and, 59. *See also* Solana, Javier

Commonwealth of Independent States (CIS), 79, 85, 108

Community Assistance for Reconstruction, Democratization, and Stabilization (CARDS), 40, 51–52, 53

conditionality, political: accession and, 30, 33–34; in Central Asia, 102, 106–8; domestic structures and circumstances and, 34–35; during Eastern accession, 18–21; follow-up on, 16–17, 25; leverage on, 25–26, 31; long-term prospects for, 34–35; Morocco and, 126–28; Romania and, 16–18, 27–30; safeguard clause and, 19–20, 29, 31, 32, 33; stabilization and association process and, 40–41; Ukraine and, 69–70. *See also* postaccession compliance

Conventional Forces in Europe Treaty, 82

Cooperation Council and Central Asia, 103

Copenhagen conditions, 18, 41

corruption: in Balkans, 17; in CEE, 34; in Iraq, 156–57; in Latvia, 24–25; neopatrimonialism as, 112; in Nigeria, 175–76, 182, 184; ratings of, 24; in Romania, 27, 28–30, 31, 32–33, 34; in Slovakia, 24

Cotonou Agreement, 176, 179, 181, 186

Council of Europe, 21

Council of European Union. *See* European Union Council

critical theory perspective on foreign policy, 5

Croatia, 38–39, 41

Czech Republic, 50, 161

DCI (Development Cooperation Instrument), 100, 105

deep free trade with Ukraine, 66, 73, 74

de Mistura, Staffan, 156, 172n28

democracy promotion: in Balkans, 40, 51–52; case studies of, 3–4; in Central and Eastern Europe, 9, 16–17; in Central Asia, 99, 101–3, 104–5, 112; definition of, 3; as demand-driven and tailored, 2; enlargement of EU and, 1–3, 16, 68; governance reform compared to, 12–13; in Gulf region, 140–43; in Iraq, 154–55, 156, 161–62, 169; limitations of, 5–8, 13; in Morocco, 115–18, 123–26, 131–32; in Nigeria, 175–78, 191–92; OSCE and, 78–79, 84–85, 89–95; in Ukraine, 61–64, 74. *See also* European Initiative/Instrument for Democracy and Human Rights

Denmark, 162

Department for International Development (DFID, UK): Iraq and, 158; Nigeria and, 177, 188–89, 190

development aid: GCC and, 139–40, 142–43; Iraq and, 164–66

Development Cooperation Instrument (DCI), 100, 105

Dhi Qar reconstruction team, 158

dialogue commitments in Central Asia, 101–2, 103–4, 110, 112

Diena (newspaper), 23–24, 25

Division, interethnic, 50–51, 52–53, 154

Dodik, Milorad, 48, 54

domestic political structures: in Central Asia,

109–10; foreign policy and, 11; in Morocco, 118–20; political conditionality and, 34–35; donations: extrabudgetary, to OSCE, 92–93; to Nigeria, 179–80
Dzurinda governments, 22, 24

Eastern Partnership, 59, 73, 91
EC. *See* European Commission
Economic and Financial Crimes Commission (EFCC), 177–78, 185
EIDHR. *See* European Initiative/Instrument for Democracy and Human Rights
EITI (Extractive Industries Transparency Initiative), 178, 183–84, 190
election monitoring: in GCC, 151–52; in Iraq, 167; in Morocco, 129; in Nigeria, 177, 185–88; ODIHR and, 86–89; OSCE and, 82–83
elections: in Bahrain, 152n4; in Central Asia, 107; in Morocco, 119, 125–26, 129; in Nigeria, 175, 185–86, 191
EMP (Euro-Mediterranean Partnership), 135, 137–38
energy security: Central Asia and, 109; GCC and, 146–48; Iraq and, 168–69; Morocco and, 122
English School theory and foreign policy, 5
enlargement of EU, 30, 74; CEE and, 60; democracy support and, 1–3, 16, 68; doubts over, 2–3; and enlargement fatigue, 47–50; financial crisis and, 48, 50; model for, 55; problems during, 46; Ukraine and, 60–61. *See also* post-accession compliance
ENP. *See* European Neighborhood Policy
ENPI. *See* European Neighborhood and Partnership Instrument
essential elements clause, 107–8
Estonia, 90
ethnic divisions, 50–51, 52–53, 154
EU. *See* European Union
EUJUST LEX, 159, 160, 161, 165–66
EU Monitoring Mission, 91
EU-Moroccan Association Council, 127
Euro-Mediterranean Committee for the Barcelona Process, 103
Euro-Mediterranean Partnership (EMP), 135, 137–38
European Commission (EC): Balkans and, 49; Central Asia and, 100; delegation in Riyadh, 137; EU Council and, 44; Gulf region and, 139; Iraq and, 165; Morocco and, 123; Romania and, 32–33; strategy paper, and, 164; Ukraine and, 70, 73. *See also* European Neighborhood Policy
European Economic and Social Committee, 72
European Economic Community, 136
European Initiative/Instrument for Democracy and Human Rights (EIDHR): Central Asia and, 102, 105–6; Gulf region and, 142–43; Iraq and, 169–70; Morocco and, 117, 128–29; Nigeria and, 188; OSCE and, 83; Ukraine and, 63–64
European Neighborhood and Partnership Instrument (ENPI): Morocco and, 128–29, 130–31; Ukraine and, 63
European Neighborhood Policy (ENP): conditionality and, 126; Georgia and, 91; Morocco and, 116, 117, 123–25, 126–27; new generation of agreements of, 131; problems of, 79; Ukraine and, 62, 65–66, 67–68, 69–70
European Parliament: Balkans and, 49; Morocco and, 125, 126; Ukraine and, 67–68
European security and defense policy missions, 44
European Union (EU): absorption capacity of, 48; model of inclusiveness of, 4–5; OSCE and, 83–84. *See also* enlargement of EU; European Commission; European Parliament; foreign policy of EU
European Union Council: EC and, 44; Gulf region and, 139; Iraq and, 165
EU-Ukraine Action Plan, 62, 65–66, 69–70
external governance, democracy promotion as, 4–5
Extractive Industries Transparency Initiative (EITI), 178, 183–84, 190

Ferrero-Waldner, Benita, 104, 116, 168
FES (Friedrich Ebert Foundation), 189–90, 191
Fico government, 23, 24
field missions of OSCE, 86, 89–93, 95–96
financial crisis and enlargement, 48, 50
Finland, 67
foreign direct investment in Gulf economies, 144, 151

foreign policy of EU: assessment of, 3; duality of, 1–4; idealism of, 4–5, 13; limitations of, 5–8; toward GCC, 135–36, 150–52; toward Iraq, 155–56; toward Western Balkans, 44–47; variations in, 8–11. *See also* democracy promotion; human rights promotion
France: Gulf region and, 148; Iraq and, 157, 159–60; Morocco and, 120–21, 122, 129–30; Nigeria and, 180, 181; Ukraine and, 62, 67
free trade areas: GCC and, 136, 140, 143–46; Morocco and, 122; Nigeria and, 181; Ukraine and, 66
Friedrich Ebert Foundation (FES), 189–90, 191

GCC. *See* Gulf Cooperation Council
Georgia, 59, 78, 80, 91
Germany: Gulf region and, 142, 148; Iraq and, 162–63; Nigeria and, 180, 181, 189–90; OSCE and, 84; Ukraine and, 62, 67; Uzbekistan and, 107, 108–9
Gomes, Ana, 165
Governance Facility of ENP, and Morocco, 126–27
governance reform: in Balkans, 51–52; in Central Asia, 102–3, 104–5, 110, 111; democracy promotion compared to, 12–13; GCC and, 145–46; in Nigeria, 183–85, 188–91; and OECD-UNDP good governance initiative, 142; OSCE field missions and, 92
Greece, 42, 49–50
Gulf Cooperation Council (GCC): bilateralism in, 138–40; democracy promotion and, 140–43; energy policy and, 146–48; foreign policy toward, 135–36, 150–52; and institutional obstacles to, 139–40; Partnership and Cooperation Agreement with, 136–38, 143–44; regime security and, 140–41; security interests and, 148–50; trade with, 136, 140, 143–46
Gulf of Guinea Energy Security Strategy, 183
Gulf region, European involvement in, 136–38

Harabin, Stefan, 23
Heinrich Böll Foundation (HBF), 189–90, 191
human rights promotion, 1, 6. *See also* European Initiative/Instrument for Democracy and Human Rights
Hungary, 60

incentives for Morocco, 117, 126–28
Independent National Electoral Commission (INEC), 185, 187–88
India, 138
institutional structure: in Balkans, 55; and foreign policy, 10–11; GCC and, 139–40; of OSCE, 95; in Ukraine, 64–66
Institution Building Partnership Program, 105
Instrument for Cooperation with Industrialized and other High Income Countries, 142–43
Instrument for Preaccession Assistance (IPA), 40, 52, 53
interethnic divisions: in Balkans, 50–51, 52–53; in Iraq, 154
International Energy Forum, 147
International Reconstruction Fund for Iraq (IRFFI), 164, 165, 166, 169
International Security Assistance Force, 108
investment, 144, 151
IPA (Instrument for Preaccession Assistance), 40, 52, 53
Iraq: Basra reconstruction team, 157–58; commitments to, 157–63, 170–71; democracy promotion in, 154–55, 156, 161–62, 169; Dhi Qar reconstruction team, 158; energy security and, 168–69; EUJUST LEX and, 159, 160, 161, 165–66; foreign policy toward, 155–56; security interests and, 154; strengthening role in, 166–70; subcontracting engagement in, 164–66, 167; trade relations with, 168–69
IRFFI (International Reconstruction Fund for Iraq), 164, 165, 166, 169
Islamists: EU and, 6; in Gulf region, 141; in Morocco, 118, 121–22
Istanbul Charter, 81
Istanbul cooperation initiative, 148, 149–50
Italy: Gulf region and, 148; Iraq and, 157, 158, 160–61; Nigeria and, 181

Japan: Gulf region and, 138, 144; Iraq and, 171
Joint Council meetings, and GCC, 141–42
joint donor basket for Nigeria, 187, 188, 190
Jordan, 165, 168
judicial reform: in Central Asia, 101, 102, 110, 111–12; in Latvia, 23–24; in Romania, 28, 29; in Slovakia, 22–23

Karadžić, Radovan, 43
KAS (Konrad Adenauer Foundation), 189–90, 191
Kazakhstan: EIDHR and, 105; election observation in, 88; energy reserves of, 109; EU delegation to, 104; governance of, 92, 100; OSCE and, 79, 91, 93; Policy Advice Program and, 105; rule of law initiative in, 111
Konrad Adenauer Foundation (KAS), 189–90, 191
Kosovo, 39, 43, 46–47, 49
Kouchner, Bernard, 159–60
Kuwait, 141, 142
Kyrgyzstan, 93, 100, 105, 108

Lajèák, Miroslav, 42, 54
Latvia, 23–25, 90
Lavrov, Sergey, 82
leverage: GCC and, 138, 139, 141; Morocco and, 117–18, 126, 132; Nigeria and, 177; political conditionality and, 25–26, 31; Ukraine and, 75
Lipsic, Daniel, 22
Lisbon Treaty, 48, 50
Lithuania, 61
Loskutovs, Aleksejs, 25

Macedonia: CARDS funds in, 52; EU membership of, 41–42, 45, 48; reform process in, 39, 53
Macovei, Monica, 22, 29, 31, 32
makhzen (Morocco), 118–20, 122
Maliki, Nouri al-, 155, 156, 166
market economy, 63
MEDA program, 128, 129, 130–31
Melescanu, Teodor, 161
Merkel, Angela, 48
Middle East and North Africa (MENA), 6, 9, 115, 132. *See also* Morocco
migration: Morocco and, 120–21; Nigeria and, 180–81
military cooperation, 180
Mladiæ, Ratko, 43, 45
MNF-I (multinational force–Iraq), 157, 161, 163, 170
Mohammed VI, 116, 117, 118, 128, 129
Moldova, 59, 90, 92
monitoring capacities of OSCE, 85–89, 94
monitoring of external pressure: overview of, 21; in Romania, 33–34; in Slovakia and Latvia, 26
Montenegro, 43, 45
Morar, Daniel, 32
Morocco: advanced status of, 116, 117, 122, 127, 131, 132; conditionality, incentives, and, 126–28; contrasting interests in, 120–22; democracy promotion in, 115–18, 123–26, 131–32; elections in, 119, 125–26, 129; energy security and, 122; *makhzen* in, 118–20, 122; myth of model of, 118–20; political aid to, 128–31, *130;* semiauthoritarianism of, 132
Moscow Mechanism, 85
multinational force–Iraq (MNF-I), 157, 161, 163, 170

NATO: Bulgaria, Romania, and, 19; Iraq and, 160, 161, 163, 170; Istanbul cooperation initiative, 148, 149–50; Ohrid Agreement, 41, 56n22; OSCE and, 10, 79, 81–82; Ukraine, Georgia, and, 60, 68
Netherlands: Balkans and, 44–45; election monitoring in, 88; Iraq and, 162, 163; Serbia and, 43; Ukraine and, 62, 67
NGOs. *See* nongovernmental organizations
Nigeria: commitments to, 178–85; corruption in, 175–76; democracy promotion in, 175–78, 191–92; elections in, 175, 185–88, 191; governance assistance projects in, 188–91; military cooperation with, 180
Nigeria-EU Joint Way Forward, 176
Nnamani, Ken, 187
nongovernmental organizations (NGOs): in Central Asia, 110–11; in Morocco, 123, 128–29; in Nigeria, 186–87; as pressure agents, 21–22; in Romania, 31–32
Northern Ireland, 55

Obama, Barack, 3, 83, 138, 141
Obasanjo, Olusegun, 179, 183, 185, 186
OECD-UNDP good governance initiative, 142
Office for Democratic Institutions and Human Rights (ODIHR) of OSCE: Central Asia and, 106; democracy assistance by, 89–90; description of, 81; election observation by, 86–89; internal disputes and, 95; United States and, 82–83

Ohrid Agreement, 41, 56n22
oil and gas sector: in Central Asia, 109; in Gulf region, 146–48; in Nigeria, 176–77, 180, 181–83
Oman, 142, 145
Orange Revolution in Ukraine, 59, 60, 61, 64, 73
Organization for Security and Cooperation in Europe (OSCE): assistance through, 80–81; Central Asia and, 104; challenges and expectations of, 93–96; democracy promotion and, 78–79, 84–85, 89–95; description of, 78; EU and, 83–84; extrabudgetary donations to, 92–93; field missions of, 86, 89–93, 95–96; monitoring capacities of, 85–89; as paper tiger, 79, 96; Parliamentary Assembly of, 88–89, 90, 95; problems of, 79; reform and divergent interests of, 80–84; Russia and, 78, 80, 81–82, 93, 95; U.S. and, 82–83; work of, 96n2. See also Office for Democratic Institutions and Human Rights (ODIHR) of OSCE

Paris Club, 179
Parliamentary Assembly of OSCE, 88–89, 90, 95
Partnership and Cooperation Agreements (PCAs): with Central Asia, 100, 103–4, 107; with GCC, 136–38, 143–44; with Ukraine, 59, 62
Partnership for Peace, 79, 149
patronage: in Central Asia, 110, 112; in GCC, 145, 150; in Iraq, 156–57; and *makhzen* in Morocco, 118–20, 122; in Nigeria, 189
Patten, Chris, 104
personnel of OSCE field operations, 91–92
Piebalgs, Andris, 168
Poland, 60, 61, 161
police reform: in BiH, 42; in Iraq, 159, 160, 161, 165–66
Policy Advice Program, 105
political conditionality: accession and, 30, 33–34; in Central Asia, 102, 106–8; domestic structures and, 34–35; during Eastern accession, 18–21; follow-up on, 16–17, 25; leverage on, 25–26, 31; long-term prospects for, 34–35; Morocco and, 126–28; Romania and, 16–18, 27–30; safeguard clause and, 19–20, 29, 31, 32, 33; stabilization and association process and, 40–41; Ukraine and, 69–70. See also postaccession compliance

political parties: in Latvia, 23; in Morocco, 118–19, 121–22; in Romania, 27, 28–29; in Slovakia, 22; in Ukraine, 60–61, 67
postaccession compliance: dynamics of, 20–21, 26–27; in Romania, 30–34; in Slovakia and Latvia, 21–27
pressure for reversal: overview of, 20–21; in Romania, 33; in Slovakia and Latvia, 26
Prouse, Anna, 158
PSD (Social Democratic Party), 27, 28–29
public policy perspective on foreign policy, 5
Putin, Vladimir, 81, 82, 87, 108

Qatar, 148
quick-start assistance package to Nigeria, 179

reformist ministers, 26
refugees, 38, 51–52
Rehn, Olli, 19, 49
Repse government, 24
Republika Srpska, 39, 54
Ribadu, Nuhu, 185
Romania: accession of, 60; compliance after accession, 30–34; compliance during accession, 27–30; conditionality and, 16–18, 19–20; corruption in, 24, 27, 28–30, 31, 32–33, 34; Iraq and, 161; judicial reform in, 28, 29
routinization and status quo bias: overview of, 20; in Romania, 33; in Slovakia and Latvia, 26
rule extension, 5
rule of law initiative in Central Asia, 101, 102, 110, 111–12
Russia: Central Asian states and, 108; democracy in, 10, 79; democracy monitoring and, 85; EU response to, 68; field missions of OSCE and, 90–91; gas supplies from, 147; *korenizatsiya* in, 112; ODIHR and, 87–88, 89; OSCE and, 78, 80, 81–82, 93, 95; Single Economic Space and, 60

SAAs (stabilization and association agreements), 39, 42–43, 49, 54
safeguard clause and political conditionality, 19–20, 29, 31, 32, 33
SAP. See stabilization and association process
Sarkozy, Nicolas, 121, 122, 125–26, 177
Saro-Wiwa, Ken, 179
Saudi Arabia, 139, 146, 148–49

scenarios of postaccession dynamics, 20–21, 26, 33–34
sectarian conflict. *See* interethnic divisions
security interest: in Central Asia, 104; foreign policy and, 11; GCC and, 148–50; in Iraq, 154; in Morocco, 121; in Nigeria, 180, 182–83. *See also* Organization for Security and Cooperation in Europe
security sector governance and OSCE, 90
Serbia: EU membership of, 43, 47, 48; Montenegro and, 45; OSCE field mission in, 92; SAA and, 39, 49
Shell, 179, 181, 182
Slovakia, 22–23, 24, 60
Slovenia, 41
Social Democratic Party (PSD), 27, 28–29
socialization processes: Central Asia and, 112; Ukraine and, 70–71
social learning: overview of, 21; in Romania, 34; in Slovakia and Latvia, 26–27
Solana, Javier: Central Asia and, 104; Gulf region and, 139; Iraq and, 155, 165, 166; Morocco and, 126; Ukraine and, 61
Southern Iraq Employment Program, 157–58
South Ossetia, 91
Spain: Iraq and, 163; migration from Morocco to, 120; Morocco and, 121, 122, 130; Ukraine and, 62, 67
Spencer, Oliver, 89
Spiric, Miroslav, 42
stabilization and association agreements (SAAs), 39, 42–43, 49, 54
stabilization and association process (SAP): in Balkans, 38, 39, 40–44, 47; lessons from, 53–55
statut avancé of Morocco: energy sector and, 122; ENP and, 116, 131; integration with EU and, 127; leverage and, 117, 132
Strategy for Africa, 176
Straw, Jack, 165
Sweden: Balkans and, 50; banks in, 184; Gulf region and, 142; Iraq and, 161–62; Ukraine and, 67

Tadiæ administration, 47
Tajikistan, 91, 100, 105, 108
Tariceanu government, 29

technical reforms: GCC and, 151–52; to OSCE, 81, 94
terrorism, war on: Central Asia and, 108–9; Morocco and, 121
Topcagic, Osman, 46
trade relations with Iraq, 168–69. *See also* free trade areas
Treaty of Amsterdam, 21
Treaty of Friendship, Partnership, and Cooperation, 160–61
truth commission in Morocco, 128
Turkey, 24, 49
Turkmenistan, 95, 100, 109
Tusk, Donald, 161
Tymoshenko, Yulia, 60, 63

UK. *See* United Kingdom
Ukraine: accession and, 60–61, 66–68; Association Agreement with, 59, 66, 67–75; deep free trade with, 66, 73, 74; democracy promotion in, 61–64, 74; democratic consolidation in, 64–66; Institution Building Partnership Program and, 105; lack of unity on, 74; and market economy, 63; membership prospective of, 66–68; Orange Revolution in, 59, 60, 61, 64, 73; Partnership and Cooperation Agreement with, 59, 62; political parties in, 60–61, 67
UN Assistance Mission for Iraq, 164
United Arab Emirates, 148
United Kingdom (UK): Balkans and, 44–45; Gulf region and, 142, 148–49; Iraq and, 157–59; Nigeria and, 180, 181, 189, 190; OSCE and, 84; Ukraine and, 67
United States: Bahrain, Oman, and, 145; democracy aid from, 64; Gulf region and, 148; Iraq and, 170; Nigeria and, 182; OSCE and, 82–83. *See also* Obama, Barack
Uusitalo, Ilkka, 165
Uzbekistan: Andijan massacres in, 85–86, 107, 108; democracy in, 100; energy reserves of, 109; OSCE Tashkent Center in, 91; Partnership and Cooperation Agreement with, 103; rule of law initiative in, 111–12

van den Berg, Max, 185
Verkhovna Rada Resolution, 61
visa facilitation agreement with Ukraine, 71–72

Western Sahara conflict, 121
White, Stephen, 159, 166
World Trade Organization (WTO), 66, 143

Yanukovych, Viktor, 60
Yar'Adua, Umaru, 178, 186, 187

Yeltsin, Boris, 81
Yugoslavia, 85
Yushchenko, Viktor, 60, 63

Zagreb summit, 40
Zapatero, José Luis, 121, 130, 163